Palgrave Studies in the Future of Humanity and its Successors

Series Editors
Calvin Mercer
East Carolina University
Greenville, NC, USA

Steve Fuller
Department of Sociology
University of Warwick
Coventry, UK

Humanity is at a crossroads in its history, precariously poised between mastery and extinction. The fast-developing array of human enhancement therapies and technologies (e.g., genetic engineering, information technology, regenerative medicine, robotics, and nanotechnology) are increasingly impacting our lives and our future. The most ardent advocates believe that some of these developments could permit humans to take control of their own evolution and alter human nature and the human condition in fundamental ways, perhaps to an extent that we arrive at the "posthuman", the "successor" of humanity. This series brings together research from a variety of fields to consider the economic, ethical, legal, political, psychological, religious, social, and other implications of cutting-edge science and technology. The series as a whole does not advocate any particular position on these matters. Rather, it provides a forum for experts to wrestle with the far-reaching implications of the enhancement technologies of our day. The time is ripe for forwarding this conversation among academics, public policy experts, and the general public. For more information on Palgrave Studies in the Future of Humanity and its Successors, please contact Phil Getz, Editor, Religion & Philosophy: phil.getz@palgrave-usa.com.

More information about this series at
http://www.palgrave.com/gp/series/14587

Roy Jackson

Muslim and Supermuslim

The Quest for the Perfect Being and Beyond

palgrave
macmillan

Roy Jackson
University of Gloucestershire
Gloucestershire, UK

Palgrave Studies in the Future of Humanity and its Successors
ISBN 978-3-030-37092-3   ISBN 978-3-030-37093-0   (eBook)
https://doi.org/10.1007/978-3-030-37093-0

This Palgrave Macmillan imprint is published by the registered company Springer Nature Switzerland AG.
The registered company address is: Gewerbestrasse 11, 6330 Cham, Switzerland

To Annette: The Perfect Being!

CONTENTS

CHAPTER 1

Introduction: The Future of the Human

The Irish playwright George Bernard Shaw's (1856–1950) philosophical comedy drama *Man and Superman* contains a long third act, the 'Dream scene' (sometimes also referred to as the 'Hell scene') which, due to its length, is—sadly, but understandably—often omitted from stage productions. This act involves a philosophical debate between Don Juan/Jack Tanner and the Devil. Despite its frequent omission, it is an important part of the play. As Shaw himself stated:

> I took the legend of Don Juan in its Mozartian form and made it a dramatic parable of Creative Evolution. But being then at the height of my invention and comedic talent, I decorated it too brilliantly and lavishly. I surrounded it with a comedy of which it formed only one act, and that act was so completely episodical (it was a dream which did not affect the action of the piece) that the comedy could be detached and played by itself. (Shaw 1987, Preface)

An interesting phrase in the quote above is 'Creative Evolution'. The philosophical underpinning of the play is Shaw's own contentious interpretation of the French philosopher Henri Bergson's (1859–1941) concept of 'orthogenesis', of evolution motivated by *élan vital*, humanity's natural creative impulse (Bergson 1983), combined with the German philosopher Friedrich Nietzsche's (1844–1900) concept of the *Übermensch*, the 'Overhuman'. In the Dream scene, heaven and hell are metaphors for

© The Author(s) 2020
R. Jackson, *Muslim and Supermuslim*, Palgrave Studies
in the Future of Humanity and its Successors,
https://doi.org/10.1007/978-3-030-37093-0_1

two opposing attitudes towards life on earth. On the one hand there is the diabolical, represented by hell, where no improvement in the human condition is possible and, consequently, no hope or salvation. Heaven, on the other hand, symbolises something much higher and nobler in which human improvement and progress is indeed achievable (Wisenthal 1971, p. 299). The Devil cynically argues that the power that governs the earth is not Life, but Death, for 'Man measures his strength by his destructiveness' (Shaw 1970, p. 654). The Devil considers man (as opposed to the gender neutral 'Man') as 'the most predatory and destructive expression of life' (Gibbs 1976, p. 170), whereas Don Juan argues for the potential for man to achieve 'higher … organisation and completer self-consciousness' (Shaw 1970, p. 660). Don Juan does go on to differentiate between masculine and feminine forms of creativity in a somewhat reductive and essentialist manner, but in a more metaphorical sense the marriage of Don Juan/Jon Tanner to Ann Whitefield can be seen as 'a union of contemplative and primary forms of creativity' (Gibbs 1976, p. 172).

At root in Shaw's play is an optimism in the human, whether this be male or female, to *evolve*, hence the title *Man and Superman*. This confidence in the human to progress is also the main ingredient of this book, and this is the reason for the title *Muslim and Supermuslim*, for 'Man' can readily be substituted for 'Muslim'. One is synonymous with the other. If I may be perhaps overly simplistic for a moment by defining philosophy as concerning itself with the 'big questions', surely one such 'big question' is what does it mean to be human? This philosophical preoccupation with the human, going back in western philosophy to the ancient Greeks, is also a concern for Muslim believers. Whilst it has been conventionally accepted within the Islamic tradition that there has historically been some degree of animosity and suspicion towards the philosophical, as opposed to the theological and legal, tradition, this work will set out to show that, in actual fact, philosophy is, and has been through most of its history, *central* to Islam. Given this, it is only right that we should consider what the Islamic tradition can contribute to one of the most important questions for today: the future of the human.

The existential menace that looms over humanity's identity and existence has become more imaginable in recent years, certainly since the detonation of the first atomic bomb on July 16, 1945, from which point humankind has the power to cause its own extinction. The term 'Anthropocene' is not yet recognised or properly defined officially by anthropologists, although it is becoming increasingly used in modern parlance to refer to a new geological epoch which is marked by significant human impact upon the Earth's ecosystem (Waters et al. 2014). The Anthropocene Working Group is currently occupied in accumulating evidence in arguing for the case for the Anthropocene to be recognised as an official geologic epoch. This is yet to be ratified. One of the issues is that even if the term is accepted, agreement needs to be reached as to when was the official beginning of this epoch. For example, does it begin with the testing of the first atom bomb in New Mexico, or further back to, say, the Industrial Revolution?

Officially we are still in the Holocene ('recent whole'), the post-glacial geological epoch that began some 10,000–12,000 years ago, but the call for a new epoch, the Anthropocene, is growing (Crutzen and Stoermer 2000). The term 'Anthropocene' itself is a combination of *anthropos*, the Greek for 'human', and '-cene', which is the suffix used in names of geological epochs. The word was first used by the ecologist Eugene Stoermer in the early 1980s to describe what he observed of the industrial pollution on the wildlife of the Great lakes that separate Canada from the US (Lovelock 2019, p. 37), but as early as 1926 the Russian geologist V.I. Vernadsky acknowledged the growing power of the human when he wrote 'the direction in which the processes of evolution must proceed, namely towards increasing consciousness and thought, and forms having greater and greater influence on their surroundings'. In 1924 the term 'noösphere', the 'world of thought', was coined by the French Jesuit Teilhard de Chardin and E. LeRoy (Crutzen and Stoermer 2000). Geologists tend to see earth history in terms of millennia, and so to apply an epoch to humans—who in geological terms have only been around during a metaphorical blink of an eye—may seem like hubris but, whether officially recognised as an epoch or not, there is no denying the impact human activity has had on the earth's system. In particular, the damaging effects such as global warming, oceanic acidification, habitat loss, and so on have increased the concern that *Homo sapiens* as a species is a detriment not only to other species but to itself. This concern has prompted ecology movements to engage in self-scrutiny and to lobby governments and corporations, who might not always be so scrupulous in their anxiety for the environment, to alter their policies and practices. Islam, for its part, has a growing body of research and groups in the field of ecology (though still in its infancy), often citing the call for Muslims to live up to their responsibilities as *khalifa* (Qur'an 6:167), or guardians, of God's creation for the sake of future generations. The concern for the environment, therefore, is seen as an act of religious worship and a duty. The role of humanity as 'guardian' suggests a paternalism towards other species, but transhumanism takes the status of *Homo sapiens* into a new territory, not so much as protectors of the planet, rather a possible enemy to itself and others that need to be overcome.

This 'overcoming' of the human is where transhumanism comes in: a school of thought that is increasing in terms of scholarly research and importance. Yet, transhumanism is a catch-all term: how this 'overcoming' is to be understood covers a very broad spectrum of views within the transhumanist movement, from the less radical enhancement of the human species that will allow the humans to adapt, survive, and thrive more readily to the changing environment, to the more drastic where *Homo sapiens*, if they survive at all, will be the cousin, perhaps the poorer cousin, of a new Humanity 2.0. This more radical school of thought inevitably raises important religious questions, particularly concerning the status of humankind in relation to God and creation. Whilst Islamic authority can be found and utilised in a way that encourages Muslims to protect the planet, it may be more difficult to argue that Islam can justify the possible extinction or, at best, depreciation, of the current human species (i.e. Humanity 1.0) in its quest to achieve such environmental goals. Having said that, however, whilst difficult to argue, this is not the same as saying that it is impossible, provided one is careful in the articulation of terms, most especially when dealing with such generalist words as 'transhumanist' and 'Islam'.

In Chap. 2, therefore, I will clearly focus on a *particular expression* of transhumanism and how this can be applied to a *particular expression* of Islam. The reasons for this should be obvious, for nothing adds more to confusion and misunderstanding than a liberal use of general terms that can mean many different things to different people. I begin by examining what is meant by 'transhumanism' in the modern context and what assumptions are made in terms of the nature of the human and the antagonism towards religious belief. The middle way approach between transhumanism and religion more generally is something that is already being engaged in, and has been for some years now. Transhumanists have certainly been willing to embrace the 'eastern' religions, especially Confucianism and Buddhism, which may allow for the perception—all depending of course on how interpreted—of the human being as at one stage in an evolutionary process. Going back to 2003, an informal meeting took place between the World Transhumanist Association (WTA, now known as Humanity+) president, Nick Bostrom, and the Templeton

Oxford Summer Seminars in Christianity and the Sciences. This discussion led to an informal working paper entitled, 'A Platform for Conversation: Transhumanism and the Christian Worldview'. What has Islam contributed so far? Frankly, very little, and the problem is that when Muslims address issues that arise in transhumanism they do tend to look to the *prescriptive* paradigmatic religious sources of, primarily, the Qur'an, and its kin, the hadith and shari'a for answers. This book subscribes to the view presented in Shahab Ahmed's (1966–2015) ground-breaking work *What Is Islam?* (2016), which cogently looks to a *creative* and *explorative* explication of Islamic sources which are all too often ignored (by Muslims and non-Muslims alike), yet they provide so much guidance in terms of meaning and value. An awareness of the complexities and diversity of Islamic belief is key to understanding the relationship between Islam and transhumanism. Many transhumanists—what I refer to as the secular transhumanists—are wary of a possibility for any positive contribution that can emerge from religious traditions, especially the Abrahamic, due to a prevalent, particular of theology that believes, hopes, and prays for a better *next life*, and/or relies upon supernatural forces for a better *this life*. Recent scholarship in the Jewish and, more prominently, Christian traditions, have set out to alter this perception. What I set out to demonstrate is that there are other forms of Islam that, certainly prior to the mid-nineteenth century, were dominant in the Islamic world and, when these are considered in modern light, also show that secular transhumanists need not be so distrustful and suspicious here.

The primary concern of this book, then, is to see what how Islam can confront and respond to the challenge of secular transhumanism. In the battle of ideas, there are far too many misunderstandings between what are regarded as separate and distinct disciplines, no more so than that between religion and science. What I want to consider in Chap. 3 is whether or not questions that arise from the transhumanist debate are to be kept firmly within a secular, empirical, scientific arena and, if this were the case, is science sufficient in answering those kinds of questions that do arise? If it is not sufficient, then where else might we look for guidance? How far can the boundaries be stretched before they begin to tear? Whilst many transhumanists, our secular transhumanists, are quite prepared to be 'interdisciplinary' in their methodology, hence allowing such disciplines as philosophy and, indeed, the 'arts', within these boundaries, there is still, alas, some robust resistance to religion which, I believe, is understandable, but also misplaced.

Chapter 4 focuses on the 'trans' element of transhumanism in terms of 'surpassing' or 'going beyond' human boundaries and, indeed, whether there *are* such boundaries. Secular transhumanism targets religion, especially the Abrahamic tradition, as 'closed' to possibilities of 'transgression', yet this bias belies the complexity of religious belief. However, Islam itself contains within it a reification, primarily as a response to modern, secular, and western challenges to its identity. The resultant literalism and closing in of itself only plays into the hands of the accusations made by secular transhumanists, whereas if the spotlight was pointed instead towards its acknowledgement of the perplexity and paradoxical nature of religion in the relation to the human, as well as it 'mystery' and the need to express this through metaphor, poetry, and so on, then the seeming divisions between Islam and transhumanism start to blur.

Science, despite its attempts to be otherwise, cannot be entirely objective, if only because it still operates through the human. This is the paradox faced by transhumanism, for in order to transcend the human species, the scientists have to operate within human values, however much the secular transhumanist might prefer to brush such values under the carpet. Ziauddin Sardar has argued that science is not value-free and looks to the Muslim world for an 'indigenous science' that reflects Islamic values. This 'Islamization' of knowledge, which will be examined in Chap. 5, has its origins with the Traditionalist, or Perennialist, school of thought with René Guénon (1866–1951) and Frithjof Schuon (1907–1998), and then passed on to the mighty figure of Seyyed Hossein Nasr (b. 1933), who champions a totalising of all knowledge under the umbrella of Islam. That is, science, history, anthropology, philosophy, and so on are all to be found—and sought—in divine revelation, as this constitutes perennial truth. Therefore, the claims of modernity, which would include evolutionary theory, are to be disputed if they are not part of this perennial truth. Stefano Bigliardi, a scholar of philosophy, specialising in Islam and science, has devoted a number of years examining the debates on Islam and science, and claims that we can now talk of a 'new generation' of scientific thinkers.

In the further pursuit of blurring the perceived lines that the secular transhumanist seems to want to create between the goals of transhumanism and religion, we must steer away from the presumed 'clash of civilisations' thesis: that Islam and the west are too 'other' to be able to engage in any meaningful exchange of ideas. Yet, when we get beyond the reified, modernist expression of Islam, we can see just how rich Islam is in terms of philosophy and culture. In Chap. 6, I look to one work of fiction, the philosophical tale *Hayy ibn Yaqzan*, written by the Muslim philosopher Ibn Tufayl (1105–1185) and how this is a literary expression of *ishraqi* (Illuminationist) thought in Islamic philosophy.

In Chap. 7, we shall see how transhumanist philosophical thought has its own 'spiritual' dimension, and I will draw parallels between this concept of philosophy and that of the works of important Muslim thinkers such as al-Ghazali, Ibn Rushd, Muhammad Iqbal, and Rumi. The key point in this final chapter is that, in the case of transhumanism, human nature is seen as dynamic and changeable: in the same way Ibn Tufayl resorted to fictional narrative through the protagonist Hayy ibn Yaqzan for his *bildungsroman*, the Indian poet and philosopher Muhammad Iqbal (1877–1938) used poetry primarily to express his conception of *Khudi* (Selfhood). We look to our scientists to tell us what is technically possible for the human to become, but we—and by 'we' I mean scientists too—look to our visionaries, our philosophers, religious thinkers, poets, and so on, for what it means to become something other than what we are or how we perceive ourselves. Islamic thought has its visionaries too, and Iqbal presents a paradigm that resonates with the vision of transhumanism. This is all-important in respect of the transhumanist debate because Iqbal's Perfect Being (importantly it is a trope that can be found in other Islamic thought, notably that of Rumi's *Mard-e-Haqq*) and Nietzsche's *Übermensch* (which greatly influenced Iqbal's thought) are paradigms of human transformation towards a 'better human'. In addition, both Nietzsche and Iqbal recognised the 'religiosity' of being human and of how our language and understanding of our world are driven and frame-worked by religious ideals. By 'religion' and 'religiosity' here I mean it in its, for want of a better term, anti-realist sense, or the 'spiritual' or 'mystical' sense, that even certain transhumanist writers, such as Giulio Prisco, hope for. In the case of both Nietzsche and Iqbal, the self is seen in this fluctuating, fluid, and changing manner. There is an existential quality to the extent that the Self is always in a process of becoming, for to 'be' is to cease to be creative and cease to challenge and create. I conclude by returning to my opening references to the Anthropocene in the Introduction and briefly consider James Lovelock's optimistic call for a new epoch, the Novacene, before making some modest Affirmations for a Muslim Transhumanist Association.

Bibliography[1]

Books

Ahmed, Shahab. 2016. *What Is Islam? The Importance of Being Islamic*. Princeton and Oxford: Princeton University Press.
Bergson, Henri. 1983. *Creative Evolution*. Translated by F.L. Pogson. New York: Harper Torchbooks.
Lovelock, James. 2019. *Novacene: The Coming Age of Hyperintelligence*. London: Allen Lane.
Shaw, George Bernard. 1970. *Bodley Head Bernard Shaw: Collected Plays with Their Prefaces*. Edited by Dan H. Laurence. London: Bodley Head Ltd.
———. 1987. *Back to Methuselah: A Metabiological Pentateuch*. London: Penguin.
Waters, C.N., et al., eds. 2014. *A Strategical Basis for the Anthropocene*. London: Geological Society Publication (GSL).

Journal Articles and Book Chapters

Crutzen, Paul, and Eugene F. Stoermer. 2000. The 'Anthropocene'? *IGBP Newsletter*, no. 41.
Gibbs, A.M. 1976. Comedy and Philosophy in Man and Superman. *Modern Drama* 19 (2): 161–175.
Wisenthal, J.L. 1971. The Cosmology of Man and Superman. *Modern Drama* 14 (3): 298–306.

[1] *Note*: All quotes from the Qur'an are from the translation by M.A.S. Abdel Haleem, Oxford University Press, 2005.

CHAPTER 2

Blurring the Boundaries

The future of the human must be, for humans anyway, the most important philosophical and religious issue. Perhaps it always has been, yet much recent scholarship on what is referred to as 'transhumanism' lays claim to the question of the future human as a new issue and seeks to define it within a narrow secular arena that shuts all doors to the religious. Like all '-isms', there are many variants of 'transhumanism' and what we are witnessing is a new transhumanism with its own rules, which, in this book, shall be referred to as *'secular transhumanism'*. This secular transhumanism displays many of the same tendencies as new, or 'militant', atheism, most especially in its antipathy towards religious belief, while being more open to other scholarly disciplines. *Why* religion is so excluded will be examined later on, and particular emphasis will be on the religion of Islam, especially as—if not explicitly stated—Islam often seems to represent all that is 'bad' about religious beliefs so far as the militant atheist (and, by implication, the secular transhumanist) is concerned.

The transhumanist debate is both fascinating and extremely important and, in the future, it is destined to increase in importance with technological change. Islam, for its part, should be a part of this debate, and so here I want to *reclaim* the debate, to show that others can play the transhumanist game, that the doors to the arena should be open and should welcome contributions from the non-secular. Note I use the term 'reclaim', not 'introduce', for, as shall be shown, in many ways Islam has, through most of its history, been involved in one way or another in the transhumanist

© The Author(s) 2020
R. Jackson, *Muslim and Supermuslim*, Palgrave Studies
in the Future of Humanity and its Successors,
https://doi.org/10.1007/978-3-030-37093-0_2

debate, whilst it may not specifically use the term 'transhumanism' or understand it in the stricter sense that secular transhumanists are seeking to define it. The postmodern world in which we find ourselves is confronted by a myriad of emotional and intellectual responses to the rapid developments in technology. Some of these responses are fearful and perplexing, while others are more embracing and exciting. What unites them all is a questioning of what it means to be human. This questioning, this *re-questioning*, is nothing new in terms of concerns for the future of humankind, and the transhumanist movement readily acknowledges its debt to the intellectual past, at least as far back as the European Enlightenment.

Steve Fuller and Veronika Lipinska define transhumanism as 'our seemingly endless capacity for self-transcendence, our "god-like" character, if you will' (Fuller and Lipinska 2014, p. 1) and this is a definition I wholly subscribe to, for it succinctly presents two key characteristics of the transhumanist movement: firstly, the 'endless capacity for self-transcendence', with the emphasis, for me, on 'endless'. Secondly, our 'god-like' character. Where transhumanism appears more radical is that technology in the future, in perhaps the near future, will result in greater 'displacement' of the human condition. We are talking here of a much more radical stage in evolution, from one species of the genus *Homo* to a whole new species. This more radical form of transhumanism breaks away from the four-billion-year-old process of natural selection (assuming one accepts natural selection as a scientific fact and, as we see later, not everyone does) and now puts evolution in the hands of scientists. We are talking about animals becoming gods as a result of their own intelligent design and leaves seemingly no room for the divine, for *Homo sapiens is* divine.

But if humans are indeed to *become* gods, then it is vital to understand what it means to *be* a God. After all, such an exploration may also raise the question of whether such an evolution is desirable. Religion is often considered to be distinct from science and technology—in itself a debatable point as I shall argue—but, even if it were so distinct, that does not mean that it should remain silent on issues that arise from science and technology, especially when it relates so directly to the transformation of the human being. So 'becoming divine' is not synonymous with leaving the divine behind, rather it brings the divine front of stage. By evolving, what are we leaving behind? To answer that question, we need to understand what being human actually involves. Whilst religion does not have exclusive rights to the question of the nature of existence and humankind's place within it, it has, nonetheless, been central to religion for, quite possibly, as long as religions have existed. The quest for what it means to be human consists of a vast battlefield with various forces, sometimes allied, sometimes opposed. Philosophy, going back at least as far as the pre-Socratics, has also reflected upon the natural world and the human within, while 'natural philosophy' has often worked alongside philosophy, to the extent that they are not always that distinguishable. Stemming from this is the empirical modern sciences. These varying traditions are not easily pigeon-holed, at times working together with the same goals and methods, while at other times in serious conflict. In fact, when we look to ancient Greek thought it is not always too romantic a view to see human flourishing and spiritual nourishment as the overriding aim, making full use of philosophical, empirical, and religious insights to achieve that aim (see, e.g. Hadot 1995). A spectator from a distance may understandably be puzzled as to who is fighting who in this battle of ideas.

There is an undeniable tension that exists between many transhumanists and religious believers. On the one hand, the transhumanist emphasis on enlightenment origins, on science and technology, and on 'reason' is seen by transhumanists as antithetical to religious tenets. On the other hand, those with strong religious views themselves see transhumanism as opposed to religion. Here I want to unpack these assumptions some more and see if some middle ground can be found.

TRANSHUMANISM AS INTERDISCIPLINARY

Nick Bostrom, a philosopher at the forefront of transhumanist scholarship, gives us perhaps the best attempt to present the core and corollary values of transhumanism:

Core Value: Having the opportunity to explore the transhuman and post-human realms

Basic Conditions
- Global security
- Technological progress—Wide access

Derivative Values
- Nothing wrong about "tampering with nature"; the idea of hubris rejected
- Individual choice in use of enhancement technologies; morphological freedom

- Peace, international cooperation, anti-proliferation of WMDs
- Improving understanding (encouraging research and public debate; critical thinking; open-mindedness, scientific inquiry; open discussion of the future)
- Getting smarter (individually; collectively; and develop machine intelligence)
- Philosophical fallibilism; willingness to re-examine assumptions as we go along—Pragmatism; engineering- and entrepreneur-spirit; science
- Diversity (species, races, religious creeds, sexual orientations, life styles, etc.)
- Caring about the well-being of all sentience
- Saving lives (life-extension, anti-aging research, and cryonics). (Bostrom 2002)

In the above it is significant that religious belief is not precluded and a recognition of diversity, including religious, is stated. The primary concern of this work is with the *transhuman*, as opposed to the 'posthuman', yet these two terms seems to be frequently interchangeable in the literature available, and so it is important to be clear in our terms. Perhaps the best way to distinguish transhumanism from posthumanism is to see the former as 'clinging' to the human, whereas the latter is entirely set free from any such ties. Transhumanism adopts an interdisciplinary approach to enhancing the human condition (primarily through technological advances), not escaping from it. Humanism, as a school of thought, looks to societal change and educational improvement in order to make us better humans based on the assumption that this life is the only one we have (see the 2002 Amsterdam Declaration for the widely accepted definition of humanism). Therefore, humanists are not religious believers, but see the world through an empirical lens. Transhumanists, to a large extent, are equally empirical and non-religious (although, as we shall see, this is not always so clear-cut), but want to go beyond the limitations of human biology and genetic inheritance. In other words, humans are not an end in themselves, but something that can be overcome through further evolutionary change. In this respect, the 'human condition' is not a fixed entity. The reason, therefore, that posthumanism is often equated with transhumanism is that the boundary between what is human and when humans cease to be 'human' is not so clearly delineated. Given that transhumanism is regarded as a continual process, and perfection is not a defined, set goal, then there are, by definition, no limits. In this existential, epistemological, and technological sense, the human is always in a process of change (although, inspired by the writings of Ayn Rand, some transhumanists subscribe to a foundationalist epistemology. See Murnane 2018), and so you have self-declared transhumanists talking of, for example, 'uploading' minds to non-biological substrates, which does seem to leave behind pretty much all that would be regarded as 'human'. As we shall explore, this rests with the philosophical notion of personal identity, of what makes us distinctively human. If we are to argue that all that is necessary and sufficient to be human is our psychological existence, then 'posthuman' seems something of a redundant term. Rather, 'we' are always in a process of transcending, for to be 'post' human is equivalent to ceasing to exist, which seems synonymous with death. From this, therefore, I do not make use of the term 'posthuman' at all in this work. My view is that posthumanism is not at all desirable, for to be 'free' from the human is synonymous with no identity, with *death*. For the posthuman, the human is something as an obstruction, something that is an enemy of the planet and, consequently, such hubris needs to be reined in at the very least. This notion of the posthuman perhaps fits better with certain eastern religious traditions such as Buddhism whereby, for example, the concept of *anatta*, of 'non-self', is a goal, but what of 'me' will remain here? For me there is nothing consoling in lacking an 'I', whatever form that may take, for what am I if I do not retain my memories, personality, hopes, desires, and so on? What makes us human is wanting to cling on to these things, even if in reality they are 'bundles' of self, rather than a self as such.

Another helpful definition of transhumanism comes from Max More:

> Transhumanism is a class of philosophies that seeks the continued evolution of human life beyond its current form as a result of science and technology guided by life-promoting principles and values. Transhumanism promotes an interdisciplinary approach to understanding and evaluating the opportunities for enhancing the human condition and the human organism opened up by the advancement of technology. (More and Vita-More 2013, p. 1)

There are a couple of points in the above quote that are worth highlighting in terms of the debate in this book. First of all, the view that transhumanism 'seeks the continued evolution of human life'. The assumption is obviously made that human life has already been through a process of evolution and what needs to be addressed to begin with is the extent to which Islam, or rather certain strands of Islam, may well be resistant to this idea. Secondly, the quote moves on to state that this evolution goes 'beyond its current form as a result of science and technology'. The Islamic belief that humankind was created by God in His/Her image may well conflict with what can be perceived as hubristic to go *beyond* its current form. Further, it begs the question *why* humans should go beyond their current form as a result of science and technology. What, therefore, is the role of science and technology, particularly in relation to faith? In addition, the quote goes on to say that this evolution is to be 'guided by life-promoting principles and values'. This requires considerable unpacking from an ethical standpoint, for how are we to determine which principles and values are 'life-promoting'? What can Islamic ethics contribute here? The final sentence states that transhumanism 'promotes an interdisciplinary approach', and therefore it will be, hopefully, enlightening to examine what the discipline of Islamic thought has to offer to this understanding.

The need for an interdisciplinary approach to transhumanism is the recognition that, as stated at the very beginning of this chapter, this is an '-ism' and, what is typical of '-isms', this is a catch-all. Having said that, all '-isms' have certain central characteristics that distinguishes them (Islam should be no exception here, as explored below). The quote by More above helps to illustrate what the term refers to, and More elaborates on his own definition by aligning this worldview with that of secular humanism and Confucianism in the sense that these do not rely or require a belief in the supernatural in order to have practical implications. In fact, it seems that one essential feature of transhumanism is its rejection of the supernatural, of the divine. Given this, what possible contribution can any religion make to a worldview that rejects religion? As we see below, there is a danger of a 'clash of civilisations', with Islam rejecting entirely transhumanism, and transhumanism rejecting Islam, but it is sincerely hoped that this work will help to bridge a perceived chasm here. More has associated transhumanism with euphraxsophy, a term introduced by Paul Kurtz (1925–2012) in 1988 which literally means 'good practice and wisdom'—from the Greek roots *eu* (good, well); *praxis* (practice, conduct); and *sophia* (wisdom)—and is a philosophy that seems to widen the gap between religion and science even more by offering a secular vision that is an ethical *alternative* to religion. Euphraxsophy draws from philosophy, science, and ethics for this vision, but does not acknowledge any contribution from religious traditions, although an exception is made for Confucianism which Kurtz, in line with the viewpoint of More, did not consider a religion as it does not, in Kurtz' view, rely on the transcendent or supernatural (Kurtz 2012). However, this view, somewhat typical of new atheist thinking generally, tends to adopt a rather simplistic notion of religious belief, so that painting a black and white, dualistic vision of philosophy as something *separate* from religion ignores the complexities and the historical interactions *between* religion and philosophy. If we were to adopt the stance of transhumanism as a euphraxsophy, then the debate ends at this point, for Islam has nothing to offer.

Some transhumanists are considerably more 'militant' in their beliefs. The cognitive scientist Marvin Minsky (1927–2016) was the author of a number of works on artificial intelligence (AI) and philosophy and, in a contribution to an anthology of articles on transhumanism (More and Vita-More 2013), he said the following:

> And so Pascal's Wager: either you believe in God or you don't; if there is no God it can't do any harm to believe in him because he's not going to punish you because he doesn't exist; on the other hand if you don't believe in him and there is one then he'll be mad at you and you won't get eternal life. The argument convinced a lot of people that it didn't do any harm to believe in religion. But in fact it did them harm and it's what killed them all because if they had believed in science instead of religion 2,000 year ago we would all be immortal now. (Minsky 2013, p. 169)

It is simply wrong to assert that Pascal's Wager 'convinced a lot of people that it didn't do any harm to believe in religion' and betrays a simplistic and naive understanding of the complexity of religious belief. Similarly, the assertion that it is an 'either/or'; either you believe in science or you believe in religion, does not hold up to historical scrutiny, as we shall see when looking at science in Islam. Whist, admittedly, the Minsky contribution comes across as considerably less scholarly and more careless compared with many other contributions in the anthology, his views represent this strand of secular transhumanism. By way of another example, we have Zoltan Istvan, who was also the first Presidential candidate for the Transhumanist Party during the 2016 US Presidential Election. He wrote a novel, *The Transhumanist Wager* (Istvan 2013), which tells the story of the transhumanist Jethro Knights who establishes a floating city, Transhumania, populated by like-minded individuals. These are primarily scientists, and the enemy, not surprisingly, are fanatical religious groups, including the mystic Zoe Bach. The book proudly proclaims on the back cover that it was, 'Scorned by over 500 publishers and literary agents around the world', which it seems to see to its credit because of the view its rejection by so many publishers was due to its controversial content, whereas I suspect that it was more likely due to the poor quality of writing.

This, it must be said, is no *Atlas Shrugged*. However, it is indicative of the concern amongst many transhumanists that the enemy of its goals is religion. Religion, it is argued by many transhumanists, is *the* major stumbling block towards scientific progress. As the theologian Ted Peters states, 'Through the eyes of today's transhumanists, religion looks like a roadblock, an obstruction. What the transhumanists think they see in religion is an atavistic commitment to the past, to the status quo, to resistance against anything new' (Peters 2011, p. 159). One other example of this perception of religion as 'atavistic' is Simon Young who states that, 'The greatest threat to humanity's continuing evolution is theistic opposition to Superbiology in the name of a belief system based on blind faith in the absence of evidence' (Young 2005, p. 324). The assumption made here are that faith is 'blind', whatever that may mean (blind to what exactly?), and that this is the antonym to 'evidence', whatever is meant by that!

In terms of the intellectual origins of the use of the terms 'transhumanism' in some form or other, we can go back to the fourteenth century, to Dante's *Divine Comedy* in 1312 to be exact, who used the term *trasumanar* to refer to passing beyond the human in a religious or spiritual manner, and T.S. Eliot used the term 'transhumanized' in *The Cocktail Party* (1935) in the sense of a mystical 'illumination'. For modern transhumanists, neither of these fit, given that Dante and Eliot do not relate the 'going beyond' to any technological transformation. The 'secular transhumanists' look to Julian Huxley as the starting point, as he had a brief chapter entitled 'Transhumanism' in his work *New Bottles for New Wine* (1957), although this was not a well-developed philosophical position: for that we need to look more recently with Max More's 1990 essay 'Transhumanism: Toward a Futurist Philosophy'. However, strands of transhumanist thought in the technological sense are numerous and varied, and just a few are mentioned here. For example, we have the 'proto-transhumanists'—the alchemists of Europe from around the thirteenth to the eighteenth centuries—which inspired Mary Shelley's *Frankenstein* and a concern that Mankind was 'playing God'. Another precursor was Nikolai Fedorovich Fedorov (1829–1903) who argued for the use of technology to achieve life extension and, indeed, immortality. Fedorov went further in advocating resurrection of the dead. Importantly in the context of this work, Fedorov was a Russian Orthodox Christian and part of the Russian cosmism movement which combined elements of religion with eastern and western philosophy. Fedorov was a deeply religious man who believed that God had created humankind for a purpose and that our mortality is a result of ignorance and discord which is antithetical to God's purpose. Science and reason, for Fedorov, are not opposed to faith, but all part of what makes us human, yet it is curious that the secular transhumanists disregard the religious aspect. It is worth pointing out that Fedorov's transhumanist ideas also influenced the esotericist Peter Ouspensky (1878–1947) who, though he did not subscribe to one particular religion, was certainly a believer in the metaphysical and mystical. Interestingly, his novel *Strange Life of Ivan Osokin* (2012, originally published 1915) is a narrative for explaining his philosophy through Friedrich Nietzsche's concept of the eternal recurrence which, from a psychological perspective, emphasises the importance of personal responsibility and transformation. The secular transhumanists tend to consider such existential angst as alien to religion, but this need not—and often is not—the case.

Twentieth-century transhumanists (or proto-transhumanists) include Robert Ettinger (1918–2011) who founded the Cryonics Institute. His work *Man into Superman* (1972) used the term 'transhuman', though perhaps the most idiosyncratic transhumanist was Fereidoun M. Esfandiary (1930–2000) who changed his name to FM-2030, partly in the hope that he would like to live to be 100 (i.e. in 2030) but also in a rejection of traditional naming conventions. Many of these figures were, therefore, from a number of disciplines, not just the sciences. One current notable transhumanist writer is Natasha Vita-More, the author of the *Transhuman Manifesto* (1983), followed by the *Transhuman Arts Statement* (1992, revised 2002) is a designer and artist. As we have seen, some were writers of fiction, perhaps, inevitably, science fiction in many cases and, as will be constantly reinstated, one other discipline that has contributed is the *religious* tradition, and so it seems curious that this is now frequently considered to be *outside* of the transhumanist debate. Vita-More states that 'Transhumanism's proposed elevation of the human condition involves technology *and* [her own emphasis] the arts' (Vita-More 2013, p. 18). If the arts can enter the arena—and not just science or 'reason'—then why should religion be excluded? As Vita-More goes on to say,

> New media's interpretation of the human form, visual landscapes, literary narratives, and musical scores move us from one mental state to another—offering experiences that shift perceptions of ourselves and the world around us. (Vita-More 2013, p. 18)

Does not religious narrative, experience, and other expression of religious thought 'move us from one mental state to another—offering experiences that shift perceptions of ourselves and the world around us'? Vita-More is opening the door to other, more 'creative' or 'humanistic' disciplines, if you will, yet there seems to be a degree of 'religion-blindness' going on here, and to some extent this is certainly understandable, for religion, as presented to the public, tends not to do itself any favours, and Islam especially takes centre-stage when people who wanted to criticise religious belief for its dogmatism and resistance to scientific advances are looking for an easy target. However, as religious scholars, we need to try harder than this, and to look beyond the superficial public image, in the same way transhumanists need to break away from new atheist militancy.

The first fully explicit transhumanist organisation is the Extropy Institute (Ex1) which began in the late 1980s. It has its own periodical, *The Journal of Transhumanist Thought*, and has run conferences since 1994. At its very first conference, Extro 1, a precursor of transhumanism that was praised was the Renaissance philosopher Pico della Mirandola (1463–1494). As Max More states in his reference to Mirandola:

> In his 1486 piece, *Oration on the Dignity of Man*, he portrays God as the Craftsman explaining to humanity its nature in a way that sounds much closer to transhumanism than to the religious worldview it emerged from. (More 2013, p. 9)

Again, the 'religious worldview' is seen as separate from 'transhumanism'; as two opposing forces, rather than noting that one 'emerged from' the other. Mirandola himself, one suspects, would not have been too impressed in this hijacking of his name for the cause of secular transhumanism, whilst putting his religious sensibility in the shadows. Despite Mirandola's *Oration on the Dignity of Man* being considered a manifesto of the Renaissance, he sought to downplay the more radical 'pure' humanism and, in fact, considered himself indebted to the writings of such Islamic thinkers as Ibn Rushd (1126–1198, Latinised as 'Averroes') and Ibn Sina (c. 980–1037, Latinised as 'Avicenna'). As we shall see later on in this work, it is these Islamic thinkers, and others besides, who represent an important strand of Islamic thought that has much to offer to the transhumanist manifesto. Giulio Prisco provides us with some insightful writings on what he calls a 'transhumanist religion' and the quote below sums up what the intentions of this book signify:

Many transhumanists with an ultra-rationalist approach have a very hard time considering parallels between transhumanism, spirituality, and/or religion. Good interpretations of religion have done great good to many people, and following William James (1896) I think a modern transhumanist religion, with religion's contemplation of transcendence and hope in personal resurrection, but without its bigotry and intolerance, can be a powerfully positive force in the life of a person, which is what really matters. (Prisco 2013, p. 238)

We must not be too rash in painting all transhumanists with the same brush, in the same way we must not do likewise for all Muslims. As noted by Mark Walker and Heidi Campbell: 'At the heart of the transhumanist project is an interpretation (or re-interpretation) of what it means to be human. This leads to questions about humanity's relationship to other entities, including the transcendent or divine' (Campbell and Walker 2005, p. i). As we have seen, many transhumanists recognise the importance of this relationship, although there are others who are hostile towards religion, and dismissive of any claims it may make in the transhumanists debate.

Transhumanist Dialogue with Religion

The middle way approach between transhumanism and religion more generally is something that is already being engaged in and has been for some years now. Going back to 2003, an informal meeting took place between the World Transhumanist Association (WTA, now known as Humanity+) president, Nick Bostrom, and the Templeton Oxford Summer Seminars in Christianity and the Sciences. This discussion led to an informal working paper entitled, 'A Platform for Conversation: Transhumanism and the Christian Worldview'. This is a start, with a recognition that transhumanism and religion—or Christianity at least—have shared values such as a desire for eternal life, the elimination of pain and suffering, and the creation of better human beings, although it did also highlight some of the dissonance between them, particularly, from the religious scholars, that of hubris and of 'tampering with nature'. Following on from this, which had resulted in considerable traffic on the WTA list, a more public one-day conference was held in 2004, the Transvision Conference in Toronto entitled 'Transhumanism, Faith and Hope'. There was also a 'pre-pre-conference event' at Green College in Oxford in July 2004 to allow those unable to get to Toronto to engage in dialogue. Various papers were delivered both for and against the ideals of transhumanism, and participants came from WTA members, as well philosophers and theologians. Debates up until this point seem to be largely monopolised, however, by Christianity in terms of a religious response. As for the Toronto conference, this has been considered to be somewhat 'uneven' (Campbell and Walker 2005, p. iv), especially during an open discussion which revealed a number of transhumanists' distaste for religion and a view that it is the religious believers who need 'converting' to secular transhumanism. This attitude to religious believers as essentially 'weak-minded' is also a recurring theme on transhumanists' email lists.

Therefore, there is still quite some way to go in finding common ground, and this is perhaps more difficult with the Abrahamic religions, with the accompanying view of human beings as being created by God as originally perfect, and, *even more so* with Islam than with Judaism and Christianity, for a number of reasons that will be explored in this work. As noted, transhumanists have certainly been willing to embrace the 'eastern' religions, especially Confucianism and Buddhism, which may allow for the perception—all depending of course on how interpreted—of the human being as at one stage in an evolutionary process. Interestingly, the Mormons have been reasonably positive about transhumanism, as the idea of immortal bodies and becoming gods is right in line with Mormon theology. In 2004 and 2005, the WTA issued a survey (Hughes 2007, p. 5) amongst its members. The survey received 1100 responses and it reflected its global membership of 45% US residents and 55% from elsewhere around the world. In response to the question 'Which best describes your religious or spiritual views?', a quarter declared themselves to be 'religious or spiritual'. The breakdown is in the table below:

Which of these best describes your religious or spiritual views?

62% Secular, atheist
30% Atheist
16% Agnostic
9% Secular humanist
7% Other non-theistic philosophy

24% Religious or spiritual
6% Spiritual
4% Protestant

2% Buddhist
2% Religious humanist
2% Pagan or animist
2% Catholic
2% Unitarian-Universalist
2% Other religion
1% Hindu
1% Jewish
1% Muslim

14% Other/DK
11% None of the above
4% Don't know

To some extent this is encouraging, although given the often-declared remark that 'I am spiritual but not religious', it is not always the case that respondents see them as synonymous. Equally, this may well be the case for Buddhism, Universalists, animists, and so on. Also, only 1% (11 people!) call themselves Muslim here, and we do not know what *kind* of Muslims these are; that is Ethnic, or 'normative' Muslims, or orthodox? Nonetheless, the important thing is that there is *dialogue* and it is promising that the annual American Academy of Religion conference has held a 'Transhumanism and Religion Group' since 2006. Books that make the connection between transhumanism and religion are on the increase, and in August 2005 the *Journal of Evolution and Technology* devoted a special issue to 'Religion and Transhumanism'. There is still very little specifically when we look to Islam, hence the need of this work and, it is hoped, more to come from other Islamic scholars.

I ask you to imagine a large, circular table, seated at which are the current major thinkers on transhumanism. They are brought together to discuss, not so much the technological possibilities of transhumanism, for many of the participants at the table will not have much expertise in that arena, but rather to consider the *impact* of technological transhumanism: what does this reveal about our human nature? What are the moral and ethical considerations? Would the transhuman still be 'human' and, if not, why not? Here we have Nick Bostrom, Aubrey de Grey, Ray Kurzweil, Max More, Natasha Vita-More, Giulio Prisco, Ben Goertzel, and many more of what are largely secular transhumanists. Representing Christianity would be Ted Peters, for Buddhism we have Derek F. Maher, and others representing Judaism, Daoism, Confucianism, Hinduism, Mormonism, and many other religions. Imagine, also, a spokesperson for Islam. *The prime intention of this book, then, is to see what Islam can bring to this 'Transhumanist Table'.*

As I have already pointed out, the dialogue with religion has been going on for some years in the transhumanist scholarly world, and so we should begin by seeing what Islam has contributed so far. Frankly, it has been very little, and what there is would likely as not leave others at the table feeling that the chair could be better utilised. The problem is that when Muslims address issues that arise in transhumanism they do have a tendency to look to Qur'an, hadith, shari'a for answers and, therefore, see Islam as essentially *prescriptive*. If you cannot find guidance in the authoritative texts, then there can be no answer. Further, if you can find guidance in the authoritative texts, then *that* is the answer. For example, the Islamic contribution by Aisha Musa to an anthology entitled *Religion and the Implications of Radical Life Extension* (Maher and Mercer 2009) looks to the Qur'an because 'it is the most authoritative source of knowledge about divine commands relating to life, death, the here, and the hereafter' (Musa 2009, p. 123). Musa, therefore, goes on to say that 'A basic understanding of life and death is clearly articulated in the Qur'an. God predetermines an individual's life span prior to his or her birth' (ibid., p. 124), and then looks to characters such as Noah for 'hints' as to how long that predetermined life span may be.

I want to look at this methodology some more, for it raises important issues as to how we approach the Qur'an; for the Qur'an, as an authority, can be used either to condone or condemn transhumanism depending upon one's understanding of the tradition, and this applies as much to any religious tradition as much as it does to Islam. Let us then consider the quote that refers to Noah: 'We sent Noah out to his people. He lived among them for fifty years short of a thousand but when the Flood overwhelmed them they were still doing evil' (29:14). Therefore, one human being at least, the Prophet Noah (Nuh) lived for at least 950 years. How long Noah lived in total differs from one scholar to the next. The Andalusian Qur'anic commentator al-Qurtubi (c. thirteenth century) notes that these views go from 'only' those 950 years, to a total of 1650 years (Al-Qurtubi 2003). Regardless, we are talking here of a long lifespan indeed, even if it is something of an exception. In terms of how this is interpreted, we can, for example, look to the Islamic scholar Fakhr al-Din al-Razi (1149–1209). Al-Razi continues to be esteemed highly in the Islamic world, especially his great works *Mabahith al-mashriqiyya fi 'ilm al-ilahiyyat wa-'l-tabi'iyyat* (*Eastern Studies in Metaphysics and Physics*) and *al-Matalib al-'Alya* (*The Higher Issues*). Equally important is his commentary on the Qur'an, *Mafatih Al-Ghayb* (*Keys to the Unseen*). Al-Razi is a philosopher who adopted Mu'tazila[1] methodology to some extent, especially with his commentary on the Qur'an where he believed that the interpreter needs to exercise independent reasoning in the struggle to understand its meaning. In relation to the Qur'anic verse concerning Noah's longevity, his following comment is interesting:

> Some physicians say that human life span does not exceed one hundred and twenty years, but the verse indicates the opposite of their statement, and reason agrees. Indeed, survival of the human body is possible; otherwise, he [Noah] would not have survived. ... Their words go against reason and tradition. We say: "There is no dispute between us and them because they say that the natural life span is not greater than one hundred and twenty years, and we say this life span is not natural, rather it is a divine gift." (Ibid., pp. 124–125)

What we can take from al-Razi's commentary on Noah is that he is prepared to accept the possibility of an extended life and, indeed, it is a 'divine gift' rather than seen as an act against God. Other accounts of extended life can also be found in the Qur'an, for example sura 8 which recounts a tale of a group of believers who were seeking refuge from religious persecution. God 'sealed their ears [with sleep] in the cave for years' (8:11) before awakening them. How many years this was is not given, but it can conjure an image of some kind of 'divine cryogenic suspension'. However, in a sense, that is the central point here in that life extension ultimately depends on *divine grace*: the physical aspect of human nature is entirely contingent, and it is the spiritual aspect that is ultimately controlled by God. There are, of course, many references in the Qur'an to God's power to resurrect the dead and, whilst our physical bodies are contingent, for Muslims we are also ensouled, and so we are able to experience spiritual life for an eternity. For the secular transhumanist, of course, there is no 'spiritual' element to concern us; hence, no 'mystical' attach-

---

[1] Briefly and, inevitably, somewhat simplistically, Mu'tazila (or Mu'tazalite) is a theological school of thought dating back to the eighth century. Its methodology referred to here involves the use of analogy and human reason in an effort to determine the meaning of the Qur'an, rather than a strict literalist interpretation.

ment to ageing, but for the Muslim our physical nature is not all that there is and so, it may be suggested, by extending life we are encroaching upon God's power. That may be one way of reading God's power in the Qur'an, whilst another reading may see this as allowing for us to conceive of the possibility of life extension; of, to some extent, 'endorsing' it as a concept. However, I will argue later (see Chap. 5) how problematic it can be in this approach of looking to the Qur'an to 'endorse' scientific exploration.

We might look to the Qur'an for guidance as to whether or not humans *should* go beyond the laws of nature and defeat death: in the Qur'an it states that 'Every soul will taste death' (3:185; 29:57) and 'Death will overtake you no matter where you may be, even inside high towers' (4:78). Eventually, then, we must all face death, but how soon? Are we talking in hundreds of years, or thousands, or millions? The Qur'an as a source is, like all religious texts, subject to ambiguity and various interpretation, so that even references to death may be seen as metaphorical, referring to— not a literal, physical death of the body—but a death of the self and a subsequent spiritual, more knowing and enlightened, renewal, and so we cannot take the Qur'anic references to death at face value, for to do so is to fall into the fundamentalist trap. Similar, anti-realist, interpretations of the Qur'an can be found with reference to life after death and an eternity in heaven or hell. Ahmad Parvez considered the Qur'anic reference to Heaven and Hell as psychological, not literal, and states: 'Heaven (*Jannah*) stands for fruition coupled with glowing home for the future. Hell (*Jahannam*) is the experience of frustration tinged with remorse and regret' (Parvez 2008). Aisha Musa quotes the Dutch Muslim thinker Arnold Yasin Mol who certainly adopts an anti-realist position towards the Qur'an, seeing *Jannah* as a metaphor for the state of evolution of the human and society, rather than any metaphysical phenomenon. Similarly, *Jahannam* is when the individual and society fail to evolve and develop. Mol sees the concept of *Akhira* (the afterlife) in the more concrete way of the next stage in the evolution of the physical universe. Such interpretations of scripture are extremely common in Christianity, and currently less so in Islam, but what I find curious is Musa's conclusion from this: 'Such a radical redefinition of Heaven, Hell, and the Hereafter, if it gained acceptance, could make the sort of practical immortality that might result from RLE acceptable as well' (Musa 2009, p. 128). The idea that RLE (Radical Life Extension) may only be 'acceptable' to Muslims when a sufficient number of them accept a 'radical redefinition' of central concepts of *Jannah*, *Jahannam*, and *Akhira* strikes me as an erroneous conclusion to make. To say that the technology associated with transhumanism is 'acceptable' in this sense is to say that it is okay because the Qur'an—interpreted in some ways anyway—*says* it is okay. This is problematic for a number of reasons, for example there are many Muslims who interpret the Qur'an in a way that would regard transhumanism as unacceptable for Muslims, and so the question then arises as to who has the 'right' interpretation. Musa considers the possibility that a 'wider acceptance' of a particular interpretation along the lines of Parvez and Mol could make RLE acceptable, but by this criterion the majority wins, regardless of whether or not the majority have understood the Qur'an 'correctly'. Such a populist approach to Qur'anic exegesis is dangerous territory, especially today when many people's understanding of the Qur'an derives from tweeted hadiths and other forms of social media. It may be that the 'wider acceptance' applies only to those in the field of Islamic scholarship, but that still leaves the question open as to whether those scholars in the minority are, by definition, failures in their field because of their minority view. As Willem B. Drees says,

> "Islam and science" cannot but be a part of the wider struggle as to which Islamic voices will have the upper hand, schematically a traditional and mainly antimodern version or a more liberal one. Who speaks for the Church? Who speaks for the Muslims, for the Hindus, for the Jews, or for the Buddhists? The definite article in such singulars hides a plurality of voices and opinions. Having science on one's side can be valuable. That is not just the case for liberals and modernizers; quite a few of the orthodox or fundamentalists seek to have science on their side as well. In the controversies over evolution advocates of a creationist understanding of their tradition do not just give up on science; they rather argue that science is misunderstood and dominated by a particular ideology, and that they represent the more genuine scientific spirit, which thus in the long run will be on their side. (Drees 2013, p. 736)

We can 'use' the Qur'an to be on 'our side', whatever that side may be. This is certainly one approach Islam can adopt in its contribution to issues in transhumanism, but seems to me rather misguided and somewhat pointless. The question of whether we should break the laws of nature as they are understood cannot be deemed as answerable by looking to the Qur'an as being a source for what is 'acceptable' or not. However, this is not the same as saying that the Qur'an should be *ignored*. I cannot stress enough how important it is that we question this approach because, surely, we want Islam to be taken *seriously*. As shown, transhumanists are, for the large part, not Muslim and not monotheists; in fact, mostly not religious at all. The concerns that transhumanists raise are important, they raise what it means to be human and the very future of *Homo sapiens*. Also, transhumanists are, with some exceptions, open to debate with non-scientists on these issues. The sad fact is that if all that Islam can bring to the table is to open up the Qur'an because it is, in the words of Musa, 'clearly articulated' in there what we can and cannot do and, further, we have the story of Noah to help us, it is no wonder that transhumanists remain at best sceptical and, at worst, antagonistic towards Islam.

As a *literary device*, therefore, what can the Qur'an tell us about what it means to be human and, by implication, to go beyond the human? The key thesis throughout this work is that Islam provides us with a series of heroic acts and events if you will, that act as paradigms for what it means to be human. Even if one is not a Muslim and does not believe in the Qur'an as divine revelation, the possibility remains that the Qur'an none-theless has something important to contribute to the transhumanist debate. The Muslim believer may well take the accounts of lengthy lifes-pans of characters such as Noah in the Qur'an in a literal sense, or see this as endorsing RLE, but perhaps these are 'myths' in the sense, not as false-hoods, but as stories that help us to understand our human nature and what we can aspire to be. For example, the account of the lengthy lifespan of Noah is, rather, a literary device to make him seem larger than life. The heroes of not only the Qur'an, but the Bible, the Greek and Norse myths, and so on, are seen as strong, healthy, living often incredibly long lives or even immortal, and possessing various super-powers.

There is another anthology, a 'sequel' if you will, by the same editors, called *Transhumanism and the Body* (Mercer and Maher 2014). Again, there is a chapter contribution on the Islamic view, entitled 'God's Deputy: Islam and Transhumanism', in this instance by Hamid Mavani. He begins by citing Abd al-Hakim Murad (aka Timothy Winter) who has argued that the most important issue is not the clash of civilisations or religious funda-mentalism, but the scientific excesses that may lead to the end of the human species as we know it and a new, to use his preferred term, 'posthu-man'. On this, I could not agree more, yet Mavani's opening 'argument' consists of one quote after another from the Qur'an in the literal sense, without pause for hermeneutic reflection, hence 'Each person has been commissioned to actualise the divine purpose: to obey God and to have an intense and profound sense of his cognisance (*ma'rifah*), love Him, and establish an egalitarian and moral-ethical public order without transgressing the boundaries set out by Him' (Mavani 2014, p. 68). Already, in this early paragraph, we have 'boundaries' and the dangers of 'transgression'. Whilst both Mavani and Musa can be seen as bastions against the conservative elements that are fundamentally against transhumanism in *any* form—and for this we should be thankful for their contribution—they, neither of them, go anywhere near far enough, other than to declare, in a reflexive manner, that the Revealed Sources can be read as sanctioning various transhumanist aims, whilst stressing the importance of remaining within certain ethical boundaries. Frankly, you do not need a Muslim to tell you that. Yet another anthology, *Religion and Transhumanism: The Unknown Future of Human Enhancement* (Mercer and Trothen 2014), was published a few months later and which has one of the editors, Calvin Mercer, who edited the previous two works. Yet, it should not be too surprising that in this anthology Islam, in any explicit way, has been left out altogether. In the Introduction to this more recent work, the editors state that 'unfortunately' most of the contributions come from Christianity, but 'We sought out scholars from traditions other than Christianity and are fortunate to offer three chapters from experts in Judaism, East Asian traditions, and Chinese religions' (Mercer and Trothen 2014, p. x). Have we exhausted all that Islam can offer on the subject after just two chapters in two anthologies? Can Islam give anything *more*?

ISLAMIC AUTHORITY AS EXPLORATIVE

Obviously, given I have written this book, the answer to the question of what more Islam can offer is that yes, indeed, it can offer much more. However, for it to do so requires us to understand Islam in a different way from the prescriptive manner that is more commonly adopted. Rather, I subscribe to the Islamic scholar Shahab Ahmed's (1966–2015) approach that, in his own words,

> has presented a historical scenario of significant societies of Muslims who *thought* and *lived* in a manner that destabilises any reflexive conceptualisation we might have of Islam having been constituted by the overweening supremacy of those sources of Revealed Truth that we moderns are intellectually conditioned to regard as primary: the Qur'an, Hadith or Islamic law. … We have seen, rather, that Islamic philosophy *subordinates the Qur'an* to the supremacy of reason—which is to say not merely that the *text* of the

Qur'an is read rationally; rather the *concept* of the Qur'an as the text of divine revelation is contracted and read subject to the demands of a total Truth-matrix elaborated by reason in which reason/philosophy is the higher truth and the text of revelation the lower. (Ahmed 2016, p. 97)

To look at what Islam can contribute we need not restrict ourselves to the Qur'an, but can look to creative and explorative explication for which all too often is ignored, yet they provide so much meaning and value. What, for example, did the Muslim writer and philosopher Ibn Tufayl (1105–1185), through the medium of his novel *Hayy ibn Yaqzan* (which I will explore in much more detail in Chap. 6), have to say about the human condition and what humans can overcome has as much value as the Qur'an or hadith. Similarly, Rumi's (1207–1273) poetry, for which his *Masnavi* is 'a Qur'anic exegesis *by other means*' (Ahmed 2016, p. 307), deserves its place at the table in the discourse with transhumanists, as does other works of poetry, by the likes of Muhammad Iqbal (1877–1938, see Chap. 7). Musa adopts the safe, literal approach of addressing a modern issue by *reflexively* going straight to the Qur'an for answers. My concern with this approach is not, of course, to deny the importance of the 'sources of Revealed Truth', but that the *approach* to these sources is where many modern Muslims have gone astray. As Amir Latif states, '*Tafsir* should be seen both as genre and as process and, regarded in this fashion, studies of Qur'anic interpretation done outside the *tafsir* genre … the study of poetic and creative writings, therefore, deserves a prominent place in the field of Qur'anic interpretations' (Latif 2009, pp. 106–107). By seeing Islam as *prescriptive*, as governed primarily by the law, we are seeing Islam as nothing *more than* law, denying the importance of the discursive tradition of theology, philosophy, poetry, and so on, as important sources of authority:

But can we not conceive of other forms of authority that not only are *not* prescriptive, but that are actually at odds with prescriptive authority? I suggest that, to understand the discursive tradition of Islam, we must conceive not only of prescriptive authority, but of what I should like to call *explorative authority—the authority to explore.* (Ahmed 2016, p. 282)

Ahmed is not plucking this idea of explorative authority out of thin air, but is based on Islam as an historical phenomena in, roughly, the period 1350–1850, in what Ahmed calls the 'Balkans-to-Bengal complex', by which time one could see in the Islamic world a structured community with established constitutions, which included as part of its canon the concepts and vocabularies of philosophers, poets, Sufis, and musicians. Importantly, these are not *marginal* to the Islamic paradigm, but *central*. During this period the translation, circulation, and transposition of philosophical concepts had been integrated into larger modes of thinking, as well as the hermeneutics of Islam. It is only after 1850 we see Islamic reification (see Chap. 4) and a *salafi* inclination to look for a mythical notion of an Islam that was believed to have existed before the fourteenth century. In terms of philosophy, of *falsafah*, it was not long before this discipline was integrated into the Qur'anic-Arabic notion of *hikmah* (in Persian, Ottoman, and Urdu: *hikmat*), which the major Islamic thinker Ibn Sina refers to as '*a real-true* philosophy (*falasafah bi-al-haqiqah*): a *first* philosophy which imparts validation to the principles of the rest of the sciences and that is Wisdom in Real-Truth (*al-hikmah bi-al-haqiqah*)' (Ibn Sina 2005, p. 3). Therefore, 'Revealed Truth' is seen through the lens of the 'Real-Truth'. *Hikmah* has the same semantic roots (*h-k-m*) as *hukm*, or 'rule', and so philosophy, in a Platonic sense, reveals the rules of the universe, as well as determining the ethical rules to live by. Let us not forget that Ibn Sina, like many Islamic thinkers of his time, was a polymath and, in his case, as much a physician as a philosopher, and so the physical sciences work *hand-in-hand with philosophy* in revealing universal truths. This, then, is how the Muslim must approach issues of transhumanism: *not* as Qur'anic scholars, with the Book before us looking for answers, but as philosopher-scientists, as *hukama* (sing. *hakim*).

The Essence of Islam?

An awareness of the complexity and diversity of Islamic belief is key to understanding the relationship between Islam and transhumanism. There are 'many Islams', and no one book can possibly hope to represent all Muslims or all aspects of Islamic teaching. The concern over religion for many transhumanists is based upon a particular understanding of religion that hopes and prays for a better life in the *next life*, or relies upon supernatural forces for a better life in *this life*. Of course, there is no denying that many Muslims, as with other religions, do 'use' religion in this manner, but this is one of many kinds of Muslim. Whilst, as will be considered later, it would be stretching it too far to argue that secularism is central to Islam—despite the existence of 'cultural Muslims' in, as an example, the quote concerning Bosnian Muslims below—this does not mean going to the other extreme of rejecting human autonomy and placing all responsibility on God. There can be something of a 'middle way' which sees religion in a Nietzschean sense; a more 'existential' approach to religion and Islam in particular that does allow for engagement with the transhumanism debate. A commonality between transhumanism and the transcendental is the Latin prefix '*trans*'; a recognition at the very least by both that human beings can go 'beyond'. What that 'beyond' might be is where things become more convoluted, of course.

Given this picture, it is important to tread gently and carefully before making assertions as to what one belief system, philosophical system or scientific system, 'believes' to be the case, especially in this postmodern world of competing and overlapping beliefs, or, to use a metaphor of sociologists, this age of 'liquid modernity', where everything is in a state of continuous change (Bauman 2000). Likewise, to look back in history it is also important to avoid stark contrasts, for things are always more nuanced. Whilst opposing views have often raised themselves above the parapet, what lies beneath may well be subtler. Whilst being so wary, one need only scan the literature to be aware that apparent conflicts are brought to our attention and, further, when looking to the western world, the conflict of ideas, or the 'clash of civilisations', is frequently presented as a sharp contrast between western modernism, globalisation, and postmodernism with that of the Islamic reluctance or downright stubbornness to embrace the modern world. The extent to which this conflict is 'real' or not largely depends on your perspective. There are 'hardliners' on all sides of these perceived clashes who draw strict boundaries as to what the 'west' is, what 'Islam' is, and so forth. At the centre of these perceptions is the role and status of the human being, with subsequent ethical and political concerns regarding the 'essence' of the human, if indeed there is such a thing, and the best political system in which human beings can flourish. It raises very broad questions revolving around authority in terms of that of the divine and the human. In the case of Islam, divine authority through the medium of scripture may or may not take precedence depending upon the views of Islamic scholarship. Amongst some Islamic scholars, Islam in essence is universal and therefore beyond the realm of reform. For example, the scholar Hamid Enayat (1932–1982), to name but one of many, argues that the 'Islamic essence' relies upon idioms which are unchangeable, eternal, and beyond the realm of reform. What takes precedence is the Qur'an as something that is inviolate and perfect; no mere 'whims' of mankind can be so accommodated within the will of God. This, as will be explored, is by no means an exclusive view. Shireen Hunter is one critic of an essentialist, ahistorical culturalism, pointing out that, 'Understanding Islam and analysing its relationships to other ideas and civilisations can be accomplished correctly only within *specific frames of time and space* [my italics]. Any other approach leads to incomplete and hence inaccurate generalities that would represent only one aspect of Islam, not its totality' (Hunter 1998, p. 17). Hunter, looking at Islam from a political perspective, sees the religion encompassing a full range of symbols that can just as much point to absolutism and hierarchy, as towards democracy and egalitarianism. In terms of its attitude towards science, then, one can equally identify 'many Islams' containing a full spectrum of views.

The criticism by transhumanists of religion generally and Islam specifically is based on a particular 'kind' of Islam. Now, this inevitably leads to the question, what, then *is* Islam? Once more, we can look to Shahab Ahmed's excellent work, *What is Islam?*, for an exploration of this contentious issue, but, to summarise here, he successfully picks holes in a number of attempts to define Islam. It has already been noted that to see Islam as prescriptive is to omit so much of what is valuable in terms of what makes us *human*, let alone a Muslim. This prescriptive view of Islam is summed up by Jacques Waardenburg:

> "Normative Islam" is that form of Islam through which Muslims have access to the ultimate norms that are valid for life, actions and thought. ... In classical terms, normative Islam is the *Shari'a*. (Waardenburg 2002, p. 97)

This understanding of Islam is echoed in the writings of various Muslim and non-Muslim scholars, including such luminaries as Wael Hallaq, Joseph Schacht, H.A.R Gibb, G.E. Von Grunebaum, and Ernest Gellner. However, Shahab Ahmed has, in my view, clearly demonstrated that this was not 'normative' at all through most of Islamic history, up until the mid-nineteenth century anyway and, as he states,

> This totalizing "legal-supremacist" conceptualisation of Islam as *law*, whereby the "essence" of Islam is a phenomenon of prescription and proscription, induces, indeed *constrains* us to think of Muslims as subjects who are defined and constituted by and in a cult of regulation, restriction and control. (Ahmed 2016, pp. 119–120)

In line with a number of my scholarly colleagues, I consider Ahmed's work ground-breaking, and which is astounding in its synthesis of Islamic philosophy, history, law, politics, poetry, fiction, and so on. This certainly helps me in paving the way for adopting this approach to how Islam should be perceived. His book on the Satanic Verses affair (Ahmed 2017) reveals a side of Islam that is frequently ignored or denied, an Islam that for centuries considered the Satanic Verses incident—in which the Prophet Muhammad was supposedly deceived by Satan into believing that it was God who told Muhammad to praise the three goddesses Lat, Uzza, and Manat—was true and open to debate, not the defensive and fearful closing of shutters and a refusal to engage in such possibilities which seem more indicative of the modern response that Islam adopts. For Ahmed, Islam is much more than a religion, and so to define what we mean by Islam we have to look at what Muslims *do* and this must include its creative forms, from poetry and music, to art and philosophy.

The *fear* that many Muslims have of breaking away from the shackles of prescribed law, given its authority from the Qur'an and—almost on an equal level—the hadith, prevents Islam from contributing anything dynamic and creative to the transhumanist table. It is perhaps not surprising that modern Islamic discourse is dominated by what the law has to say, for modern humans more generally seem to be increasingly defined as legal entities, as *Homo juridicus*, rather than determined by other authoritative sources. By seeing ourselves this way it becomes a self-fulfilling prophecy; we are unable to see the human in any other way. If, however, what is Islam is not—or *should* not—be defined by *shari'a*, then what? The *shahada* (the declaration of belief in one God and Muhammad as the seal of the prophets) may provide a basic framework, but when you attempt to unpack it, we are left with a series of complex, philosophical, and theological concepts that only result in obscuring what we mean by Islam: what do we understand by God? In what way is the Prophet the 'seal'? Without elaborating here, Andrew Rippin (1950–2016), for example, has demonstrated that each of the Five Pillars of Islamic faith raises problems in terms of their origins and how they are to be understood (see Rippin 2018, Chap. 7).

The *Cambridge History of Islam* states that, 'Islam is a religion. It is also, almost inseparably from this, a community, a civilisation and a culture' (Gardet 1970, p. 569). However, these seemingly innocent opening lines are deeply problematic conceptually. To what extent is the religion separable from community, civilisation, and culture, given that Gardet says it is 'almost inseparable', and what would remain if it is separated?

What do we mean by culture and how is this different from the religion? What do we mean by 'civilisation' and how is this different from culture or religion? Ditto the concept of 'community'! The historian of Islam Marshall Hodgson (1922–1968) gives us his renowned distinction between 'Islamic' as referring to faith or religion, contrasted with 'Islamdom' or 'Islamicate' which he regarded as its historic culture and society. Shahab Ahmed spills considerable ink on Hodgson, rightly so, but the central point is that, 'In order to function, Hodgson's schema, like any sliding scale, requires an independent unit of measure: to distinguish Islamic from Islamicate, we have to know what religion=Islam is and how to gauge its presence' (Ahmed 2016, p. 160). Needless to say, we do not seem to have an 'independent unit of measure'. Indeed, this attempt to separate a kind of 'pure' Islam from its historical, social, and culture accretions falls into the very hands of the fundamentalists as well as those proponents of a clash of civilisations thesis. It ignores the important contribution that other cultures, religions, and philosophies have made to what we now call 'Islam', which is why this book makes no excuses for tapping into those 'other' cultures, for they not as 'other' as might be supposed. As Shahab Ahmed parenthetically says (and I agree entirely): 'human and historical Islam is arguably almost as Neo-Platonic as it is Muhammadan' (Ahmed 2016, p. 173). Hodgson's distinction between Islamic and Islamicate certainly has some value; for example in describing Moses Maimonides (c. 1135–1204) as 'Islamicate' rather than 'Islamic' I get what he means, for I also make reference to Maimonides in this work as an important contributor to Islamic thought. Maimonides was brought up and educated in an Islamic environment and his philosophy is imbued with Islamic concepts, but he is not an 'Islamic' thinker in the sense that he was Jewish, although, in fact, he combined his Jewish philosophy with that of Islam. As Sarah Stroumsa said when writing on Jewish theology, 'The development of Jewish systematic theology takes places under Islam and mostly in Arabic. ... As Arabic came to replace Hebrew and Aramaic as the main cultural language of the Jews, the intellectual activity of eastern Jews became an integral part of the intellectual Islamic scene' (Stroumsa 2003, p. 73), and, as Sarah Pessin points out in relation to Maimonides' work *Guide for the Perplexed*, 'As is clear from the representative quotes from Islamic sources cited throughout ... understanding the Islamic philosophical context of the Guide is key for understanding the intricacies of Maimonides' thought' (Pessin 2014).

However, this does not resolve the problem of what exactly do we mean by 'Islamic' in any pure sense of the term. The history of the discipline of Religious Studies shows us that it is difficult enough to define what we mean by 'religion'! In the case of Islam, there is no one all-encompassing authority, such as the Pope in Catholicism,[2] that can lay down decrees as to what is 'Islamic' and what is not and so, inevitably, we have individuals and groups that look to a number of authoritative sources for guidance. Perhaps for this reason, it makes no sense to talk of a 'reformation' in Islam, because it is in its very nature to always be in a process of reform as the various conflicting bodies struggle for their supremacy of ideas in values in a Nietzschean will to power kind of way. The trouble is, we seem no nearer to knowing what Islam is, and perhaps we are led to the conclusions of Hamid Dabashi:

> We need to relieve a view of the vast and diversified Islamic heritage that is irreducible to Islamic *doctrinal* beliefs. … Positing Islam as a cosmopolitan worldliness … will have a conclusively transformative impact on the way we ordinarily think of the terms "Islam" or "Islamic". (Dabashi 2013, pp. 13–14)

Perhaps, but I am not convinced this really helps us to understand what Islam or a Muslim is, any more than I really know what someone who has an outlook of 'cosmopolitan worldliness' would actually *believe*. And, as I have already pointed out, even the basic doctrinal beliefs that are attributed to Islam are open to much dispute and interpretation. It is unavoidable that in using terms such as 'religion', 'science', 'Islam', 'secular', and so on, we are creating boundaries that are, in reality, blurred. As will become evident in this work, we are trapped by our vocabulary; striving to explain the paradox and complexity that is the human experience with words that fail us. I must, however reluctantly, be also compelled to use labels, but always with the proviso that these are labels of convenience rather than to be strictly defining. For example, I make no apologies for employing the insights of so-called 'western' philosophers to inform the debate on what 'Islam' can contribute to transhumanism. Note here the need to use the terms 'western' and 'Islam' which, in itself, suggests that they are two separate and distinct systems of thought. They are not. Islam,

---

[2] This may apply less to Shi'a Islam than Sunni, which really just emphasises my point that there are 'many Islams'. I do, incidentally, tap into Shi'a Islam, Sunni Islam, and Sufism (and not may be Shi'a or Sunni) throughout this book.

for its part, would not be recognisable today if it were not for the influence of Greek philosophy, for example, and, likewise, 'western' thought owes much to Islam, ancient Greek thought to 'eastern' philosophy and religion, and so on. This is why I prefer to use the term '*hikmah*' as a kind of Islamic *Weltanschauung*, for there is a saying attributed to the Prophet, 'Hikmah is the believer's straying camel; he takes it from wherever he may find it; and does not care from what vessel it has issued' (Arberry 1956, p. 34). This magpie-like accretion of knowledge from whatever source and making it your own is typical of Islam, as with many other belief-systems, and flies against this idea of a *salafi* 'pure Islam'. There are always tensions, of course, yet, at the same time, in the *hikmah* tradition, it is Aristotle who is known as the 'First Teacher', and there is also the 'Divine Plato' (*Aflatun-i ilahi*). The non-Islamic philosophical tradition likewise 'uses' Muslim philosophers, preferring to Latinise their names; to refer to Ibn Sina as Avicenna, or Ibn Rushd as Averroes. Such an adoption perhaps makes these Islamic philosophers less 'Islamic' in the sense of being more 'global'. Islam, for its part, does the same, hence Aristotle is Aristu, Plato is Aflatun, Galen is Jalinus, and so on. These philosophers, in being acquired in this way, become 'Islamic' in the sense that, for example, Musa is an Islamic prophet and, in some ways, different from Moses, or Isa differs from Jesus. The difference, however, is that the prophets would be considered as 'Muslims', whereas the philosophers are not Muslims, but they are Islamic. This cannot be stressed enough, for Islamic philosophers of the past have often been accused of merely 'copying', or even stealing, the philosophical views of the Greeks, but it is really the Islamisation of knowledge, which is not the same thing at all. Ibn Rushd's 'Aristotelian' philosophy is not the philosophy of Aristotle, but the philosophy of Aristu.

Let us then see what Islam can contribute to the transhumanist table in its *explorative* sense. We may have a copy of the Qur'an on the table, but also Rumi's *Masnavi*, Muhammad Iqbal's poetry and philosophy, Ibn Tufayl's philosophical fiction, Maimonides' *Guide for the Perplexed*, Ibn Rushd's commentary on Aristotle/Aristu, the writing of Muslim scientists such as Mehdi Golshani, Mohammed Basil Altaie, Bruno Guiderdoni, Nidhal Guessoum, and so on. Here we will see that Islam does not *prescribe*, it does not say what is forbidden and what is allowed, but it *reveals*, through its generations of creativity, what it means to be human and, as a consequence, what it means to be transhuman.

Bibliography[3]

Books

Ahmed, Shahab. 2016. *What Is Islam? The Importance of Being Islamic.* Princeton and Oxford: Princeton University Press.
———. 2017. *Before Orthodoxy: The Satanic Verses in Early Islam.* Cambridge, MA: Harvard University Press.
Arberry, A.J. 1956. *Revelation and Reason in Islam.* London: George Allen & Unwin.
Bauman, Zygmunt. 2000. *Liquid Modernity.* London: Polity Press.
Dabashi, Hamid. 2013. *Being a Muslim in the World.* New York: Palgrave Macmillan.
Fuller, Steve, and Veronika Lipinska. 2014. *The Proactionary Imperative: A Foundation for Transhumanism.* Hampshire: Palgrave.
Hadot, Pierre. 1995. *Philosophy as a Way of Life: Spiritual Exercises from Socrates to Foucault.* Oxford: Wiley-Blackwell.
Hunter, Shireen T. 1998. *The Future of Islam and the West.* Washington, DC: The Centre for Strategic and International Studies.
Ibn Sina. 2005. *The Metaphysics of the Healing.* 2nd ed. Translated by Michael E. Marmura. Chicago: University of Chicago Press.
Istvan, Zoltan. 2013. *The Transhumanist Wager.* Nevada: Futurity Imagine Media LLC.
Kurtz, Paul. 2012. *Meaning and Value in a Secular Age: Why Eupraxsophy Matters – The Writings of Paul Kurtz.* Edited by Nathan Bupp. London: Prometheus Books.
Maher, Derek F., and Calvin Mercer, eds. 2009. *Religion and the Implications of Radical Life Extension.* New York: Palgrave Macmillan.
Mercer, Calvin, and Derek F. Maher, eds. 2014. *Transhumanism and the Body: The World Religions Speak.* New York: Palgrave Macmillan.
Mercer, Calvin, and Tracy Trothen, eds. 2014. *Religion and Transhumanism: The Unknown Future of Human Enhancement.* Santa Barbara, CA: Praeger.
Murnane, Ben. 2018. *Ayn Rand and the Posthuman: The Mind-Made Future.* New York: Palgrave Macmillan.
Parvez, G.A. 2008. *Islam: A Challenge to Religion.* Lahore: Talou-e-Islam Trust.
al-Qurtubi, Abu 'Abdullah Muhammad. 2003. *Tafsir al-Qurtubi.* Vol. 1. London: Dar al-Taqwa.
Rippin, Andrew. 2018. *Muslims: Their Religious Beliefs and Practices.* 5th ed. Oxon: Routledge.
Waardenburg, Jacques. 2002. *Islam: Historical, Social and Political Perspectives.* Berlin: Walter de Gruyter.
Young, Simon S. 2005. *Designer Evolution: A Transhumanist Manifesto.* New York: Prometheus Books.

---

[3] *Note*: All quotes from the Qur'an are from the translation by M.A.S. Abdel Haleem, Oxford University Press, 2005.

JOURNAL ARTICLES AND BOOK CHAPTERS

Campbell, Heidi, and Mark Walker. 2005. Religion and Transhumanism: Introducing a Conversation. *Journal of Evolution and Technology* 14 (2): i–xiv.

Drees, Willem B. 2013. Islam and Bioethics in the Context of 'Religion and Science'. *Zygon* 48 (3): 732–744.

Gardet, Louis. 1970. Religion and Culture. In *The Cambridge History of Islam, Volume 2B: Islamic Society and Civilisation*, ed. P.M. Holt, Ann K.S. Lambton, and Bernard Lewis, 569–603. Cambridge: Cambridge University Press.

Latif, Amer. 2009. *Qur'anic Narratives and Sufi Hermeneutics: Rumi's Interpretation of Pharaoh's Character*. PhD Dissertation. New York: Stony Brook University.

Mavani, Hamid. 2014. God's Deputy: Islam and Transhumanism. In *Transhumanism and the Body: The World Religions Speak*, ed. Calvin Mercer and Derek F. Maher, 67–84. New York: Palgrave Macmillan.

Minsky, Marvin. 2013. Why Freud Was the First Good AI Theorist. In *The Transhumanist Reader*, ed. Max More and Natasha Vita-More, 167–176. Chichester: Wiley-Blackwell.

More, Max. 2013. The Philosophy of Transhumanism. In *The Transhumanist Reader*, ed. M. More and N. Vita-More. Chichester, West Sussex: Wiley-Blackwell.

More, Max, and Natasha Vita-More. 2013. Roots and Core Themes. In *The Transhumanist Reader*, ed. Max More and Natasha Vita-More. Vols. 1–2. Chichester: Wiley-Blackwell.

Musa, Aisha Y. 2009. A Thousand Years, Less Fifty: Toward a Quranic View of Extreme Longevity. In *Religion and the Implications of Radical Life Extension*, ed. Derek F. Mhaer and Calvin Mercer, 123–131. New York: Palgrave Macmillan.

Peters, Ted. 2011. Transhumanism and the Posthuman Future: Will Technological Progress Get Us There? In *H+/−: Transhumanism and Its Critics*, ed. Gregory R. Hansell and William Grassie, 147–175. Philadelphia, PA: Metanexus Institute.

Prisco, Giulio. 2013. Transcendent Engineering. In *The Transhumanist Reader*, ed. Max More and Natasha Vita-More, 234–240. Chichester: Wiley-Blackwell.

Stroumsa, Sarah. 2003. Saadya and Jewish Kalam. In *The Cambridge Companion to Medieval Jewish Philosophy*, ed. Daniel H. Frank and Oliver Leaman, 71–90. Cambridge: Cambridge University Press.

Vita-More, Natasha. 2013. Aesthetics: Bringing the Arts & Design into the Discussion of Transhumanism. In *The Transhumanist Reader*, ed. Max More and Natasha Vita-More, 18–27. Chichester: Wiley-Blackwell.

WEBSITES

Bostrom, Nick. 2002. Transhumanist Values. Accessed July 26, 2019. http://www.nickbostrom.com/ethics/values.html.

Hughes, James J. 2007. *The Compatibility of Religious and Transhumanist Views of Metaphysics, Suffering, Virtue and Transcendence in an Enhanced Future.* Institute for Ethics and Emerging Technologies. Accessed July 26, 2019. http://ieet.org/archive/20070326-Hughes-ASU-H+Religion.pdf.

Pessin, Sarah. 2014. The Influence of Islamic Thought on Maimonides. In *The Stanford Encyclopaedia of Philosophy.* First published Thu Jun 30, 2005; Substantive Revision, Wed May 28, 2014. Accessed June 7, 2018. https://plato.stanford.edu/entries/maimonides-islamic/.

CHAPTER 3

Secular Transhumanism as Scientism?

Whilst acknowledging that there are many strands to the bow of transhumanism, the concern with this work is with its more secular form, in particular the fact that it denies the possibility of any contribution that religion can make to the issues that arise from transhumanism. The dangers of this attitude are obvious, for it inevitably results in divisiveness that can only lead to misunderstandings and conflict. Rather than a dualistic picture of 'religion versus science', we have three seemingly diverse ways of thought that, at times, work together, at other times are hostile: religion, science, *and* philosophy. All three have themselves to blame to some extent, creating their own boundaries for which no aliens shall cross. In terms of the disjunction between science and religion, the Indian-born physicist Rustum Roy (1924–2010) provides a good illustration:

> Every major religion has within its followers a segment of dogmatically committed fundamentalists, supported by a distorted interpretation of its theology. Fundamentalism affirms that only their beliefs—often coded in a written text rather than oral traditions—are true. On a small planet with an ineluctably polymorphous cast, now forced by technological developments to interact with each other, all fundamentalisms are dangerous, and the more powerful, the more dangerous. Science-and-technology is the most powerful force under human control; hence, scientific fundamentalism is the most dangerous. (Roy 2005, p. 836)

© The Author(s) 2020
R. Jackson, *Muslim and Supermuslim*, Palgrave Studies
in the Future of Humanity and its Successors,
https://doi.org/10.1007/978-3-030-37093-0_3

Therefore, not only does religion have its 'fundamentalist' element, but so does science. Likewise, philosophy on occasion likes to have its own boundaries. Bernard Williams (2006) has argued that philosophy is a humanistic discipline that is unique in that it tries to make sense of ourselves and our place within the world, whereas the realm of science is concerned with the world in itself, with a 'view from nowhere' to use that well-worn Thomas Nagel (Nagel 1986, p. 70) phrase. Williams' views here are interesting because, whilst to a large extent representative of the analytic tradition in philosophy and, therefore, one might expect him to see philosophy as a bedfellow of science, he is asserting the independence of philosophy from science. In other words, philosophy is a *contrast* with scientism, not a discipline that shares its seeming 'intellectual authority' (Williams 2006, p. 188). Philosophy is humanistic in a sense that the sciences are not, for science gives us a picture of the universe that would be the same whatever species has the sufficient intelligence to determine it, whereas the same cannot be said for what it means to be human; only *humans* necessarily can do that.

Building boundaries around Islam, that is its 'reification', which will be the primary focus of the next chapter, is an example of attempts to 'rationalise' religion. That is, to show that religion does not need science or any other form of thought. It is self-contained and can be understood in its entirety. This concept of religion is far removed from the mysterious, paradoxical belief by, for example, Søren Kierkegaard (1813–1855). Rather, what we have is an 'onto-theology' which, as Martin Heidegger (1889–1976) understood it, is utilising God for our own purposes and design, rather than God as something *beyond* our thought. Onto-theology, therefore, is much more than a matter of theology, but is a concern for a metaphysical grounding in a more general sense. In Derridean terms this is his 'metaphysics of presence', and, indeed, Jacque Derrida (1930–2004) is an important critic of onto-theology, but less in the 'theological' understanding and more in the non-religious way, which is why some scholars adapt the term as 'onto-theo-logy': hence, onto (being), theo (highest), and logy (thought), or the 'highest thought of being'. In the context of secular transhumanism, we have here a non-religious example of onto-theology (or, if you prefer, onto-theo-logy) as a form of scientism. The accusation made against scientism by various philosophers and theologians is that it still represents a desire for ground, and that it sets out to present a worldview that supports the adherents of that worldview, rather than be open to other possibilities. Scientism sets out to be the master of the world through the power of science and reason and so, in this way, it does not differ in its intention from religious onto-theology, for they are both intent on manipulating the world to serve their own purposes which can be seen as an 'epistemological violence'.

Is such an accusation against scientism a fair one to make and, if it is, does secular transhumanism fall into this category? In terms of how this relates to Islamic thought there are two major considerations here. First of all, there is the question of how 'scientific' Islam is. This will be explored in considerably more detail later on in this book, but, for the moment, it needs to be kept in mind that I am not wishing to present a picture of Islam versus science, as if these are two opposing world-views. As will be demonstrated, Islam as an intellectual tradition is not, by any stretch of the imagination, averse to scientific thought and progress although, at the same time, there have been in the past, and continues to be so today, some serious tensions, and we need to consider why these tensions exist and how justified they are. Secondly, just how all-inclusive is science anyway? That is to say, does science have all the answers or, at least, have answers to the things that matter? This second question is key to what we understand by the accusation of scientism: that it is guilty of hubris, of a belief that there are no other forms of knowledge that really count as 'knowledge'.

Yuval Noah Harari has made this interesting observation about us *Homo sapiens*:

> Legends, myths, gods and religions appeared for the first time with the Cognitive Revolution. Many animals and human species could previously say, "Careful! A lion!" Thanks to the Cognitive Revolution, *Homo sapiens* acquired the ability to say, "The lion is the guardian spirit of our tribe". This ability to speak about fictions is the most unique feature of *Sapiens* language. (Harari 2011, p. 27)

Importantly, Harari is not limiting these 'fictions' to religions, but also includes public limited companies as a fiction, using the 'Legend of Peugeot' (Harari 2011, p. 28) as an example of a 'body' that unites people under a common goal, yet does not 'exist' as such. Likewise, our moral system, our belief in human rights, is another such 'imagined reality', hence we live in a 'dual reality' of 'the objective reality of rivers, trees and lions; and … the imagined reality of gods, nations and corporations' (Harari 2011, p. 36). One would presumably class science as dealing with the objective, whilst 'non-science' is concerned with the 'imagined'. If this is how we understand this epistemological duality, then Rustum Roy's quote above, equating 'science-and-technology' with religious fundamentalism, seems inaccurate or, at best, misleading, for whilst indeed science is a very powerful force today, the 'fundamentalist' tag seems to be stretching the analogy too far.

However, accepting a duality, and leaving aside for the moment whether one can say which side of this duality is 'better' than the other, this at least means that science does not have the answers to *everything*. Philosophically, this is pointed out by the empirical philosopher David Hume's (1711–1776) famous claim that you cannot derive an 'ought' (moral premises) from an 'is' (non-moral premises), which suggests that morals cannot be derived from reason (Hume 1978, 3.1.1). Science, therefore, has nothing to offer for what must surely be one of the most important facets of being human, and presumably would still be important for the transhuman, and that is fundamental moral questions; how we *ought* to live our lives.

There are a variety of responses to this. Perhaps the most extreme view is to simply declare that as morality is not objective, it is therefore meaningless. However, to regard our moral viewpoint, and those defenders of human rights, as 'meaningless' seems to jar with our perception of the world and the human place within it: certain human acts *are* evil, and we want to declare them as evil in a way that is meaningful. This is not the same as saying an act is *objectively* evil, or good, but it is also not the same as saying it has no meaning in the sense of having 'value'. This gets down to the crux of the matter when we go back to Harari's 'duality of realities', for he acknowledges just how important imagined realities are for *Homo sapiens* and, without getting into the detailed arguments here, we would not have thrived—or perhaps even survived—as a species without them.

So moral rules are important and are not, in this sense, 'meaningless' or 'illegitimate'. However, another, much stronger, response is to side with Hume when he stresses that science *alone* cannot provide us with a moral code, but this is not the same as saying that science cannot contribute in some, or even in a big, way. For this book, this argument is extremely important in terms of the aim to break away from such dualities; to look, in a Nietzschean sense, *beyond* faith and reason. As the philosopher Stephen Law notes:

> Science remains capable of playing an important role in justifying and challenging many moral beliefs, most obviously those whose justification depends in part upon empirical assumptions. If I believe women ought not

to have the vote because I believe both that people of low intelligence ought not to have the vote and that women are of low intelligence, then my justification can be straightforwardly shown to fail by scientific evidence that women are not of low intelligence. (Law 2017, p. 123)

And, indeed, it may well be that, in the future, science can discover more about our moral sense as we learn more about human nature. In fact, some would go so far as to argue that science can have a much greater hegemony over moral beliefs and not just a supporting role. Sam Harris' book *The Moral Landscape* (2010) reveals its intentions in its subtitle *How Science Can Determine Human Values.* Harris argues that there is nothing special about morality in terms of knowledge and, therefore, science will, in time, reveal how we ought to live. In fact, science already knows a sufficient amount about neuroscience to be able to make moral assertions. It's an interesting argument that is critical of moral relativism, for if morality can be determined by science—in the same way science can determine other objective facts about the world—then, following Harris' logic, there is no such thing as Muslim morality, in the same way there is no such thing as Muslim algebra; there is just algebra!

Harris' argument is problematic on a number of levels, not least is that his somewhat Aristotelian concept of wellbeing as flourishing is itself subjective. Whilst certainly an interesting argument, such writers as David Eagleman and Oliver Sacks appreciate that to determine what a good human is requires a 'story' of a person's inner being, intentions, and desires, and here we are back to our 'imagined reality' again, whereas Harris relies on empirical data. Some might well argue for another option, of course, which is to state that even if science cannot contribute to moral values, then religion cannot contribute anything either: given that morality is relative, then it all comes down to one person's or group's opinion on the matter. This, however, strikes me as foolishly and naively dismissive of thousands of years of religious endeavour in the search for human wellbeing. It does typify a new atheist attitude towards religion as having had its time (and, for the new atheist, what an awful, barbaric time that was), and as an irrelevancy for the modern age. Let me stress: whether religious traditions actually reveal a 'Truth' (in the objective sense) or not is not really an issue I am concerned with here, but rather whether religious traditions, even if they are 'imagined realities', help us to understand what we are as human beings, and surely religious tradition can contribute here, in the same way many other 'imagined realities' can?

Bernard Williams' view that philosophy sits outside the scientific arena is not really that damaging for secular transhumanism. As we have seen from some definitions given earlier, the transhumanists are not averse to defining themselves as interdisciplinary and as a series of 'philosophies'. Therefore, whilst driven to a great extent by scientific innovation, it does not leave aside the philosophical issues that arise from such technology. In this respect, surely we can assert that transhumanism cannot be accused of 'scientism', unless it is shown that transhumanism *assimilates* philosophy to the aims of the sciences. If we are talking of assimilation rather than cooperation, then this is where Williams is right to assert that philosophy is not a part of the goal of scientism. The English philosopher Simon Blackburn defines scientism as, 'the belief that the methods of natural science, or the categories and things recognized in natural science, form the only proper elements in any philosophical or other enquiry' (Blackburn 1996, p. 344). However, this definition suffers to some extent because 'natural science' is not by any means a fixed system for it has changed over time and will continue to do so, whereas the American analytic philosopher William Quine's (1908–2000) definition is that the only point of view that philosophy can offer is 'the point of view of our own science' (Quine 1981, p. 182) by which he means our *present* science. This, too, seems unsatisfactory, for Quine sees philosophy's task to *react* to science by helping to clarify and explain it. This, perhaps, puts too much onus upon the philosopher to do a job that scientists are far more qualified to do.

More significantly is this assertion that philosophy is one thing and science is another. Going back to Williams, by defining philosophy in the way he does, Williams is also limiting it, for if philosophy were to make any declarations that are objective, then this must be 'science' and not philosophy. Yet, are we right to say that science describes the world as it *actually* is? As the philosopher Michael Dummett asserts, 'science is in large part an attempt to answer [the question] what things are like in themselves, as opposed to how they appear to us' (Dummett 2010, p. 43). Is such a dichotomy justified? This notion seems outdated to us; a relic of the Aristotelian age that has, since the time of Galileo, been renounced. Science, therefore, does not give an account of the world as it is *in itself* but, at best, describes phenomenal properties of the world in a Kantian sense. As already granted, our moral values are not independent of scientific discoveries in the sense that we may well adjust our moral outlook according to what science reveals about the world, but this does not just work in one direction. Not only can values be affected by 'facts', but 'facts' can be affected by values. However hard we try, we cannot 'step out' of ourselves, for human beings, by their very nature, are not objective automatons. In all our actions we are guided by a set of values, and this does not exclude entirely the scientific hypotheses about the world.

Whilst I am sceptical concerning a great deal of what the contentious biologist Rupert Sheldrake[1] has to say concerning what science can do in the future, he does also make some decent observations concerning science as it currently exists, for example he states that 'the very idea of a *law* of nature is anthropocentric. Only humans have laws' (Sheldrake 2012, p. 84). The point being made here is that humans *value* laws, and the view that there are eternal laws has its origins in the belief in a God as an eternal law giver. Yet there is really no reason to be certain that the universe does operate according to eternal laws and, leaving aside Sheldrake's views, the idea that the laws of the universe have evolved in the same way the universe itself has evolved is gaining more ground in the scientific community. As Albert Einstein once said, reading the laws of physics is like reading the mind of God. But can God *change* his mind? Scientists seem more open to the varying of numerical constants than they are to the possibility of changes to the laws of physics themselves, but theoretical physics does seem to be recently producing increasingly bizarre theories which is leading some scientists, admittedly a small minority (e.g. Stuart Kauffman, Lee Smolin, and Andreas Albrecht), to doubt the immutability of physical laws.

Perhaps the quest for eternal laws tells us more about *ourselves* than it does about the universe: the fact that human beings look for order and patterns. Plato displayed this awareness that human beings strive towards perfection, but this is constantly derailed by the need to survive, and by the harsh and unforgiving nature of our environments. As Plato states, 'the decoration of the heavens should be used as paradigms, to help with the learning that leads to those other objects; it's just as if we happened to come across diagrams exquisitely painted and worked by Daedalus, or some other craftsman or painter' (Plato 2012, 529a–520a), while also acknowledging that such patterns may never be possible to recreate on Earth. The human here is humbled when confronted with the struggle for perfection, and this led Plato to suppose that there is such a thing as

---

[1] Academically speaking, Sheldrake is extremely well-qualified in biological science and his ideas have appeared in a number of prominent scientific publications, but his interest in Indian philosophy especially, which has impacted upon his scientific views, has drawn considerable criticism from the scientific community.

perfection. Swapping the 'is-ought' to 'ought-is', we might wonder if just because we *ought* to seek perfection (if, indeed, this is a given, which is debatable), it follows that there *is* perfection. The nature writer Richard Mabey provides an instructive and illuminating example of what, it seems, nature can 'reveal':

> The big oak at the end of our Norfolk garden is a kind of coda, a flourish of contrapuntal woodiness that says decisively: cultivation ends here. [...] It was a long time before I could bring myself to do anything as mundane as put a tape measure round its trunk. [...] Working my way round the trunk, I could see that the main side branches [...] were at right angles to each other, and all left the trunk at close to forty-five degrees to the vertical. Some way along each of these slanting ribs, secondary branches sprung out horizontally, at forty-five degrees below the supporting branch. And so it went on to the outermost twigs, an alternation of upward and downward forty-five degree divisions. [...] Of all the oaks in all of Norfolk I seemed to have the one designed by Pythagoras.
>
> If I had more of a surveyor's skills and temperament. [...] I might have found that the numbers of main branches followed the Golden Ratio, with five in the lowest layer, three in the next, two at the top. This is a proportion found throughout nature, in the spiral form of tornadoes and the efflorescent growth of crystals just as much as in the organic world. (Mabey 2015, pp. 95–96)

In the same way, Plato looks to the human struggling to seek this perceived cosmic perfection, and Mabey goes on to say,

> Yet in the real world these are only ever ideal models, approximations to a pattern. Living plants are subject to unquantifiable and unpredictable stresses. They're bent in the wind, raddled by fungus, shaded by their neighbours. Every Platonic pure intention is overthrown by the realities of life, which is not to achieve perfect form but to survive. (ibid., p. 97)

These observations may well support the view that science does indeed reveal 'paradigms', but it is not to be argued here that the universe does *not* display order and law but, rather, two important points. Firstly, the fact that there are laws at present does not, in true Humean empirical fashion, mean that those laws were the same in the past or will continue to hold in the future. In this respect, it may be overly ambitious for scientists to hope for a unifying 'theory of everything' and, in fact, to be fair to the scientific community, many would not subscribe to this anyway. Secondly, and more importantly here, even if the human has 'revealed' the laws of the universe as they currently are, the 'are' here is still from a *human perspective at this moment in time*. As already stated, science is crossing new boundaries all the time, and our future understanding of the universe may require a paradigm shift that is more profound than changing numerical constants but, the stronger point here, is that this is still nonetheless from a human perspective. Human beings see the world in a human way: a way that is different from how other creatures on this planet see the world. As Immanuel Kant (1724–1804) points out, our knowledge is something 'which is peculiar to us, and which therefore does not necessarily pertain to every being, though to be sure it pertains to every human being' (Kant 1998, A42/B59) and, as reiterated by the philosophical novelist and creator of 'imagined realities' Italo Calvino (1923–1985), science may make 'efforts to escape from anthropomorphic knowledge', but our 'imagination cannot be anything but anthropomorphic' (Calvino 1988, p. 90).

Returning to Bernard Williams' assertion that philosophy differs from science because the latter describes the world 'as it is in itself', we have no reason to suppose science really can do this. At best, it can give us a human picture of the world as it is currently understood. An alien creature, with different senses and facilities from the human, may well perceive the cosmos as very different from how humans perceive it. In this way, science is as much a humanities discipline, not separate from it. As noted by the analytic philosopher of language Carlo Cellucci,

> Philosophy is not essentially different from the sciences, on the contrary, it is akin to them, being an inquiry which aims at acquiring knowledge about the world, including ourselves. In carrying out such inquiry, philosophy may even give birth to new sciences. (Cellucci 2015, p. 268)

Cellucci and Williams, when using the term 'philosophy' here, are limiting themselves to a discipline as understood as exclusive to the 'western' world, given that the philosophers they cite—Kant, Husserl, Quine, and so on.—are all part of this 'western tradition', but I am including Islamic thought as 'philosophical'; that is, as being able to engage in philosophical discourse that is equal to any discourse engaged in by western philosophers. In fact, I try to resist, as best as I can, this 'east-west' dichotomy entirely, for it is a false one. To create a dichotomy is to underplay the interaction of thought that has taken place between the Islamic and non-Islamic civilisations. Granted, as we shall see, there are tensions that exist between philosophy, theology, and law within the Islamic tradition, but that does not deny the existence of a philosophical tradition. The word 'philosophy' does, of course, derive from the ancient Greek '*philosophia*', meaning 'love of wisdom', and so the Greek origins for this discipline is acknowledged here and debt duly noted, although even then this excludes, for example, Hinduism and Buddhism from 'philosophy' if understood in this way, which seems somewhat unjust and irrationally western-centric. The difference between Islamic philosophy and that of the philosophy of Hinduism and Buddhism is the former does more directly derive from the Greek tradition. Hence, Islamic philosophers such as Ibn Sina, Ibn Rushd, and so on, refer to Greek philosophy as their 'compass' and methodological scaffolding. For this reason, the 'foreign' science of philosophy (*falsafah*) is considered less 'Islamic' than the sciences of theology (*kalam*), jurisprudence (*fiqh*), and law (*sharia*), hence this tension between what is perceived as the inclusive and the foreign, although this is often alleviated by the well-known, frequently-quoted hadith 'pursue knowledge even to China, for its pursuance is the sacred duty of every Muslim'.

Leaving aside the derivation, philosophy *today*, whether it is of a secular nature, Islamic, Hindu, Buddhist, Christian, and so on, all borrow from each other and are all addressing the same questions such as what can we know for sure, what does it mean to be good, is there a mind that is separate from the body, and so on. Some Islamic traditionalists, as we shall see, may well try to argue that Islam is (or can be) entirely self-contained and, therefore, does not need to 'borrow' its knowledge from elsewhere, but, as hopefully will be demonstrated, this is nothing less than damaging, if not fatal, for Islamic intellectual thought. Like religion, philosophy is incredibly diverse in its methodology and what it prioritises with, perhaps, the contrast that exists between the analytic and continental traditions although, even here, this contrast is not always so stark, with a number of philosophers diluting these boundaries and, of course, the analytic/continental distinction is a relatively recent one, considering the long history of philosophy, and does not always help us when looking to philosophers before the twentieth century. To what extent, for example, would Kant be considered an analytic philosopher, or at least a forerunner? In this work I adopt an all-embracing approach to the philosophical tradition that blurs the lines not only between the analytic and the continental but also between philosophy and religion. Even if we wish to limit ourselves to philosophy in the 'western' sense as being but a series of footnotes to Plato, as the British philosopher A.N. Whitehead (1861–1947) famously declared, then it is worthwhile stressing that for Plato and other philosophers of that period, 'there was no separate word for religion. Spirits, gods and demi-gods were believed to be everywhere and in everything' (Hughes 2010, p. 27).

The scientific view of the world that has become dominant is as reified as some religious dogmas, if not more so. To that extent, it is fair to assert that science is a religion of its own. As the naturalist philosopher John Searle states:

> There is a sense in which materialism is the religion of our time, at least among most of the professional experts in the fields of philosophy, psychology, cognitive science, and other disciplines that study the mind. Like more traditional religions, it is accepted without question and it provides the framework within which other questions can be posed, addressed and answered. (Searle, cited in Goetz and Taliaferro 2008, p. 9)

It does indeed provide a framework, and it is certainly a framework that works in the sense of allowing humans to manipulate the world, but this does not make it true and objective. I want to be clear that science is a good thing, I like science and what it can achieve, and I would rather live in a world where science is allowed to progress in order to cure sickness and disease. In everyday life we function as empirical animals and would struggle to get through the day if we did not. I am not denying any of those common sense facts about the world. At the same time, it should be understood that science is as much an imagined reality as religion, and it bases its methodology on a series of assumptions. The problem is when science and scientists assert that their imagined reality is not imagined at all and, therefore, is in this way a superior form of knowledge to other frameworks on offer out there. Frankly, it should not be a competition for hegemony, but a cooperation; yet it is quite understandable for science to 'win' the epistemology race because of the treasures it opens up to us all. Yet, in staring in awe at the shiny diamond-studded ark of the covenant, we ignore at our peril the contents of the dull, brown goblet in the corner. By way of illustration, it is worth considering some examples of this biased assumption that science makes, and what better way to start by looking to that most severe critic of religion, including Islam of course, Richard Dawkins. Consider this statement from that well-worn book *The God Delusion*:

Any creative intelligence, of sufficient complexity to design anything, comes into existence only as the end product of an extended process of gradual evolution. Creative intelligences, being evolved, necessarily arrive late in the universe, and therefore cannot be responsible for designing it. God, in the sense defined, is a delusion. (Dawkins 2007, p. 52)

Scientists argue that we must always look for evidence, yet where is the evidence in this assertion? How can we be so sure the creative intelligences are evolved and come as the end product? Is this not more of an assumption than an empirical fact? The Christian philosopher of religion Keith Ward asks us to consider the possibility that it could be the other way around, that creative intelligence comes first, followed by matter:

are there not good reasons for thinking that the ultimate character of the universe is mind, and that matter is the appearance or manifestation or creation of cosmic mind. (Ward 2008, p. 19)

Keith Ward has, of course, written many books on the relationship between science and religion, but I would argue that you do not, like Ward, have to be motivated by religious beliefs. For example, the philosopher Thomas Nagel, no believer in God himself, nonetheless questions the exclusivity of reductive materialism. When considering the answer to the question of the origins of life, Nagel states:

My skepticism is not based on religious belief, or on a belief in any definite alternative. It is just a belief that the available scientific evidence, in spite of the consensus of scientific opinion, does not in this matter require us to subordinate the incredulity of common sense … everyone in our secular culture has been browbeaten into regarding the reductive research program as sacrosanct, on the ground that anything else would not be science. (Nagel 2012, pp. 6–7)

While I am not personally convinced by these specific arguments of Ward and Nagel, I nonetheless recognise their methodology of questioning scientific assumptions. Therefore, leaving aside whether or not you believe in God, at the very least we should be justified in questioning the authority of scientific reductionism to find the answers to everything. Dawkins, of course, believes that whether God exists or not is a scientific question. Dawkins rejects Stephen Jay Gould's (2002) NOMA ('non-overlapping magisteria') which sees science and religion as dealing with different questions and different approaches to these questions which prevents them from overlapping, whereas Dawkins believes that if a question is not a scientific one then it has no value whatsoever. Whilst I also do not subscribe to NOMA, neither do I endorse Dawkins' dogmatism: the questions raised by science and religion do overlap with each other, and both disciplines have much to contribute to providing answers to these big questions. I also think Keith Ward, following on from Richard Swinburne (2004, pp. 35–45), is right to stress the value of personal explanation:

> If you want to explain how it is that I am writing these words, you could do so by showing that I am aware of some possible future states (I can stay in bed, have a coffee, or write these words), I evaluate one of them as desirable (I want to finish this book), I set in motion a causal process to bring about what I desire (I get out of bed), and finally I enjoy what I am doing, because it is what I wanted and decided to do. This is personal explanation. It is a perfectly satisfactory form of explanation, and it does not seem to be reducible to scientific explanation. (Ward 2008, p. 23)

There is a danger that explaining something in a 'personal' way can be suggestive of an extreme subjectivity that opens the door to all kinds of beliefs, and this is something Dawkins picks up on in his reference to celestial teapots, tooth fairies, and so forth. We are not here all nodding in agreement that there are teapots orbiting the earth, but we are tapping into common experiences of self-awareness, of consciousness. These are direct experiences, not claims to some empirical objects outside of ourselves, and they are also experiences that, frankly, do not lend themselves to scientific reductionism, whatever Dawkins may claim.

If our bodies can be reduced to our physical parts, as transhumanists claim, then our subjective experiences, our 'personal explanation' for the what we believe, hope, desire, and so on, are purely physical, yet this seems to fly against the wind of our experience as if such things do not matter. It is important, because I want to believe that if my 'self' is uploaded onto a computer then it really will continue to be me, yet, though I am sceptical about many non-empirical claims, I am not quite so trusting that this will be the case. My experiences of hope, love, creativity, and joy do not seem readily reducible to brain states. Nor, for that matter, can the spiritual joy experienced by religious mystics be equated simply with monoaminergic neurotransmitters (serotonin and dopamine), otherwise drugs would always provide us with this sense of fulfilment and 'oneness', and so on, that are attempts to describe the 'indescribable'. William Dembski in his article 'Kurzweil's Impoverished Spirituality' has, as this title suggests, declared the impossibility of a machine possessing a 'spiritual' side: 'In place of talking cures that address our beliefs, desires, and emotions, tomorrow's healers of the soul will manipulate brain states directly and ignore such outdated categories of beliefs, desires, and emotions' (Dembski 2002, p. 108).

When the British philosopher Gilbert Ryle (1900–1976) famously criticised Cartesian dualism as a 'ghost in the machine' he rightly raised the problems of this form of dualism that proposes a mind, or spirit, that is independent of the body, to the extent that the body has little purpose. Such dualisms seem counter-intuitive and raise a series of problems that seem intellectually questionable, and I am closer to subscribing to Charles Taliaferro's 'integrative dualism', which he describes so:

> Integrative dualism affirms that the embodied person thinks, sees, looks, glimpses, smells, tastes, touches, and so on, as truly embodied. It fully recognises the united character of personal life, and does not leave the body and person dangling in scandalous disarray, picturing the person as inhabiting the brain or delivering commands to the brain from some remote, mental theatre. (Taliaferro 1994, p. 121)

Whether this 'spiritual' expression of myself can survive the death of the physical body does become a matter of faith for which I am on less firm ground, but my more modest declaration that what constitutes 'me' is a *qualia* that is not reducible to data seems intelligible and, as such, raises concerns for me that my 'computer me' would not be me at all, but a pale and incomplete copy.

Methodological Naturalism

We need to confront the proverbial elephant in the room. It was noted above that secular transhumanist are more open to, for example, Confucianism, because it is perceived as not dependent upon supernatural entities. Transhumanism is concerned with the human, and with overcoming the human, through natural means. To introduce the supernatural into the equation is, for the secular transhumanist, side-tracking, irrelevant, and even obstructing. Yet, for any Muslim to deny the supernatural is to deny being a Muslim. Many transhumanists, and many philosophers for that matter, subscribe to *metaphysical* naturalism (or philosophical materialism, or metaphysical materialism) and deny entirely the existence of supernatural entities, but what the views of a person are in terms of a belief in God or not are less significant here than the fact that modern transhumanism, as a *scientific* enterprise, engages in *methodological* naturalism (MN). As Phil Stilwell points out, MN 'does not deny the possibility of supernatural entities', rather:

> MN is a provisional epistemology and ontology that provides a framework upon which to do science. These parameters are merely provisional. MN does not entail philosophical naturalism, but instead entails out of pragmatics and precedent that science begin each particular inquiry with the assumption that any explanation will fall within the existing matrix of established material definitions and laws. ... MN also implies that, if a natural explanation does not immediately emerge from the inquiry, we do not default to a declaration of a supernatural cause. (Stilwell 2009, p. 229)

This view had been echoed by the likes of Massimo Pigliucci (2010) and Barbara Forrest (2000), and more fervently by Niles Eldredge: 'If there is one rule that makes an idea scientific, it is that it must invoke naturalistic explanations for phenomena, and those explanations must be testable solely by the criteria of our five senses' (Eldredge 1982, p. 82). In other words, leave the divine out of it. How, therefore, can Islam engage in the transhumanist debate without bringing God into it? Ultimately, this will, as has already been argued, depend on what 'Islam' we are talking about, and what we mean by God. As will be demonstrated later in Chap. 5, the more 'Traditionalist' approach to the relationship between Islam and science has at its root a tendency to defer to God as the ultimate arbiter in all matters, including the scientific, and this strand of Islam continues today with the likes of Zaghloul El-Naggar and Harun Yahya who, when there is any scientific doubt, would look to the Qur'an and hadith as providing the answers. This, of course, goes against the grain of scientific method, the adoption of Occam's Razor, or the principal of parsimony. Science, in explaining the world, *works*; at least in explaining natural phenomena. Where science cannot declare absolute certainty on a natural phenomenon, then this does not result in the abandonment of MN and a resort to the divine for the scientist but, rather, further empirical studies and technological development to bridge those gaps. Whilst Provisional (or Pragmatic) MN (PMN) does not rule out the possibility of supernatural phenomena (unlike Intrinsic MN, see Boudry et al. 2010, 2012;

Fishman and Boudry 2013), it is very much a last resort when all empirical methods have been exhausted. It can be seen how this is a problem for Muslims who see God as acting in the world, whether as the Creator, or through the act of miracles as just two major tenets of Islam, not to mention other theistic traditions.

There are, of course, many responses to this issue, which would constitute voluminous pages if explored in detail here, but a few observations can be made that will hopefully show that Islam, and religion generally, is not as a result 'excluded' from the issues and discoveries in the scientific realm. I want, first of all, to refer briefly to the prominent American philosopher Alvin Plantinga here who, though having Christianity in mind for his arguments, has views that can be applied equally to Islam. In his book *Where the Conflict Really Lies: Science, Religion, and Naturalism* (2011), Plantinga argues that in the case of evolutionary biology and physics, there is only a perceived rather than an actual conflict with theism and divine action. For example, with respect to evolutionary biology, this does not exclude the possibility of *telos* (which, for Plantinga, would be directed by God). When considering divine action, Plantinga argues that neither classical physics nor quantum physics can exclude the possibility of God intervening miraculously in a series of secondary causes to produce certain events. In his book, Plantinga goes much further in arguing that, on some issues, religion is in concord with science, for example in referring to God as providing the best explanation for mathematical structures in the universe.

I personally find these arguments inadequate and part of a tradition in philosophy of religion that is somewhat orthodox and, dare I say, 'medieval' in its approach. It is perhaps no surprise, in fact, that Plantinga has written elsewhere that much of science, including evolutionary biology, should be allowed to include 'the metaphysical or religious principles' and he calls this 'Augustinian science' (Plantinga 1996, 1997). Going back to Saint Augustine (354–430) is not the answer and is not particularly helpful. The best approach, and the one adopted throughout this work, is while accepting that many Muslims are 'traditional theists', this is but one perspective and need not be at the forefront of debate on the issue of transhumanism. The traditional theist may well comfortably adopt the PMN approach, whereby appeal to the classical theistic God may not be ruled out but, for all practical scientific purposes, serves little purpose as things stand.

However, much more importantly is not to see the rich tapestry of religion as providing answers to scientific questions, but, rather, to look to religion as helping us to *frame* scientific questions. Here religion does have much to offer in many different contexts. For example, in helping us to understand the ethical implications of transhumanism. Further, given that religion is driven by an attempt to understand the human's place in the universe, one would think it has something to contribute to transhumanism and what this means in terms of our evolutionary place. In addition, whilst empirical method 'works', and we may be wary of looking to the 'supernatural' to muddy the waters of this working methodology, it is more than fair game to question the extent to which the human is nothing *more than* an empirical agent and that the 'five senses', to go back to the Eldredge quote above, are able to provide us with the whole picture. To adopt this approach is not to muddy the waters at all, but instead to provide greater clarity. To look *beyond* the five senses and step outside reductionist materialism may strike some as appealing to the supernatural, but I do not see it this way. In a Nietzschean sense—and Nietzsche does inform much of my own methodology in this book—we need to look *beyond* the natural and the supernatural; to break down such artificial distinctions.

For example, in the quote on page 7 in Chap. 2, when Prisco expresses a hope for a 'modern transhumanist religion' that follows William James, it is perhaps these moments of what might be termed 'mystical experience' which are charging and fulfilling but also, a temporary state of ecstasy that, when it recedes, leaves us feeling lost and depressed. These transient moments, as William James pointed out, leave us craving for more. Such experiences go beyond the capacity of reason and seemingly provide us with a 'knowledge', if that is indeed the right word to use, that is intuitive. The Arabic term *marifa* (literally 'knowledge'), used commonly in Sufi literature, will be explored in more detail later on but, for now, it signifies the overlap between religion and philosophy, as well as attempts to divide these disciplines. Kant is one example of this endeavour to divide schools of thought. One of his earlier works is *Dreams of a Spirit-Seer*, published in 1776. It is a rather abnormal work in the sense that it differs from much of his later writings, being quite playful, ironic, and even relatively humorous; perhaps not something one might normally attribute to works by Kant. It is a strongly sceptical work that seems influenced by David Hume's empiricism, rather than a reaction against it. The 'Spirit-Seer' in the title is a reference to the Swedish statesman and scientist Emanuel Swedenborg (1688–1722) who, in 1745 at the age of 57, decided to make a career-change to become a theologian and a mystic visionary. The young Kant spent what, for him at the time, was a lot of money in purchasing Swedenborg's eight-volume *Arcana Coelestia* (*Secrets of Heaven*, 1749–1756), and Kant seems particularly annoyed with himself for investing such money and, indeed, time, in this work (Kant 1900).

Swedenborg, in this voluminous work, gives various accounts of journeys he claims to have made to the spirit world where he engaged in conversation with angels and demons who were the departed spirits of either human beings or aliens from other planets. In referring to Swedenborg's 'journeys', he does not see these in the geographical sense of a move from one place to another, but this move from the material to the spiritual is a change in cognition from the world of the senses to a spiritual mode (Swedenborg 2009). Kant may well have a strong case for being frustrated and critical of Swedenborg's claims, as might many of us, but we may nonetheless take up the point concerning the limitations that the world of the senses provide. Whether one is able to go *beyond* the sensual world and, if so, how this can be achieved, is, of course, a matter of contentious debate. Kant's scepticism is evident in his criticism of Swedenborg but, also, more broadly, in his damning of all mystical experience as a form of cognition. For Kant, this is a pseudo-philosophy and, relevant to Islamic epistemology, his Orientalist understanding of Islam saw the Prophet Muhammad as a Swedenborg-like figure who claimed to have mystical experiences. For Kant, as the Prophet Muhammad is the 'founder' of Islam, then the whole religion is founded upon an irrational and an unphilosophical basis. Kant defines human knowledge as 'a small land with many boundaries' (Kant, cited in Almond 2010, p. 30) and these boundaries are specifically European. Therefore, for Kant, Islamic philosophy is not philosophy at all. More than that, Kant saw Islam as an 'unspiritual creed' and a 'harsh severe dogma' (Almond 2010, p. 37), in contrast to Christianity. The latter he saw as a religion that was moving in the direction of becoming an 'invisible church', of prioritising the ethical duty that one human being has to another, whilst Islam is primarily a 'visible church' of empty ritual and observances. Kant believed that the sole purpose of religion is to act as an enabler for the human to live an ethical life, since choosing to act morally is the ultimate expression of freedom.

Kant himself was, of course, a great 'system-builder'; a philosopher who famously never left the city of Königsberg, yet delved into the deep waters of metaphysical reality. The scientists may well make a claim that it is only through empirical methods of science that can reveal what is real, not from sitting in your living room or going for long daily walks in the park. It is, however, worth reminding ourselves that Kant, in his early essay (1755) *Universal Natural History and Theory of the Heavens*, put forward the view that the Milky Way was a large disc of stars which formed from a larger, spinning cloud of gas and, also, that other nebulae may also be discs of stars. Whilst not an astoundingly original work, relying as it does on various predecessors such as René Descartes (1596–1650) and Isaac Newton (1643–1727), it is nonetheless quite an intellectual achievement for one so young (and who at this point had no official teaching position or a university degree) and demonstrates this blurred boundary between philosophy, science, and religion, given that Kant was eager to stress that his cosmological views *support* the need for God, not render Him useless as one might suppose. Scientists can retort that it took the likes of the astronomer William Herschel (1738–1832) to later give Kant's speculations empirical support. However, as Stephen Law has pointed out:

> Galileo is credited with constructing a thought experiment by which he established that the Aristotelian theory that heavier objects fall faster than lighter ones in direct proportion to their weight is mistaken. Galileo noted that Aristotle's theory predicted that two balls, one heavier than the other, should fall at different speeds: the heavier falling faster. This theory could be empirically tested of course, and some suppose Galileo tested it by dropping objects from the top of the leaning tower of Pisa. However, Galileo himself records no such experiment. What Galileo did do was perform a thought experiment. (Law 2017, p. 127)

Recall that what we are trying to determine here is whether or not questions that arise from the transhumanist debate are to be kept firmly within a secular, empirical, and scientific arena and, if this were the case, is science *sufficient* in answering those kinds of questions that do arise. If it is not sufficient, then where else might we look for guidance? How far can the boundaries be stretched before they begin to tear? As stated, whilst many transhumanists, our 'secular transhumanists', are quite prepared to be 'interdisciplinary' in their methodology, hence allowing such disciplines as philosophy and, indeed, the 'arts', within these boundaries, there is still some resistance to religion. However, as hopefully the next chapter will expand upon, this is largely down to a particular understanding of religion, which has not been helped by religion—and in this case Islam specifically—engaging in its own reification. By stating that science does 'this', philosophy does 'that', religion does the 'other', may, to some extent, be helpful in terms of differing methodologies, content, and so on, but this can also blind one to the *common* methodologies for which they share.

It is quite correct to assert that a philosopher cannot sit in his or her armchair and, by merely thinking, 'reveal' empirical facts about the universe, but this does not deny the gains that can indeed be made by armchair reflection, including from scientists. Similarly, one might well be sceptical that, say, engaging in meditation or having a mystical experience genuinely results in anything that is veridical, but, again, the experience may well tell us much about what it means to be human and what humans can experience in terms of the creation of these so-called 'imagined realities'. In addition, we must be wary of classing one thing an 'imagined reality' and another 'objective reality' for, quite simply, human beings are 'trapped' within a human framework and, in Kantian terms, must always be interpreting the phenomenal world; the noumenal is closed to us. Whether the transhuman can also transcend the human in this epistemological sense is speculation beyond the scope of this book and, indeed, the period we are living in at present. However, it seems mistaken to present a simple dualistic picture of the world in terms of the 'objective' and the 'imagined'. Let me be clear that this cosmological dualism is a worldview that is presented by religious believers and non-believers alike, although what that dualism may consist of inevitably differs. For the religious believer, it may be (though need not be) the natural and the supernatural, for the non-believer it may well be the natural (objective) and the nonsense (imagined). Religious believers may well buttress their faith by placing their own strong boundaries around the supernatural, making a clear distinction between faith and reason for which the rational mind cannot possibly understand, criticise, or comprehend the supernatural. Consequently, here arise the new atheists who claim that religion and science are not 'non-overlapping magisteria' but are rather subject to rigorous scientific investigation: the existence or non-existence of God is a *scientific* question.

This book is not concerned with such debates, and there is an abundance of words written out there for the reader to explore. Whether, through faith, a believer really does access to 'something' is not a question that can be answered here. However, we owe it to ourselves as human beings to not be so dismissive of our amazing abilities to form 'alternative realities' and our attempts through language and other forms of communication to express these. Whether or not these are 'real', or whether or not, as human beings, we can ever know what is 'real', is, to a large extent, besides the point. Rather, in the phenomenological sense, we 'experience' phenomena, and these experiences can 'reveal' what it means to be human. Here I am presenting my methodology as phenomenological in exploring meaning and understanding from the perspective of the experiencer, that is the human. The philosopher and literary critic George Steiner remarked that, 'Martin Heidegger is the great master of astonishment, the man whose amazement before the blank fact that we are instead of not being, has put a radiant obstacle in the path of the obvious' (Steiner 1989, p. 158). The fact that we *are* 'being' may well be stating the obvious for anyone who may be adopting the clichéd stance of the cold empiricist, but, more likely, most, if not all, human beings, have their 'Heideggerian' moments, however they might phrase or understand it. This 'radiant obstacle in the path of the obvious' breaks down those artificial 'real/unreal', 'objective/subjective' barriers, and do, in fact, 'reveal' what we may call existential 'truths' as truths about ourselves. As Thomas Nagel states:

> There is a sense in which phenomenological facts are perfectly objective: one person can know or say of another what the quality of the other's experience is. They are subjective, however, in the sense that even this objective ascription of experience is possible only for someone sufficiently similar to the object of ascription to be able to adopt his point of view—to understand the ascription in the first person as well as in the third, so to speak. (Nagel 1974, p. 442)

In other words, whilst the human, or even transhuman, cannot 'step outside' of one's self and see the world 'as it is' in a truly objective sense, there are nonetheless common human experiences that we share, or at the very least there appears to be. The 'hard problem' (Chalmers 1995) of consciousness continues to be a hard problem, and may well always be. Come the day that a machine can reproduce entirely a person's *qualia*—which certainly seems to be considered an attainable goal for many transhumanists—then we can start to talk about the human as something that be reduced to objective, third-person components. This still seems a long way off, however. A very clear and succinct elucidation of phenomenology comes from the German philosopher Edmund Husserl (1859–1938) who saw it as a *phenomenological attitude*, rather than a school of thought, which involves a new 'way of looking' at things. To add on to this, Maurice Merleau-Ponty (1908–1961) states that, 'True philosophy consists in relearning to look at the world' (Russell 2006, p. 71). Whilst Heidegger warns us that 'there is no such thing as *the one* phenomenology' (Heidegger 1982, p. 328), it helps to see it as an 'attitude' rather than a school of thought in terms of considering issues that arise form transhumanism, for 'attitude' requires a very *human* response: no scientist who makes claims to the pure objectivity of science would then declare that science has an 'attitude'.

If secular transhumanists appeal purely to science to answer all things, then the claim is a fallacious one, for science itself does not have all the answers. Many secular transhumanists are quite prepared to allow for the perspectives of philosophers and the creative arts, yet—being by definition 'secular'—necessarily will not go as far as looking to religion as providing any meaningful contribution, *unless* 'religion' is understood in some kind of 'eastern' non-divine kind of way, rather like a western atheist is quite happy to do a bit of yoga. Those transhumanists who seem more open to religion are also seeing it as a particular *kind* of belief; perhaps a more 'universalist' or 'mystical' belief, rather than the more 'orthodox'. This, at the very least, is encouraging, and, whilst I myself despair of the dominant zeitgeist of the Muslim 'fundamentalist', we can learn much from what is referred to here as explorative Islam and it can contribute to the transhumanist debate, in the hope that, as a result, the number of secular transhumanists will decline.

BIBLIOGRAPHY[2]

BOOKS

Almond, Ian. 2010. *A History of Islam in German Thought: From Leibniz to Nietzsche*. Oxon: Routledge.

Blackburn, Simon. 1996. *The Oxford Dictionary of Philosophy*. Oxford: Oxford University Press.

Calvino, Italo. 1988. *Six Memos for the Next Millennium*. Cambridge: Harvard University Press.

Dawkins, Richard. 2007. *The God Delusion*. London: Black Swan.

---

[2] *Note*: All quotes from the Qur'an are from the translation by M.A.S. Abdel Haleem, Oxford University Press, 2005.

Dummett, Michael. 2010. *The Nature and Future of Philosophy*. New York: Columbia University Press.

Eldredge, Niles. 1982. *The Monkey Business: A Scientist Looks at Creationism*. New York: Washington Square Press.

Goetz, Stewart, and Charles Taliaferro. 2008. *Naturalism*. Grand Rapids, MI: William B. Eerdmans Publishing Co.

Gould, Stephen Jay. 2002. *Rocks of Ages*. New York: Vintage.

Harari, Yuval Noah. 2011. *Sapiens: A Brief History of Humankind*. London: Penguin.

Harris, Sam. 2010. *The Moral Landscape: How Science Can Determine Human Values*. London: Transworld.

Heidegger, Martin. 1982. *The Basic Problems of Phenomenology*. Translated by Albert Hofstadter. Bloomington, IN: Indiana University Press.

Hughes, Bettany. 2010. *The Hemlock Cup: Socrates, Athens and the Search for the Good Life*. London: Jonathan Cape.

Hume, David. 1978. *A Treatise of Human Nature*. 2nd ed. Edited by P.H. Nidditch. Oxford: Oxford University Press.

Kant, Immanuel. 1900. *Dreams of a Spirit-Seer*. Translated by Emanuel F. Goerwitz. London: Swan Sonnenschein and Co.

———. 1998. *Critique of Pure Reason*. Cambridge: Cambridge University Press.

Mabey, Richard. 2015. *Cabaret of Plants: Botany and Imagination*. London: Profile Books Ltd.

Nagel, Thomas. 1986. *The View from Nowhere*. Oxford: Oxford University Press.

———. 2012. *Mind and Cosmos: Why the Materialist Neo-Darwinian Conception of Nature Is Almost Certainly False*. Oxford: Oxford University Press.

Pigliucci, Massimo. 2010. *Nonsense on Stilts: How to Tell Science from Bunk*. Chicago: University of Chicago Press.

Plantinga, Alvin. 2011. *Where the Conflict Really Lies: Science, Religion, and Naturalism*. Oxford: Oxford University Press.

Plato. 2012. *Republic*. Translated by Christopher Rowe. London: Penguin.

Quine, W.V. 1981. *Theories and Things*. Cambridge: Harvard University Press.

Russell, Matheson. 2006. *Husserl: A Guide for the Perplexed*. London: Continuum.

Sheldrake, Rupert. 2012. *The Science Delusion: Feeling the Spirit of Enquiry*. London: Hodder & Stoughton.

Steiner, George. 1989. *Martin Heidegger*. Chicago: University of Chicago Press.

Swedenborg, Emanuel. 2009. *Arcana Coelestia*. Vols. 1–12. Translated by John Clowes. West Chester, PA: Swedenborg Foundation.

Swinburne, Richard. 2004. *The Existence of God*. Oxford: Oxford University Press.

Taliaferro, Charles. 1994. *Consciousness and the Mind of God*. Cambridge: Cambridge University Press.

Ward, Keith. 2008. *Why There Almost Certain Is a God*. Oxford: Lion Book.

Williams, Bernard. 2006. *Philosophy as a Humanistic Discipline*. Princeton: Princeton University Press.

JOURNAL ARTICLES AND BOOK CHAPTERS

Boudry, Maarten, Stefaan Blancke, and Johan Braeckman. 2010. How Not to Attack Intelligent Design Creationism: Philosophical Misconceptions About Methodological Naturalism. *Foundations of Science* 15 (3): 227–244.

———. 2012. Grist to the Mill of Anti-Evolutionism: The Failed Strategy of Ruling the Supernatural Out of Science by Philosophical Fiat. *Science and Education* 21: 1151–1165.

Cellucci, Carlo. 2015. Is Philosophy a Humanistic Discipline? *Philosophia* 43: 259–269.

Chalmers, David. 1995. Facing Up to the Problem of Consciousness. *Journal of Consciousness Studies* 2 (3): 200–219.

Dembski, William. 2002. Kurzweil's Impoverished Spirituality. In *Are We Spiritual Machines? Ray Kurzweil vs. The Critics of Strong AI*, ed. J.W. Richards, 98–114. Seattle: The Discovery Institute.

Fishman, Yonatan I., and Maarten Boudry. 2013. Does Science Presuppose Naturalism (or Anything at All)? *Science and Education* 22 (5): 921–949.

Forrest, Barbara. 2000. Methodological Naturalism and Philosophical Naturalism: Clarifying the Connection. *Philo* 3: 7–29.

Law, Stephen. 2017. Scientism! In *Science Unlimited? The Challenge of Scientism*, ed. Maarten Boudry and Massimo Pigliucci, 121–144. Chicago and London: The University of Chicago Press.

Nagel, Thomas. 1974. What Is It Like to Be a Bat? *The Philosophical Review* 83 (4): 435–450.

Plantinga, Alvin. 1996. Science: Augustinian or Duhemian? *Faith and Philosophy* 13: 369–394.

———. 1997. Methodological Naturalism. *Perspectives on Science and Christian Faith* 49: 143–154.

Roy, Rustum. 2005. Scientism and Technology as Religions. *Zygon* 40 (4): 835–844.

Stilwell, Phil. 2009. The Status of Methodological Naturalism as Justified by Precedent. *Studies in Liberal Arts and Sciences* 41: 229–247.

CHAPTER 4

The Reification of Islam and the Rise of Tele-techno-scientific Reason

Paradigm-Shifting Challenges

What possibilities humankind has to reform, change, or even reject supposed universal, eternal laws is key to the debate on the hierarchical status given to scientific developments. The discourse that has dominated western thought for some 600 years is that of the 'Renaissance', or 'Universal', Man (*Uomo Universale*), summed up by Leon Battista Alberti (1404–1472) as a man who 'can do all things if he will'. The Renaissance, at one— admittedly simplistic—level, puts humankind at the centre of the universe with no limits to what can be achieved. This view of the human is contrasted with the religious concept of humankind as having a fixed essence given by God. Here we have one, very crucial, battle of ideas which will permeate throughout this book: the conflict over how far human beings can go before they 'transgress' the borders and, for that matter, the extent to which such borders exist and can be disputed. The Latin adjective '*trans*' in terms of 'crossing', 'going beyond', 'surpassing', and so on is key here if we are to determine what the boundaries are and, therefore, the extent to which humankind can and should 'cross' these boundaries. Here, it seems, lies the perceived division between the religious and the secular, and, more specifically, between Islam and the west.

Religions in their general sense have historically been confronted by several challenges to their beliefs systems, spearheaded by new developments in our understanding of the natural world, and coupled with

© The Author(s) 2020
R. Jackson, *Muslim and Supermuslim*, Palgrave Studies
in the Future of Humanity and its Successors,
https://doi.org/10.1007/978-3-030-37093-0_4

technological advances. Some of these developments are paradigm-shifting in their power, and, consequently, religions cannot sit back and remain silent if they are to assert relevance. The most obvious example of a paradigm shift, and, arguably, the most powerful, is the theory of human evolution, which many scientists at least would consider this today to be less a theory, and more a scientific fact. As the American geneticist Joseph Hermann Muller (1890–1967) succinctly stated:

> There is no sharp line between speculation, hypothesis, theory, principle, and fact, but only a difference along a sliding scale, in the degree of probability of the idea. When we say a thing is a fact, then, we only mean that its probability is an extremely high one: so high that we are not bothered by doubt about it and are ready to act accordingly. Now in this use of the term fact, the only proper one, evolution is a fact. (Muller 1959, p. 304)

Yet many religious believers resist this paradigm to this day. Creationism has many adherents in what is regarded as the most technologically advanced nation on Earth: in Gallup polls since the early 1980s, Americans have been asked to choose among three views of evolution: that humans 'developed over millions of years from less advanced forms of life, but God guided this process' or that humans 'developed over millions of years from less advanced forms of life, but God had no part in this process' or 'God created human beings pretty much in their present form at one time within the last 10,000 years or so'. It is the latter option that has always had the largest percentage of respondents, fluctuating in a narrow range between 40% and 47%. It should be stressed that the creationist view is considerably less prevalent amongst younger Americans and those who are more highly educated. Nonetheless, amongst regular church-goers, the creationist viewpoint was held by 69% in the 2014 poll, with 24% believing that humans evolved, but God guided the process (Newport 2014). Whilst one might fully expect God to feature in human evolution somewhere, it is interesting that such a large number reject human evolution altogether.

Such statistics always need to be treated with a degree of suspicion and an awareness that these figures do not reflect Christians *as a whole*. It is unfortunate that such a tendency to draw general conclusion from specific surveys of Muslims (e.g. Hameed 2008; BouJaoude et al. 2011a, b; Pew Report 2013) also occurs, with conclusions that the majority of Muslims also reject—or at the very least have fundamental disagreements with—evolution, yet when looked more closely, things are never quite so simplistic.

For example, in the 2013 Pew Research Report *The World's Muslims: Religion, Politics and Society* (Pew Report 2013), views differ from one country to the next: the majority of Muslims in Albania (62%) and Russia (58%) believe in evolution, whereas in Kosovo it falls to 40%. In countries such as Kazakhstan and Lebanon it is around eight in every ten Muslims who believe in evolution, whereas in Iraq 67% reject evolution. Such statistics make it difficult to come to any firm conclusions except that, like the Christians in America, the more observant believers are less likely to believe in the theory of evolution. Questions are rightly raised as to what constitutes a 'Muslim' in this respect, of course, if we are to say that the more 'observant' Muslims are less likely to subscribe to evolution, then are we saying they are—by being more 'observant'—more 'Muslim'? Islam also refers to a culture and a civilisation although, again, due to the diversity that is Islam, it is difficult to pinpoint what constitutes an Islamic culture or civilisation: there are Arabic Muslims, Persian Muslims, Chinese Muslims, African Muslims, South-East Asian Muslims, and 'western' (European and American) Muslims, amongst others. There are also 'nominal' or 'cultural' Muslims whereby identity is determined by being born to a Muslim father, much like a Jew born to a Jewish mother. Other than that, it is not required to subscribe to beliefs and practices of the faith; rather, it is a matter of ethnicity or group allegiance. In this 2013 Pew Report, Muslims in Bosnia-Herzegovina are divided quite evenly over the evolution issue, but a person is described (or describes him/herself) as a Bosnian Muslim to be distinguished from Bosnian Serbs (Orthodox) and Bosnian Croats (Catholic). Other than that, the Bosnian Muslims are,

> Drinkers of slivovitz, strong plum brandy, eaters of pork, for many Bosnian Muslims their only connections with Islam until the [Bosnian] war were that they had names like Amra and Emir and left their shoes outside their houses. Bosnian Muslims were largely secular and those that were religious emphasised that they were "European Muslims", something quite different to the Ayatollahs of Iran and the Islamic clergy of Saudi Arabia. (Lebor 1997, p. 20)

It is, perhaps, not surprising that the Muslims from Saudi Arabia and Algeria that went to Bosnia to fight in the Bosnian War were shocked by the Bosnians' lifestyle and equally the Bosnians themselves were not enamoured by the orthodoxy of these *Mujahidin*. As has been shown, the issue of what is a Muslim is a complex one, but what can be maintained from all these surveys is that the more a believer—and not just a Muslim—

'observes' their religion in the conventional, *prescriptive*, sense of regular attendance of a place of worship, faith in what are regarded as fundamental tenets of that belief (primarily in this case, God as the Creator) and engaging in other orthodox ritual activities, then the harder it seems for this believer to subscribe to the theory of evolution. In other words, there is an evident tension between an interpretation of religious beliefs in God and creation, and the scientific belief in evolution. However, again, this is just one way of understanding Islam and Muslims.

Whilst Copernicus has pretty much won the day, Darwin still has some way to go and making the further leap to the challenges of transhumanism is something that Islam—as with all the religions—should have a voice. It is the hope of this author that the 'voice' can provide an enlightened and valuable contribution to the transhumanist debate. At this point in time there are no robust surveys available on the Muslim view on transhumanism or human enhancement, but the Pew Research Centre conducted an interesting survey in America in 2016 (Funk et al. 2016) which addressed public attitudes to three particular emerging technologies: gene editing that would result in reduced risk of serious diseases, the implanting of chips in the brain to improve concentration and process information, and synthetic blood transfusion to improve human physical ability such as strength and speed. Whilst none of these technologies are currently available, they are all in research or developmental stage and are even being tested in a limited way, so one might expect these three technologies to be very 'real' in the not-too-distant future. Without going into the specifics here in terms of the general US population, suffice to say that, overall, concern for human enhancement currently outweighs enthusiasm by, roughly, 60–40. What is more relevant here is the *religious* response and, in particular, the fundamental question that was asked in the survey of whether human enhancement is 'meddling with nature' (Funk et al. 2016). It is worth quoting the results of this question:

> The survey data show several patterns surrounding Americans' wariness about these developments. First, there are strong differences in views about using these technologies for enhancement depending on how religious people are. In general, the most religious are the most wary about potential enhancements. For example, those who score high on a three-item index of religious commitment are more likely than those who are lower in religious commitment to say all three types of enhancement—gene editing to give babies a lifetime with much reduced risk of disease, brain chip implants to

give people much improved cognitive abilities and transfusions with synthetic blood to give people much improved physical capacities—would be
meddling with nature and crossing a line that should not be crossed.
Americans who have lower levels of religious commitment are more inclined
to see the potential use of these techniques as just the continuation of a
centuries-old quest by humans to try to better themselves. (Funk et al. 2016)

With regard to the 'three-item index of religious commitment' mentioned above, those with a high level of religious commitment are people
who attend a place of worship at least once a week, pray at least once a day
and state that religion is an important part of their lives. The low level of
commitment is the opposite; those who consider themselves 'religious'
but rarely, if ever, attend places of worship or pray. All others come under
the medium level of commitment. What the survey reveals reflects, perhaps not surprisingly, the surveys for evolution. That is, those with a high
commitment to religion, our more observant believers are more against
human enhancement at around 60% or more per cent, compared with
those with a low commitment who constitute around 33% on average.
However, what do we understand here by 'low commitment'? It should
be emphasised that the religious believers in this report were American
Christians, and so the reference to the 'most religious' would, for example, be referring specifically to evangelical Christians. If we were to apply
these categories to Muslims, the more observant believers would be *prescriptive*. Granted, Muslims who may not attend the mosque on a regular
basis or follow closely the precepts of the Quran are *still* Muslims, but
their 'commitment' is more *explorative*.

Evolution and transhumanism are in very many respects separate issues,
of course. Physically and intellectually, humans are not the same as they
were a million years ago, and so in that respect they have 'enhanced'
(although there are many studies that suggest that the brain of *Homo sapiens* has *decreased* in size since the age of foraging as humans are no longer
required to be so adept at survival on an individual level), but this is a
result of a period of time, adapting to the environment, not the result of
any biotechnical intervention, although this in itself raises issues if one
believes that God created Man in a state of perfection. Transhumanism,
however, is not a 'fact of nature' but, some believe, mankind going *beyond*
nature. Whilst many religious believers support the view that God uses
evolution as a 'tool', if you will, for nature to function, the issue of
transhumanism seems to be more of a tool of human making, rather than

God. A concern, therefore, is expressed that God is being left entirely out of the picture when it comes to *human* enhancement. As Christian Brugger—Professor of Moral Theology at St. John Vianney Theological Seminary in Denver, Colorado—states in response to the Pew survey:

> Is this heightened concern because religious people, especially Christians, are credulous science-fearing dupes? "Neo-Luddites" as some contemporary critics of religion believe? That's absurd: Bacon, Pascal, Mendel, Newton, Kepler, Lemaître were all devout Christians. Why is it then? Simply said, it's because they believe in God. And so they believe there are God-given limits, and if the limits are transgressed, people don't flourish. And one of those limits is respect for our bodily nature, which implies at very least that we shouldn't metamorphose that nature into some grandiose more-than-human reality. They hear in the transhumanist imperative a whisper of original sin, which is pride: "Do it and you'll be like God". (Masci 2016)

To 'be like God' is to have the power of God. This is, perhaps, one of the most common criticisms by religious believers levelled against transhumanism, genetic enhancement, and so on: we are 'playing God'. In this book I am not prone to reach immediately for the Qur'an for guidance on such matters, simply because the 'playing God' card can be used by referring to certain passages in the Qur'an, but, then again, certain passages can also be used to support transhumanism. By way of a brief example, the Qur'anic sura 67 is entitled 'Sovereignty', or in the Haleem translation, 'Control', and the first few verses are very telling:

> Exalted is He who holds all control in His hands; who has power over all things; who created death and life to test you [people] and reveal which of you does best—He is the Mighty, the Forgiving; who created the seven heavens, one above the other. You will not see any flaw in what the Lord of Mercy creates. Look again! Your sight will turn back to you, weak and defeated. (67:1–5)

God is the Creator of all things, including death and life and, importantly, there are no *flaws*. Indeed, if Man is to 'test' God, 'Your sight will turn back to you, weak and defeated'. Human enhancement can be seen as one of these 'tests', of attempts to conquer death and correct what are perceived as flaws. If human beings are created with a purpose, to what extent does human enhancement stray from that purpose, if at all? I find

Haleem's translation of sura 67 as 'Control' particularly apropos, for this is really the fundamental question throughout the whole of this work: *just how much control, in terms of individual autonomy, do human beings have?*

THE REIFICATION OF ISLAM

It is unfortunate that so many transhumanists tend to home in on the prescriptive 'bigotry and intolerance' side of religion, whilst downplaying its more positive explorative contribution to the human. The 'ultra-rationalist approach' sees religion as irrational, but this belies the complexity of religious belief. As we have seen in Chap. 2, Islam for much of its history consisted of the 'Balkans-to-Bengal' complex up until the mid-nineteenth century. Islamic modernism since that time is much to blame here with its process of reification in response to primarily modern, secular challenges. This reification process was pointed out by Wilfred Cantwell Smith (1916–2000) in *The Meaning and End of Religion*, where he argues that religion responded to antithetical systems and ideologies by transforming itself from an interior faith that is realised through religious action such as ritual, piety, and obedience, to an outward theoretical system with firm social rules that can be used to defend itself (Smith 1959). In terms of the Islamic world, reification begins with nineteenth century modernist thinkers such as Jamāl al-Dīn al-Afghānī (1839–1897) and Muhammad Abduh (1849–1905) in Egypt, and Sir Syed Ahmad Khan (1817–1898) in India. In all these cases, as a result of colonial rule, they reacted in varying degrees to the increasing economic and military might of the west with their accusations of Islam as decadent, irrational, lazy, backward, and inefficient (Said 1978) by asserting that Islam is, in fact, the bedfellow of reason, science, and progress. However, the very act of attempting to give Islam a specific and concrete definition, inevitably results in the objectification of the religion, which, in turn, results in a resistance to hermeneutical engagement with the primary religious source, the Qur'an in particular. Although this reification of Islam has its origins in the nineteenth century, it is still how Islam is largely perceived today by both Muslims and non-Muslims and, as the anthropologist Charles Lindholm rightly points out:

> Contemporary Western enmity ... is not simply a consequence of modern conflict. It is a reflection of the thousand-year rivalry between the Muslim Middle East and Christian Europe for economic, political and religious hegemony over the Western hemisphere and beyond—a contest dominated until recently by Islam. (Lindholm 1996, p. 3)

Until the nineteenth century, the military—as distinct from the commercial—advance of the west into the Muslim world was primarily limited to the Balkans and the northern and eastern shores of the Black Sea, but the real turning-point came at the very end of that century when, in 1798, Napoleon Bonaparte occupied Egypt, which was followed by rapid western intervention in other parts of the Islamic world and eventually resulting in the last great Islamic empire, the Ottomans, being declared the 'sick man' of Europe (Lindholm 1996, p. 4). It is within this context that the psychological impact on the Muslim world needs to be understood, for, previously, the Ottoman Empire prided itself in its reason, efficiency, and technology. Yet, the western 'mindset' saw Islam very differently, and this is best summed up by the remarks of Lord Cromer (1841–1917), who was the British consul-general of Egypt from 1882 to 1907. Cromer lived and worked with the Egyptian people for many years, yet, in his work *Modern Egypt* presents us with a smug and derogatory picture of this conquered nation. He observes that 'the want of mental symmetry and precision ... is the chief distinguishing feature between the illogical and picturesque East and the logical West' (Cromer 1908, Vol. 1, p. 7), and further he states that 'somehow or other the Oriental generally acts, speaks and thinks in a manner exactly opposite to the European' (Cromer 1908, Vol. 2, p. 164).

Such a view of Islam exists to this day, for example the present British Prime Minister (at the time of writing) Boris Johnson, in the final chapter to his book *The Dream of Rome* (2006), argues that there is something about Islam that has hindered its development and that it inherently inhibits progress and freedom. With such perceptions it is no wonder that one might be wary of a positive and enlightening contribution from Islam towards the transhumanist debate, and that transhumanism is considered as an essentially western, secular trope for which the illogical, irrational realm of religion can only be its opposite. As already pointed out, however, there are 'many Islams' and the observer—like Cromer—can pick and choose his or her Islam. It is not that Cromer's observations are *wrong*, for his description may well apply to many Muslims he encountered, rather the mistake is making generalisations about Islam as a whole based on selective observations taken at a particular time and a particular place. However, Islam has often been its own worst enemy in doing exactly the same with its own religion. The Islamic modernists looked to treat Islam as one fixed ideological identity so as to be more robust in challenging antithetical ideologies, and, therefore, reputing the existing rich Islamic tradition of jurisprudence, philosophy, and the spiritual/mystical aspect, to be replaced with a more direct exegesis of the primary religious sources. At first the motivation was to show that Islam could be just as scientific and rational as the west, best represented by the effort of the aforementioned Indian educator and political thinker Syed Ahmad Khan who founded the Muhammadan Anglo-Oriental College (also known as the Madrasat ul-'ulūm Musalmanān) in Aligarh in 1875, with the primary aim of promoting the education of Indian Muslims by providing them with a western-style education, hence denigrating the form of education offered by the ulama which he considered—like western commentators themselves—to be lacking in reason and logic. As Ahmad Khan's knighthood suggests, he was pro-British, and believed that Indian Muslims should support the British Raj, not rebel against them.

The founding of the Anglo-Oriental College is hugely significant for a number of reasons, for it addresses the fundamental question of Islamic identity; of what it means to be a Muslim and how a Muslim can be distinguished from the non-Muslim, yet not be seen as synonymous and, therefore, irrational and resistant to technological, political, and social change. In other words, how to be both Muslim and 'modern'. Before the coming of the Anglo-Oriental College, what other new colleges that existed in India—for example the Sanskrit College in Benares (founded 1791), the Delhi College (1792), and the Punjab University College in Lahore (1870)—all taught in the classical tradition, focusing primarily on learning the Qur'an in the belief that all knowledge could be derived from the holy text and Islamic civilisation exclusively. The intentions of Ahmad Khan's new college may, in many respects, be considered admirable, with a genuine concern that the next generation of the leaders of India needed a decent education, for, at the time of setting up his college, only about 6% of Muslims in the Northern-Western Provinces were literate. He hoped that it would be all-inclusive; alas, in reality, only the Muslim ruling classes enrolled (Khan hoped Hindus would also enrol) of which there were no women, who were not in any way encouraged to enrol, or for that possibility to be considered.

Ahmad Khan had visited Britain in 1869–1870 and what he encountered was something of a cultural shock for him when was confronted by Britain's technology and culture, which Khan contrasted with India's poverty and illiteracy. In determining why this was the case, Khan was quick to blame India's education system, with its lack of regard for technological innovation especially, and it led Khan to write his *Essay on the Question Whether Islam Has Been Beneficial or Injurious to Human Society in General* (Khan 1891). Raising such an issue regarding Islam as a whole is indicative of a concern over Muslim identity and its position in a modernising world. Khan's concerns echo throughout Islamic history and are resonant in the debate today concerning transhumanism and what Islam has to contribute here. Just as important is the attitude to be adopted by Islam towards transhumanism and, more generally, to *any* scientific advancements, especially potentially paradigm-shifting technology that gets to the very nature of what it means to be human. Ahmad Khan, therefore, represents one such attitude of a Muslim who is genuinely concerned for the identity and future of Islam which leads him to question the very existence and significance of his religion. This inevitably resulted in severe criticisms, with his adoption of western dress and his praise of British culture; al-Afghānī, for example, accused Ahmad Khan of being a materialist and even the Antichrist. In al-Afghānī's article '*al-Dahriyun fi`l Hind*' ('The Materialists of India'), published in *al Urwat al Wuthqa* in 1884, he said of Khan: 'He appeared in the guise of naturalists [materialists], and proclaimed that nothing exists but blind nature ... and that all the prophets were naturalists. ... He called himself a *neicheri* or naturalist, and began to seduce the sons of the rich, who were frivolous young men.' Curiously, al-Afghānī wrote *Refutation of Materialism* (Davies 1988, p. 59) in 1880–1881 in which he presents a venomous attack of evolutionary ideas. Yet, later on, in *The Memoir of Al-Afghani (Khatirat Jamal al-Din al-Afghani)*, he comes across as sympathetic to the views of Darwin (al-Afghānī 2002). This is somewhat puzzling, but can best be explained by the fact that al-Afghānī does not seem to have read Darwin or for that matter fully understood his evolutionary theory. Al-Afghānī's understanding of evolution seems to be a mishmash of Ernst Haeckel (1834–1919) and Jean-Baptiste Lamarck (1744–1829), amongst other naturalists. What we can glean from al-Afghānī, is that he seemed to subscribe to the view that human beings are not an ontologically fixed species, and nor are human beings radically distinctive from other animals. However, al-Afghānī was also aware of the dangers of evolutionary theory in terms of its materialism and the consequences of such a view have in terms of Islam's non-material perspective.

Ahmad Khan, for his part, saw the need for Islam to modernise if Islamic nations and Islamic civilisation were to survive and, importantly, he saw western thought, *especially* in the realm of science, as a force that should not be regarded as antithetical to Islam but, in fact, as an integral part of Islamic culture and thought. Khan was in line with his *salafi* counterparts in the Middle East—the likes of al-Afghānī, Muhammad Abduh, and Muhammad Rashid Rida (1865–1935)—in believing that Islam's survival required abandoning *taqlid*; the blind imitation of the previous Qur'anic interpreters. The Qur'an does provide guidance, but this requires a reinterpretation of the text involving less literalism and a greater understanding of the subtlety, symbolism, and allegorical nature of the text. In this respect, Khan's attitude to religious sources is more akin to Ibn Rushd or not unlike Maimonides in Judaism. Islam, therefore, is considered as much a religion of reason, and here Khan is drawing on the rationalism of the Muʿtazilites, but also not exclusively rational, as Khan was just as influenced by the more mystical 'Brothers of Purity' (*Ikhwan al-Safa*), as well as the reformism of Shah Waliullah Dehlawi (1703–1762). These differing, but interconnected, strands of Islamic epistemology will be explored in greater detail later on, but, for the moment, an appreciation of Khan's concerns and attempts to address those anxieties helps us to contextualise the Islamic response to the issues raised by transhumanism and to challenge the perceived notion that transhumanism is exclusively a topic for the rational, secular mind. Khan strived to demonstrate to his fellow Muslims that Islam could readily accommodate scientific advances and that Islam was a religion capable of relating to modernity without becoming 'westernised'.

Whilst there were many differences between the Islamic modernists such as Khan, al-Afghānī, and Abduh, they did all agree that Islam needed to confront the modern age, and that the religion needed reform in order to do this. They all blamed the ulama for Islam's weakness in the face of western ascendency, and they all believed that Islam was compatible with reason and science. They were all, therefore, part of the 'same project', in the words of Javed Majeed, which was to show to the world that Islam should not look upon itself as irrelevant—despite doubts on the part of Ahmad Khan—but was consistent with the enlightenment ideals of reason and modern science. In fact, Islam was more than just 'consistent', but rational, scientific thought was the *essence* of Islam. There was 'no fundamental incompatibility' (Majeed 2003, Vol. 2, p. 456) between modernity and Islam. Therefore, Islamic modernism should not be seen as merely a response to western hegemony, although that has to be declared an important causal factor, but the Islamic modernists would argue that islam has its own 'in-built mechanisms' of revival (*tajdid*) and reform (*islah*) which requires it to renew in times of periodic weakness. The ideal model for this reform is the Qur'an, the life of the Prophet Muhammad, and the early Muslim community. Islamic modernism, therefore, is another phase of regular renewal, an internal reformation against the ulama's resistance to change and reliance upon *taqlid*. As John L. Esposito states:

> Islamic modernists of the nineteenth and twentieth century, like secular reformers were open to accommodation and assimilation; they wished to produce a new synthesis of Islam with modern sciences and learning. Thus they distanced themselves from the rejectionist tendency of religious conservatives as well as western-oriented secular reformers who restricted religion to the private life, and they looked to the west to rejuvenate state and society. (Esposito and Voll 2001, p. 647)

Ahmad Khan believed that God's laws are identical with the laws of nature, although this did result in criticism and the perennial concern that, if indeed God's laws are synonymous with the laws of nature and that, consequently, all of morality and social ethics—not only scientific laws—can derive from these natural laws, then what is the need for revelation? Khan argued that Muslims should engage in unrestricted personal *ijtihad* (independent reasoning) of the Qur'an, although even then it would require considerable training in order to engage in *ijtihad* and so would inevitably be restricted to those sufficiently educated, hence the need for a more inclusive education, for how can illiterate Muslims know how to be true Muslims if they cannot properly understand the Qu'ran? Khan was critical of the writings of the hadith collectors and maintained the Qur'an, in its very general sense as a series of basic principles, as the only sure authority, which failed to please the conservative ulama who were not so prepared to abandon centuries of scholarly interpretation of divine texts simply in order to accommodate a scientific worldview. In addition, Khan's loyalty to Britain was seen as alienating Indian Muslims who were increasingly antagonistic towards British rule. The younger generation of Muslims especially was less generous towards their colonial rulers, and this is best illustrated by Abu Al'a Mawdudi (1903–1979). Modernists such as Ahmad Khan, whether deliberately or not, stripped Islam of most of its metaphysical dimension by aligning with the tenets of reason and thus objectified its religious content, taking away its mystery and subjective engagement. With Mawdudi this process of reification continued as he argued for an 'isolationist' epistemology: Islam possessed its own type of knowledge that was independent of, and therefore did not require, other non-Islamic forms of knowledge. On Iqbal Day in 1939, Mawdudi gave an address entitled 'War in the cause of Allah' (*Jihad fi sabil Allah*) in which he said the following:

Islam is not the name of a mere "Religion", nor is Muslim the title of a "Nation". The truth is that Islam is a revolutionary ideology which seeks to alter the social order of the entire world and rebuild it in conformity with its own tenets and ideals. "Muslims" is the title of that "International Revolutionary Party" organised by Islam to carry out its revolutionary programme. Jihad refers to that revolutionary struggle and utmost exertion which the Islamic Nation/Party brings into play in order to achieve this objective. (Mawdudi 1995, p. 5)

Islam as a 'revolutionary ideology' with 'its own tenets and ideals' excludes other ideologies and other ideals. This had political implications, of course, for,

A man who believes in Communism could not order his life according to the principles of capitalism whilst living in Britain or America, for the capitalistic state system would bear down on him and it would be impossible for him to escape the power of the ruling authority. Likewise, it is impossible for a Muslim to succeed in his aim of observing the Islamic pattern of life under the authority of a non-Islamic system of government. All rules which he considers wrong, all taxes which he deems unlawful, all matters which he believes to be evil, the civilisation and way of life which he regards as wicked, the education system which he views as fatal ... all these will be relentlessly imposed on him, his home and his family, that it will be impossible to avoid them. (Minault 1982, p. 11)

Beyond the political, being a Muslim, for Mawdudi, is also a matter of morality and epistemology. It is, in fact, an all-encompassing ideology. Mawdudi's conception of *jihad* is to contrast it with a modern notion of *jahiliyyah*.[1] Whilst having recourse to the paradigm of the Prophet Muhammad's *jihad* against the *jahiliyyah* of the pagan Arabs, Mawdudi imposes the paradigm upon contemporary events by referring

---

[1] This concept, the 'age of ignorance', as used in the Qur'an, refers to the period of time in Arabia before the advent of Islam. In its more modern context, it is a reference to any time or peoples who are also 'ignorant' of Islam and may well refer to people that refer to themselves as 'Muslim' but regarded by scholars such as Mawdudi and his followers as lacking sufficient faith and understanding to deserve this designate.

to Muhammad Ali Jinnah's (who became the founder and first Governor-General of Pakistan) Muslim League as a 'party of pagans' (*jama'at-i jahiliyya*) but, more broadly than that, *jahiliyyah* signified a state of 'ignorance' in the absence of divine revelation and included, therefore, the secular—primarily (although by no means exclusively) western—world and all that it stood for. Mawdudi presents a dualistic cosmos between the abode of peace and the abode of war; two separate realms and, for Mawdudi, it was important that the realm of *jahiliyyah* should not infect the purity of Islam, for it has nothing to offer. As pointed out by Safdar Ahmed, 'It is arguable that this duality—between Islam and ignorance—impoverishes Islam by segregating it from potentially beneficial, secular traditions of knowledge' (Ahmed 2013, p. 79). Personally, I would say this is not 'arguable' at all, but palpable, for it results in Islam closing its doors and going on the defensive. This form of Islamic modernism is what Muhammad Arkoun (1928–2010), following in the footsteps of Jacques Derrida (1930–2004), calls 'tele-techno-scientific reason'.

Arkoun is right in accusing Muslim modernists of rarely being prepared to consider the Qur'an within its historical context and that its language—like language at any time or any place—needs to be seen as affected by the society of its time. Mawdudi is a prime example of this form of modernism that Arkoun criticises, and consequently Mawdudi ignores an important part of the Islamic tradition that was prepared to engage in such debates concerning the nature of the Qur'an as 'created' or 'uncreated'. Arkoun's epistemology suggests a deconstructive approach to the language of the Qur'an in the view that, in the Derrida sense, 'there is nothing outside textuality'. Therefore, Arkoun's Islamic 'modernism' is more limited epistemologically to the text and, of particular interest here, is his dialectical approach to the history of reason in Islamic intellectual traditions, which Arkoun states has oscillated between the polarities of the 'thought and unthought'. Like Christianity's encounter with Greek rational philosophy, Islam too contended with a different way of understanding that had a massive influence on Islamic intellectual discourse. In the modern era, Islam, again like Christianity, was confronted by tele-techno-scientific reason with its accompanying technological expressions and global capitalism. Whilst many Islamic countries sought to embrace this new global force, Arkoun saw its effect on Islam's intellectual traditions as nothing short of disastrous. His concern is certainly echoed by many Islamic modernists such as al-Afghānī, but the resultant secularisation of the west also caused

Islam to be dispossessed of its philosophical richness and essential values, becoming instead reified and rationalised.

Therefore, while modernists such as Mawdudi may believe that they are asserting Islamic identity independent of western rational thought, they are, in reality, doing the exact opposite: they are rationalising a religion and submerging its more explorative, individual, subjective, mystical, and existential aspects. Mawdudi sought an Islam that was pure, that was unsullied by the non-Islamic world. Islam was perceived as a completely independent system. This idea of intellectual independence derives to a degree from Mawdudi's readings of Muhammad Iqbal's concept of *khudi* (selfhood) although, as will be shown later, this results in a misunderstanding and a narrow interpretation of what Iqbal really meant by this term, with Mawdudi preferring *khudi* as a more political creature, rather than the mystical humanism of Iqbal. Further, Iqbal, as we shall see, placed greater trust in the individual's ability to assert his or her own creative power or 'will-to-power' if you will (given the influence of Nietzsche on Iqbal), whereas Mawdudi distrusted most people's ability to *be human* in the Islamic sense, hence the political implications and the need for a Platonic overlord. This is what Mawdudi meant by the term *hakimiyya* or 'divine governance'. The majority of the population of a Muslim state would not, Mawdudi believed, be sufficiently educated to understand God's guidance and, therefore, are duty-bound to submit to a ruler who is as fully cognisant with God's will as it is possible to be. In fact, those who are given the authority to determine God's will, that is to engage in *ijtihad*, are those Muslims who have achieved the capability of interpretation, which, according to Mawdudi's own calculations, would make up no more than 0.001% of the Muslim population. Mawdudi's wariness for the genuine piety and virtue of the majority of Muslims is evident when he states that, when, 'laws are made with the will of the people, experience has shown that the common people themselves cannot understand their interests. It is a natural weakness of human beings that in most matters relating to their life they consider some aspects of the matter and overlook others; generally their judgement is one-sided' (Mawdudi 1969, p. 130).

Mawdudi was, therefore, far more reluctant in his confidence that Muslims are able to take on individual responsibility, whereas Iqbal's concept of the *khudi* is one that seemingly emerges in an evolutionary manner, rather like Nietzsche's *Übermensch*. But, in the same way suspicions have been raised regarding the moral character of Nietzsche's 'creators of values', Mawdudi might wonder why Iqbal's *khudi* would feel in any way obliged to acquiesce to the ethical requirements of Islam. The clash between the existential self and 'being moral' is a topic that the French existentialist Jean-Paul Sartre (1905–1980), for example, never satisfactorily resolved, falling back on a form of Kantian categorical imperative. However, by following the dictates of *shari'a*— as interpreted by a political elite—the individual believer engages in an impoverished form of worship in which the relationship between the human and the divine is one of submission and obedience rather than a two-way relationship involving love and a genuine faith in the Kierkegaardian sense.

LANGUAGE DEFIES REIFICATION

It is *this* reified understanding of Islam that secular transhumanism has every right to be wary of as a form of religious belief, for how can one engage in debates concerning the transhuman if there is not even any understanding of the human? Islamist modernists such as Mawdudi take away human creativity, struggle, and endeavour and replace it with blind submission to a systematised religion in which even God has become a Platonic Good that can be rationalised and understood in human, logical terms by an elite. Gone has the Kierkegaardian paradox and the mystery, the God of 'fear and trembling', or of Moses Maimonides' God of the 'perplexed'. The understanding of what it means to be human is synonymous with an awareness that human beings are not mere rational agents with specific goals and purposes, but are complex, irrational, mysterious, and contradictory creatures. Even if we accept a Feuerbachian approach to God, then presenting the divine as a rational agent is not a true reflection of what human beings are or, for that matter, necessarily what human beings aspire to be. This grounded God becomes removed from our true human nature, with His set of desires and hopes, instead becoming a distant Aristotelian God. The German philosopher Martin Heidegger (1889–1976) was right to criticise this kind of belief for, as Jim Hanson puts it, 'rationalising faith-based experience[s] of the deity' (Hanson 2012, p. 215). Mention has already been made of Moses Maimonides, and his insights on how we use language to conceive of God seem most relevant here. Maimonides' work *The Guide of the Perplexed* refers to those Jewish scholars who, despite their deep theological learning, remain 'perplexed':

Hence he would remain in a state of perplexity and confusion as to whether he should follow his intellect, renounce what he knew concerning the terms in question, and consequently consider that he has renounced the foundations of the Law. Or he should hold fast to his understanding of these terms and not let himself be drawn together with his intellect, rather turning his back on it and moving away from it, while at the same time perceiving that he had brought loss to himself and harm to his religion. He would be left with those imaginary beliefs to which he owes his fear and difficulty and would not cease to suffer from heartache and great perplexity. (Maimonides 1963, pp. 5–6)

Believers remain perplexed because the attempts to rationalise the irrational, to place square pegs in round holes, to attempt to resolve the paradoxical, are simply not possible: faith cannot be rationalised, and a literal approach to the textual sources can only take you so far in understanding. Here, Maimonides is acknowledging the importance of the esoteric, which he felt was a convention that had been lost to a more legalistic, literal tradition, hence the need to produce a *Guide* as a dissemination of esoteric knowledge before it is lost forever. The human quest for knowledge, therefore, combines faith in scripture, empirical knowledge, and the esoteric, but Maimonides' concern that the latter was being forgotten reflects the time and place he lived in. Maimonides was unfortunate in the sense that he was born at the end of the Jewish golden age in Andalusia and lived during the puritanical Almohad regime. It was a time of Jewish persecution, but also for Islam itself it was, at times anyway, dangerous to adopt a philosophical or mystical understanding of belief.

In *The Guide of the Perplexed*, Maimonides deliberately plays with language, making his text obscure and paradoxical, because he was only too aware that language has limitations and is *limiting*. Therefore, the *Perplexed* is deliberately ambiguous and conceals, but also reveals. Reading *Perplexed* is itself an exegetical strategy and a test for the reader and, even then, Maimonides is not at all persuaded that the reader will have understood him properly or, even if he or she has, will not be able to adequately communicate the message to another, hence his warning:

I adjure—by God, may He be exalted!—every reader of this Treatise of mine not to comment upon a single word of it and not to explain to another anything in it save that which has been explained and commented upon in the words of the famous Sages of our Law who preceded me. But whatever he understands from this Treatise of those things that have not been said by any of our famous Sages other than myself should not be explained to another; nor should be hasten to refute me, for that which he understood me to say might be contrary to my intention. (Maimonides 1963, p. 15)

Scripture includes a concealed layer of meaning, which is its esoteric nature, and the perplexity of the scholar results in being blind to such esotericism. This is a recognition that language cannot express the 'inexpressible'; those moments of cognition that Maimonides describes as 'flashes'. Putting such experience into words can take away from the metaphorical and can lead to idolatry. In talking of God, the very structure of language, of a subject and a predicate, is problematic; for even to say 'the Lord is One' does not make any sense as this divides God's unity into subject and predicate! All we can do then is negate attributes associated with God (*via negativa*), that is he is *not* absent, he is *not* multiple, but some interpreters have made the mistake in concluding that *via negativa* results in a greater understanding of God. However, you cannot infer any positives from these negatives. You cannot affirm the opposite. Going through a series of negations merely demonstrates how much you do not know. By making affirmations about God you, paradoxically, become more remote from Him, because you are actually imposing human categories upon him. Affirmations about God are a reference to *us*, not Him. Religious language is not providing us with the full story of being human, rather it limits. Whether God is 'real' or not is, to a large extent, not the point here, for the criticism of religious language is equally applicable to Islamic modernists as it is to, say, Christian anti-realist postmodernists such as Don Cupitt. It is this understanding that language is flawed and plays a key part in an onto-theology, and you have to bracket out language in order to have pure experience, not unlike Kant's notion of a 'disinterested' approach to the sublime and the beautiful. Importantly, Maimonides was not arguing for ascetic isolation, for the awareness that you cannot know God, for he then compels you to look to God's creations, to turn towards the world. You actually become more deeply embedded within the world, not divorced or alienated from it. Two quotes from Nietzsche, the great philologist, are particularly helpful here:

An aphorism, properly stamped and molded, has not been "deciphered" when it has simply been read; rather, one has then to begin its exegesis, for which is required an art of exegesis. (Nietzsche 1966, Preface S.8)

Just as a reader today scarcely distinguishes all the individual words (let alone syllables) on a page (of every twenty words he randomly selects five or so instead, and "guesses" the meaning that probably corresponds to those five words), so we scarcely see a tree exactly and completely, with regard to its leaves, branches, colour, shape: it is so much easier for us to dream up something approximating a tree. (Nietzsche 1998, S.192)

The first quote is referring to how Nietzsche's aphorisms are meant to be read: it is not, in fact, merely enough to read the words that are written, but an exegesis is required. Here, Nietzsche recognises, like Maimonides, that language has limitations and there is a serious concern from Nietzsche that he will be misunderstood. Nietzsche, then, in the second quote above, extends the reading of text to the reading of our environment: rather than meditate on what is in front of us, we prefer to simply fill in the gaps. We must, therefore, 'embed' ourselves within the world, for only then can we truly see. This is reminiscent of Edmund Husserl (1859–1938) who talked of a *phenomenological attitude*, rather than a school of thought, which involves a new 'way of looking' at things. Also, Maurice Merleau-Ponty (1908–1961) stated that, 'True philosophy consists in relearning to look at the world' (Russell 2006, p. 71).

Hence, the limitations of language and the realisation that human experience is something that cannot be so readily expressed or rationalised is a common enough view in many religious and philosophical traditions. For this work, focus is, of course, on the Islamic tradition, but it is important to appreciate that this is very much a *universal* human phenomenon. Just as one example here[2]: in the Christian tradition Thomas Aquinas (1225–1274) famously went 'silent' from 1273 and refused to write any more. When a friend begged him to continue he said, 'Reginald, I cannot, because all I have written seems like straw to me'. By 'straw' here, Aquinas did not mean 'gibberish'. Rather, it was a conventional metaphor for a literal reading of the Bible. It expressed the view that a straightforward reading of the Bible might provide the reader with some comfort, but that is really just a first step. So, by 'straw', Aquinas felt that he had not gone far enough; had not really understood the Scripture. He was, in the Maimonides sense, 'perplexed'. The most important things are the most difficult to explain. This goes back to Socrates: the key to wisdom is not

[2] A similar experience to that attributed to Aquinas was also experienced by the Muslim theologian and philosopher Muhammad al-Ghazali, which I will look at in more detail in Chap. 6.

how much you know but in understanding where the limits of your knowledge lie. Ultimately, an agnostic approach has to be adopted. Aquinas himself remained agnostic concerning, for example, whether it can be proved that the world has a beginning. His faith tells him so, but his intellect does not and, of course, his Five Ways were not intended to *prove* the existence of God, but, rather, to show the usefulness as well as the limits of reason. It can be seen, however, how one can move from agnosticism to a form of atheism, for some apophatic theologians have even said that to sense that God doesn't exist is actually a more profound experience than to be confident that God does exist, because the latter is too close to a human sensation.

Aquinas' new silence was not a realisation that he had somehow 'failed' in his understanding, but rather a culmination of his work. Aquinas had reached the stage that Maimonides hoped others would; the realisation of the limitations of language, and to follow the maxim in psalms 'For you, silence is praise'. This is reminiscent of the philosopher Ludwig Wittgenstein's (1889–1951) famous remark in *Tractatus*, 'Whereof one cannot speak, thereof one must be silent', and, indeed, when referring to the limitations of language, Wittgenstein is important:

> 6.4 All propositions are of equal value
> 6.41 The sense of the world must lie outside the world. In the world everything is as it is, and everything happens as it does happen: in it no value exists—and if it did exist, it would have no value.
> 6.42 Propositions can express nothing that is higher. (Wittgenstein 1961, 6.4–6.42)

The above, more 'mystical', passage from *Tractatus* suggests that Wittgenstein believes there is something outside of the facts of the world and, therefore, when we attempt to describe in language what this 'something' is we will either fail or resort to mystical or supernatural language. As he remarks in *A Lecture on Ethics*:

> My whole tendency and I believe the tendency of all men who ever tried to write or talk Ethics or Religion was to run against the boundaries of language. This running against the walls of our cage is perfectly, absolutely hopeless. ... But it is a document of a tendency in the human mind which I personally cannot help respecting deeply and I would not for my life ridicule it. (Wittgenstein 1965, pp. 11–12)

Should we therefore adhere to Wittgenstein's verdict that 'one must remain silent' when faced with such seeming hopelessness? I think not, and I am not convinced that Wittgenstein is quite so strict either. The 'obvious'—the facts that are in front of us—can be described, but so what! What is more important is what cannot be described, the *sub specie aeternitatis*. Wittgenstein finds meaning in the 'arts', for example in his love of the Ludwig Uhland poem *Count Eberhard's Hawthorn*, for which Wittgenstein said in his correspondence with Engelmann, 'The poem by Uhland is really magnificent. And this is how it is: if only you do not try to utter what is unutterable then nothing gets lost. But the unutterable will be—unutterably—contained in what has been uttered!' (Engelmann 1968, p. 7)

The poem allows the reader to 'see' the world in a way that factual language cannot. 'The facts of the world are not the end of the matter'. In this sense, Wittgenstein does not sit so comfortably in the Positivist camp when it comes to the 'unsayable'. The Uhland poem can be read from both the perspective of the person reading the poem, but also related to this is what we take from Count Eberhard's experience of the hawthorn. To appreciate this, it helps to quote the poem in full:

> Count Eberhard Rustle-Beard,
> From Württemberg's fair land,
> On holy errand steer'd
> To Palestina's strand.
>
> The while he slowly rode
> Along a woodland way;
> He cut from the hawthorn bush
> A little fresh green spray.
>
> Then in his iron helm
> The little sprig he plac'd;
> And bore it in the wars,
> And over the ocean waste.
>
> And when he reach'd his home;
> He plac'd it in the earth;
> Where little leaves and buds
> The gentle Spring call'd forth.
>
> He went each year to it,
> The Count so brave and true;
> And overjoy'd was he
> To witness how it grew.

The Count was worn with age
The sprig became a tree;
'Neath which the old man oft
Would sit in reverie.

The branching arch so high,
Whose whisper is so bland,
Reminds him of the past
And Palestina's strand. (Engelmann 1968, pp. 83–84)

The Count's care for the hawthorn tree is full of meaning. The tree acts as a reminder of both the Count's youth and his experiences, whilst also providing an ethical message of consistency and care. In terms of language, then, one can adopt a 'theological' approach to the text and appreciate the meaning *behind*, or *beyond*, the words as best as possible, or the 'onto-theological' approach to 'master' the text and to have it conform to a rational, logical understanding of the world. Surely the latter leaves out the mystery, in the same way an onto-theological approach to religion does, but secular transhumanism might declare that there is no 'mystery' to be left out. It is this reductionist approach to the human that is unsettling and a concern that has its philosophical roots in religion and, in terms of western philosophy, we can go back at least to Aristotle in his critique of the atomists.

Derrida, of course, had much to say about the limitations and corrosiveness of language. In, for example, *Speech and Phenomena*, he was critical of Husserl's 'reduction' of the importance of language. Husserl's transcendental phenomenology, in his later writings anyway, is concerned with an apparent *doubleness* between psychological subjectivity and transcendental subjectivity, and leads him to ask, 'Are "we" then supposed to be double—psychological presences, as we humans, in the world, subjects of psychic life, and at the same time transcendental, as the subjects of a transcendental world-constituting life?' (Husserl 1997, p. 171). Husserl is addressing the fundamental question that the secular transhumanist often seems to overlook in their pursuit for the transhuman dream that is *who we are*. Merleau-Ponty expresses it very clearly in his opening paragraph to *The Visible and the Invisible* when he asks, 'What is this we?' (Merleau-Ponty 1968, p. 3). Both Merleau-Ponty and Derrida seem very close in the view that when the voice speaks out beyond 'auto-affection' (i.e. beyond one's own internal monologue), the voice is no longer master of its own speech. Derrida raises a highly significant point concerning repetition, which is reflected in Nietzsche's emphasis that his aphorisms have to be read and re-read many times:

> By means of this written inscription, one can always repeat the original sense, that is, the act of pure thought which created the ideality of sense. With the possibility of progress that such an incarnation allows, there goes the ever growing risk of 'forgetting' and loss of sense. It becomes more and more difficult to reconstitute the presence of the act buried under historical sedimentations. The moment of crisis is always a moment of signs. (Derrida 1973, p. 81)

Automatic repetition in a machine-like manner divorces the text from its meaning, hence quotes from the Bible or the Qur'an, or tweets that are repeated many thousands of times. The new atheist attack on religion by selectively repeating scriptural passages is 'mastering' the text for one's own purposes. Likewise, the Islamic modernist repetition of Qur'anic or hadith passages is both 'mastering' and 'enslaving' the human in relation to the text. There is, therefore, considerable difference between *repeating* a text and engaging in a Nietzschean *exegesis* of the text.

There is a tension here, of course, between the religious believer who genuinely believes that there is something, some 'One', beyond the text, and the anti-realist who, like Derrida and Arkoun, perceive nothing 'real' beyond the text, but I do not see this as a tension that should concern us. What is more important is how the reader *reads* the text; what one 'does' with Scripture or, of that matter, other forms of communication, whether that is the religious, the secular, poetry, novels, painting, music, or other art forms. When faced with Scripture, the Islamic modernist may 'reify' the text in the belief that it must, and can, be understood (albeit by an elite few if we are referring to Mawdudi amongst others), thus 'mastering' the sacred text and God, or, alternatively—and whilst maintaining that there really is a God that exist—acknowledge that God cannot be 'understood', that God is a mystery, and that Scripture, likewise, is slippery and cannot be fully grasped. From the perspective of the anti-realist, who comes in many varieties of course, the text can still have meaning beyond the literal, whether that is 'God' in some anti-realist sense, or some 'other' in perhaps a Wittgensteinian sense; that is that which is not merely a 'fact' about the world. The secular mind too, can contextualise the text and embrace its richness and mystery; while perhaps not calling this 'God', there is nonetheless an acknowledgement of an 'other' that cannot be reduced to factual description. Alternatively, he or she can approach the text as merely a series of facts in a logical positivist way: the secular transhumanist, alas, seems to fall into this latter category.

We come again to the problems of communication when humans struggle to understand and explain that which cannot so readily be translated into limiting words. It is not just religious adherents who have been faced with this struggle and have, consequently, had to resort to metaphor, analogy, poems, riddles, stories, parables, and so on in an attempt to express the inexpressible. We have referred already to Wittgenstein, but we can go back to at least Socrates who, in *Republic*, had no choice other than to resort to a series of analogies in the hope that his interlocutors would grasp what he meant by the Good for, despite efforts to get Socrates to describe the Good, Socrates is compelled to declare that, "'I'm afraid I won't be able to manage it; I'd cut a sorry figure, eager though I'd be able to do it, and you'd laugh at me'" (Plato 2012, 506d).

The Mystery That Is Life. The Mystery That Is Death

As human beings, while we are alive we are preoccupied by thoughts of death. One essential question that the religious has concerned itself with is death and what awaits us in the hereafter, if anything at all. Further, given the fact that our lives are measured by our deaths, the task of providing meaning while we are alive has resulted in complex religious rituals, doctrines, ethical systems, institutions, and so on to provide a purposeful framework. These alternative frameworks that the different religions provide work for some, but not for others and, in the growth of modernity, many such frameworks are suffering decay or breaking down entirely. Philosophy, too, in its religious and secular sense, has endeavoured to provide the human with a response to the existential crisis of the absurd. From a secular transhumanist perspective, the issue has been more of a technical one; that is, is it technologically possible to prevent death? The question of giving meaning to the life we have, however long or short that may be, has been of secondary concern.

Consider, for example, Nick Bostrom's article 'The Fable of the Dragon-Tyrant'. This tells a nice story of a dragon that demanded from mankind thousands of men and women every day to satisfy its appetite. Having no way to defend itself against the dragon, the people acquiesced, sending its older generation to their premature deaths every day. The dragon in this fable does, of course, represent death, and the fable reveals that, in time, the people acquire technology that is able to defeat the dragon. There is, nonetheless, resistance to this technology; the expense involved, the risk of it not succeeding, other issues that some would argue need to take precedence, the general attitude that the dragon is a fact of life rather than something that is an evil, and so on. It is an enjoyable fable and its moral message deserves great attention, but there is one aspect of the article I want to question. The king decided to have an open hearing to the public to determine whether time and money should be invested in the technology to defeat the dragon. The first to speak was a female scientist who, of course, 'proceeded to explain in clear language how the proposed device would work and how the requisite amount of the composite material could be manufactured' (Bostrom 2005, p. 274). The next to speak is the king's chief advisor for morality, 'a man with a booming voice that easily filled the auditorium' (ibid.) who gives the following speech:

> Let us grant that this woman is correct about the science and that the project is technologically possible, although I don't think that has actually been proven. Now she desires that we get rid of the dragon. Presumably, she thinks she's got the right not to be chewed up by the dragon. How willful and presumptuous. The finitude of human life is a blessing for every individual, whether he knows it or not. Getting rid of the dragon, which might seem like such a convenient thing to do, would undermine our human dignity. The preoccupation with killing the dragon will deflect us from realizing more fully the aspirations to which our lives naturally point, from living well rather than merely staying alive. It is debasing, yes debasing, for a person to want to continue his or her mediocre life for as long as possible without worrying about some of the higher questions about what life is to be used for. But I tell you, the nature of the dragon is to eat humans, and our own species-specified nature is truly and nobly fulfilled only by getting eaten by it. (ibid.)

The next to speak is a spiritual sage, but instead he gives the stage to a child who says he wants the dragon killed because, '"The dragon is bad and it eats people. ... I want my Granny back!"' (ibid.). Now, while credit must be given to the spiritual sage for giving the child a hearing, the disdain shown to the moral guide by Bostrom is troubling. To what extent is Bostrom pulling at our heart strings here and engaging in disturbing stereotypes of 'woman'—represented by the scientist—as nurturing and caring, of 'child' as innocent but wise, then as the man with the 'booming voice' who attempts to deceive us whose 'phrases were so eloquent that it was hard to resist the feeling that some deep thoughts must lurk behind them, although nobody could quite grasp what they were'. Why should a moral guide be portrayed so? Are not the points he makes about 'living well rather than merely staying alive', or the importance of 'worrying about some of the higher questions about what life is to be used for', for example, worthy of consideration? One might not agree with all of his arguments, but Bostrom's portrayal of this man as engaging in deceitful obfuscation leads the reader to condemn him automatically.

I am not saying that, given the option of an extended life or being devoured by a dragon, that I would go for the dragon option and nor I am saying that I would willingly allow my granny to be dragon fodder, but I am saying that life cannot be seen merely in terms of longevity. Quality of life and meaning given to that life are important factors and should not be dismissed in the way Bostrom does, especially as numerous people do opt to take their own lives rather than continue to live. The quest for a meaning to life goes beyond the emotional response of 'I want my granny back', although it also does not deny the importance of the emotions as part of what it means to be human. Nonetheless, to give meaning we must engage our cognitive faculties. I do not agree with critics of life extension such as the influential bioethicist Leon Kass who also seems to resort to emotional outpourings, without any rational articulation. Consider, for example, his essay 'The Wisdom of Repugnance' in which he opposes human cloning:

> "Offensive." "Grotesque." "Revolting." "Repugnant." "Repulsive." These are the words most commonly heard regarding the prospect of human cloning. Such reactions come both from the man or woman in the street and from the intellectuals, from believers and atheists, from humanists and scientists. Even Dolly's creator has said he "would find it offensive" to clone a human being: 'Revulsion is not an argument; and some of yesterday's repugnances are today calmly accepted—though, one must add, not always for the better. In crucial cases, however, repugnance is the emotional expression of deep wisdom, beyond reason's power fully to articulate it. Can anyone really give an argument fully adequate to the horror which is father–daughter incest (even with consent), or having sex with animals, or mutilating a corpse, or eating human flesh, or even just (just!) raping or murdering another human being? Would anybody's failure to give full rational justification for his or her revulsion at these practices make that revulsion ethically suspect? Not at all. On the contrary, we are suspicious of those who think that they can rationalize away our horror, say, by trying to explain the enormity of incest with arguments only about the genetic risks of in-breeding. (Kass 1997, p. 18)

Something being 'repugnant' is a gut-response, not a well-articulated argument. Many people find homosexuality 'repugnant', but that does not make it morally reprehensible. I do not subscribe to the view that the possibility of immortality is a 'menacing spectre' according to the eminent biogerontologist Leonard Guarente (2003). I personally have many reasons to welcome such a possibility, although it is unlikely to be available to me before I die, although perhaps Steven Austad is correct to assert that the first 150-year-old has been alive since the year 2000 (McCann 2001, p. 8). Such debates between transhumanists and others are certainly exciting, but the point here is whether religion has anything to offer in terms of what immortality entails from a purely non-biological perspective, given that—as I hope this work demonstrates—we are not merely biological entities or, if we are, we at best cannot be so readily reduced to biological parts. Aubrey de Grey is correct, I believe, in arguing that society will, in time, overcome moral qualms it has towards curing ageing, in the same way it has towards slavery or women's equality, and he does present many cogent arguments for this. Again, however, may I interject: can religion contribute here, or is it seen rather as an obstacle or simply irrelevant? The abolition of the slave trade by British ships to the Americas was denounced by Christians, for example Richard Baxter declaring that slave traders were 'fitter to be called devils than Christians', and the Puritan Samuel Sewall who published America's first antislavery tract, *The Selling of Joseph* in 1700 (Coffey 2006). The important intervention by Christians towards the abolition of slavery is well-documented but, of course, there were also Christians who supported slavery and Christians who did not seem to care either way, but that does not mean that the arguments of these Christian critics of slavery should be ignored. Similarly, the role of religion in women's movements has been positive and negative, but, again, we should not therefore ignore the positive. For example, the suffragist Helena Swanwick (1864–1939) notes in her autobiography *I Have Been Young*, 'For—let there be no mistake about it—this movement was not primarily political; it was social, moral, psychological and profoundly religious' (Swanwick 1935, p. 187).

I do agree with the secular transhumanist view that we need to be more accepting of the technological changes that will result in radical life extension (RLE), and, perhaps eventually, immortality. I also believe that religion can contribute to this debate and, in the case of Islam, has a tradition of accepting and, indeed, embracing technological change as well as engaging with what this means for us as human beings. The rapid advance in RLE technology must, however, address the very serious ethical issues that arise from this, and that is not just a job for the scientists: philosophers, and I include in this philosophers in the Islamic tradition, can and should play a part. They are certainly not all as portrayed in Bostrom's fable, though it may bring to mind one or two individuals!

Before I look at the Islamic contribution it is important to be clear of our terms, for while I have pointed out that immortality may be a possibility at some future point, this is a different area from RLE. Michael Cerullo has stated that, 'discussions of immortality are premature at this point and only serve as a distraction from the debate regarding more credible life extension technologies' (Cerullo 2016, p. 97). However, many, including the gerontologist Aubrey de Grey, have publicly declared that the first immortal has already been born. Sceptics of such prophesies, such as S. Jay Olshansky, remind us that, 'What do the ancient purveyors of physical immortality all have in common? They are all dead' (Olshansky 2004), although the point is missed that past prophets of immortality did not have the access to technology that we have today and will have in the near future. In a way, it is difficult to separate RLE from immortality, because one implies the other; the fact that we are now able to extend life means that people may live long enough to experience the technology that extends their life indefinitely. Whilst Cerullo considers immortality a 'mythological concept' (Cerullo 2016, p. 97), it is also a *conceivable* concept. I do, therefore, think it is quite justifiable to consider the religious and ethical implication of immortality without it muddying the waters to any great extent. The bottom line is that we are talking here of extending life with, possibly, no end in sight.

IS AGEING A MYSTICAL PHENOMENON?

Aubrey de Grey states that 'there is a widespread tendency to think of aging as a mystical phenomenon, intrinsically beyond our ability to comprehend (let alone combat)' (de Grey 2009, p. 13). Is it 'mystical'? De Grey views ageing as a 'physical phenomenon' in which 'the actual nuts and bolts of aging—the difference between a younger person and an older person that cause the older person to have less time to live on average—are purely structural, definable ultimately in terms of the atoms of which the body is composed and their spatial arrangement' (ibid.). At one level, it is difficult to disagree with this. If we conceived of ageing as a sickness, as de Grey does, then the material laws of cause and effect come into play: you detect the symptoms and apply the cure. Doctors are, of course, scientists, and they adopt the scientific method, thankfully. However, any good doctor will not treat a human being in the same way he or she treats their car, for example. Why? Because human beings are not mere 'nuts and bolts'. Each human being is different, and treatments will often differ for one person's sickness to the next. Also, it is widely acknowledged amongst doctors that what brings on a physical illness cannot so readily be reduced to certain nuts and bolts, but it is interconnected at the physical *and* psychological level. De Grey is fully aware that there is a psychology underlying ageing but to reduce the concept of ageing to nuts and bolts seems too simplistic. However, it is important to study de Grey's words carefully, for he is saying that the cause of what determines a young person from an old person is a physical one, then that is stating the obvious. No one can dispute that, and those that may regard death as 'mystical' are surely not seeing it that way because time is passing and bodies decay; there is nothing mysterious about that! Rather, the mysticism is wrapped up in many layers and, by this, is meant that ageing is not reduceable to mechanical parts when we see the concept in this way. So, yes, de Grey is right at one level, but this is not what is meant when we talk of it being 'mystical'. When seen in this way, the difference between a young person and an older person are profound and, when considering what it means to be, say, a 1000 year-old person, it belittles the complexity of the human to see this merely in terms of the physics of it all. In fact, it is extremely difficult to conceive of what it would be like to be 1000 years old in terms of our psychological state, our wisdom, our memories, our emotional responses, and so on. *This* is what makes ageing 'mystical'.

Perhaps it is more conducive to discussion if we embrace the spirit of de Grey's view of ageing. That is to say, by 'mystical', it is seen as something that is a miracle of nature and, as mere humans who are dictated by the laws of nature, we are humbled by its laws. De Grey, therefore, argues that, with the advances in technology, humans can 'overcome' these natural laws: they are no longer 'mystical' in that sense because they can be understood and overcome. Just because nature 'dictates' a lifespan of roughly three score and ten, gives us no reason to follow that diktat. Historically there is no denying that all human beings have a limited lifespan so far. Today it is becoming more common for people to live to 100, and there are records of some living for 20 or 30 years more than that, although records here are less reliable. The problem with determining a natural lifespan is when technology 'interferes'. Yes, more and more people alive today can expect to live to 100 or more, but they will most likely require some medical assistance along the way, including the replacement of various body parts (hips, hearts, etc.). If we were to let nature take its own course without the use of any technology at all, then the lifespan would be shorter, however much fruit and vegetables you might consume. All evidence points to the fact that humans, like all other creatures, decay and die at some point and, generally speaking, around 70 or 80 years without the aid of medical technology seems to be the limit for most people.

BIBLIOGRAPHY[3]

BOOKS

al-Afghānī, Jamāl al-Dīn. 2002. *Khatirat Jamal al-Din al-Afghani*. Cairo: Maktabat al-Shuruq.

Ahmed, Safdar. 2013. *Reform and Modernity in Islam: The Philosophical, Cultural and Political Discourses Among Muslim Reformers*. London: Tauris Academic Studies.

Cromer, Evelyn Baring. 1908. *Modern Egypt*, Vols. 1 & 2. London: Macmillan.

Davies, Merryl Wyn. 1988. *Knowing One Another: Shaping an Islamic Anthropology*. London and New York: Mansell Publishing.

Derrida, Jacques. 1973. *Speech and Phenomena*. Evanston, IL: Northwestern University Press.

Engelmann, Paul. 1968. *Letters from Ludwig Wittgenstein, with a Memoir*. Translated by L. Furtmüller. Oxford: Wiley-Blackwell.

Esposito, John L., and John Voll. 2001. *Makers of Contemporary Islam*. Oxford: Oxford University Press.

Guarente, Lenny. 2003. *Ageless Quest*. New York: Cold Spring Harbor Laboratory Press.

Husserl, Edmund. 1997. *Psychological and Transcendental Phenomenology and the Confrontation with Heidegger (1927–1931)*. Translated and Edited by Thomas Sheehan and Richard E. Palmer. Dordrecht: Kluwer Academic Publishers.

Khan, Syed Ahmad. 1891. *Essay on the Question Whether Islam Has Been Beneficial or Injurious to Human Society in General*. Lahore: Mohammadan Tract and Book Department.

Lebor, Adam. 1997. *A Heart Turned East: Among the Muslims of Europe and America*. New York: Warner Books.

---

[3] *Note*: All quotes from the Qur'an are from the translation by M.A.S. Abdel Haleem, Oxford University Press, 2005.

Lindholm, Charles. 1996. *The Islamic Middle East: An Historical Anthropology.* Chichester: Wiley-Blackwell.

Maimonides, Moses. 1963. *The Guide of the Perplexed.* Translated by Schlomo Pines. Chicago: University of Chicago Press.

Mawdudi, Abu Al'a. 1969. *Islami Riyasat.* Lahore: Islamic Publications Ltd.

———. 1995. *Jihad fi Sabillah: Jihad in Islam.* Translated and Edited by Khurshid Ahmad. Birmingham: Huda Khattab, UK Islamic Mission Dawah Centre.

Merleau-Ponty, Mauric. 1968. *The Visible and the Invisible.* Translated by Alphonso Lingis. Evanston: Northwestern University Press.

Minault, Gail. 1982. *The Khilafat Movement: Religious Symbolisms and Political Mobilization in India.* New York: Columbia University Press.

Nietzsche, Friedrich. 1966. *On the Genealogy of Morals.* Translated by Walter Kaufmann. New York: Vintage Books.

———. 1998. *Beyond Good and Evil.* Translated by Marion Faber. Oxford: Oxford University Press.

Plato. 2012. *Republic.* Translated by Christopher Rowe. London: Penguin.

Russell, Matheson. 2006. *Husserl: A Guide for the Perplexed.* London: Continuum.

Said, Edward. 1978. *Orientalism.* London: Penguin.

Smith, Wilfred Cantwell. 1959. *The Meaning and End of Religion.* Minneapolis, MN: Augsburg Fortress.

Swanwick, Helena Maria Lucy. 1935. *I Have Been Young.* London: Gollancz.

Wittgenstein, Ludwig. 1961. *Tractatus Logico-Philosophicus.* London: Routledge.

JOURNAL ARTICLES AND BOOK CHAPTERS

Bostrom, Nick. 2005. The Fable of the Dragon-Tyrant. *Journal of Medical Ethics* 31 (5): 273–277.

BouJaoude, Saouma, et al. 2011a. Biology Professors' and Teachers' Positions Regarding Biological Evolution and Evolution Education in a Middle Eastern Society. *International Journal of Science Education* 33 (7): 979–1000.

———. 2011b. Muslim Egyptian and Lebanese Students' Conceptions of Biological Evolution. *Science and Education* 20 (9): 895–915.

Cerullo, Michael A. 2016. The Ethics of Exponential Life Extension Through Brain Preservation. *Journal of Evolution and Technology* 26 (1): 94–105.

de Grey, Aubrey. 2009. Radical Life Extension: Technological Aspect. In *Religion and the Implications of Radical Life Extension,* ed. Derek F. Maher and Calvin Mercer, 13–24. New York: Palgrave Macmillan.

Hameed, Salman. 2008. Bracing for Islamic Creationism. *Science* 322 (12 December): 1637–1638.

Hanson, Jim. 2012. Ontos and Theos: A Case for Neo-Ontotheology. *Theology Today* 69 (2): 213–224.

Kass, Leon R. 1997. The Wisdom of Repugnance. *New Republic* 216 (22): 17–26.

Majeed, Javed. 2003. Modernity. In *Encyclopedia of Islam and the Muslim World*, ed. S.A. Arjomand et al. (3 vols., 2: 456–458). London: Macmillan Reference.

McCann, J. 2001. Wanna Bet? *Scientist* 15: 8.

Muller, H.J. 1959. One Hundred Years Without Darwinism Are Enough. *School Science and Mathematics* 59 (4): 304–305.

Wittgenstein, Ludwig. 1965. A Lecture on Ethics. *Philosophical Review* 74 (1): 3–12.

WEBSITES

Coffey, John. 2006. *The Abolition of the Slave Trade: Christian Conscience and Political Action*. Jubilee Centre. Accessed July 26, 2019. http://www.jubilee-centre.org/the-abolition-of-the-slave-trade-christian-conscience-and-political-action-by-john-coffey/.

Funk, C., et al. 2016. *U.S. Public Wary of Biomedical Technologies to 'Enhance' Human Abilities*. Pew Research Centre Report. Accessed July 26, 2019. http://www.pewinternet.org/2016/07/26/u-s-public-wary-of-biomedical-technologies-to-enhance-human-abilities/.

Masci, David. 2016. *Q&A: Two Perspectives on Human Enhancement Technologies and How the Public Views Them*. Pew Research Centre. Accessed January 25, 2018. http://www.pewresearch.org/fact-tank/2016/07/27/qa-two-perspectives-on-human-enhancement-technologies-and-how-the-public-views-them/.

Newport, Frank. 2014. *In U.S., 42% Believe Creationist View of Human Origins*. Accessed January 26, 2017. http://www.gallup.com/poll/170822/believe-creationist-view-human-origins.aspx.

Olshansky, S. Jay. 2004. *Don't Fall for the Cult of Immortality*. Accessed February 11, 2018. http://news.bbc.co.uk/1/hi/uk/4059549.stm.

Pew Research Centre Report. 2013. *The World's Muslims: Religion, Politics and Society*. Accessed January 16, 2017. http://www.pewforum.org/2013/04/30/the-worlds-muslims-religion-politics-society-overview/.

CHAPTER 5

The Perennial Human and Beyond

How is it that hardly any major religion has looked at science and concluded, "This is better than we thought! The Universe is much bigger than
our prophets said, grander, more subtle, more elegant?" Instead they say,
"No, no, no! My god is a little god, and I want him to stay that way". A
religion old or new, that stressed the magnificence of the Universe as
revealed by modern science, might be able to draw forth reserves of rever-
ence and awe hardly tapped by the conventional faiths. (Sagan 1997, p. 35)

It is not the intention here to provide a broad survey of the Islamic contribution to science, for there are plenty of books out there on that subject and
it is a fairly uncontested view that the Islamic world contributed greatly to
scientific progress. Rather, the concern here is with Islam in the modern
world and where it goes from here in terms of the prevailing debate on what
it means to be human and, in this broader sense, what this tells us about the
Islamic response to modernity. Central to this is the idea that science is, can,
or should be 'Islamicized'. This project of Islamisation, which does not limit
itself to just the sciences, but to all knowledge, was a very lively intellectual
debate during my early student days in the 1980s of the last century,
although such debates began to decline during the 1990s. There is such an
abundance of scholarship on this issue, that any reasonable treatment would
be beyond the ambitions of this current work, but it is nonetheless important to raise some issues that spring from this 'Traditionalist' approach

© The Author(s) 2020   95
R. Jackson, *Muslim and Supermuslim*, Palgrave Studies
in the Future of Humanity and its Successors,
https://doi.org/10.1007/978-3-030-37093-0_5

to the sciences that will help us understand where Islam can move on from this stage in its intellectual thought.

The Traditionalist, or Perennialist, school of thought champions a totalising of all knowledge under the umbrella of Islam. That is, science, history, anthropology, philosophy, and so on are all to be found—and sought—in divine revelation, as this constitutes perennial truth. Therefore, the claims of modernity, which would include evolutionary theory, are to be disputed if they are not part of this perennial truth. They are effectively falsehoods, which is synonymous with un-Islamic. This movement has its origins with René-Jean-Marie-Joseph Guénon (1886–1951, aka ʿAbd al-Wāḥid Yaḥyá) and Frithjof Schuon (1907–1998 aka Īsā Nūr al-Dīn), and then passed on to the mighty figure of Hossein Nasr (b. 1933).

THE ISLAMIC ENLIGHTENED MAN

As noted in Chap. 2, transhumanism as a movement looks back to the European Enlightenment for its intellectual foundations, and these Enlightenment values are seen by secular transhumanists as antithetical to religious values. Coupled with this is the concept of the Renaissance Man, or the *Uomo Universale*, as a rational agent, as the centre of the universe who can achieve whatever he or she wants. There are no limits. Again, secular transhumanists see religion as placing limits on the human and stifling human goals. Islam especially is often targeted by secularists and militant atheists, as well as the media and politicians, as fundamentally incapable of possessing modernist values that seem to come natural to the west. The question is often asked if Islam can, in actual fact, boast its own Enlightenment or, for that matter, whether to talk of Islam as requiring an 'Enlightenment' in the western context makes little sense, for Islam has always had within its armoury its own forces for renewal and regeneration.

The western world can boast household names such as Voltaire, Rousseau, Descartes, Spinoza, Locke, Hume, Kant, Mozart, Beethoven, Humboldt, Adam Smith, and so on. All of these figures were prepared to challenge existing dogmas, and many were paradigm-shifting in their ideas. Can Islam lay claim to such a pedigree? Christopher de Bellaigue has argued that Islam has its own indigenous figures of regeneration and modernity, putting forward a lengthy list of examples of scientists, philosophers, politicians, and so on during the eighteenth and nineteenth centuries in, especially, Cairo, Istanbul, and Tehran, in an attempt to match what the west has produced. For example, there is Hassan al-Attar

(1766–1835), who was the Grand Imam of Al-Azhar and wrote various works on logic, medicine, and science. Another figure is the Egyptian writer Rifa'a al-Tahtawi (1801–1873) who also attended Al-Azhar, but spent five years in Paris where he studied such Enlightenment figures as Voltaire, Rousseau, and Montesquieu. On his return to Egypt in 1831 he made it his task to modernise Egypt and encouraged scholars to translate European works so they would be readily accessible. Other names cited by Bellaigue include the Turkish polymath Sanizadeh Ataullah who is still famous today in Turkey at least for his writings on medicine, notably his work on modern anatomy *Mirror of the Body*.

However, it is one thing to show that Islam is, by some at least, able to embrace western Enlightenment thought, but that is not the same as saying that such Enlightenment ideals are already embedded within Islam. In other words, can Islam only be *reactive* in response to external forces, or can it also be *proactive* due to its own internal drives, irrespective of what occurs in the non-Islamic world? For example, al-Tahtawi was a moderniser, but also an imitator; taking ideas of a western origin and applying them to Egypt with seemingly little regard as to the extent it is 'Islamic' or not. Such application of what might be considered alien ideas onto a different culture do not always prove beneficial, in the long run anyway. Similarly, Bellaigue praises Ataullah for introducing modern anatomy to the Muslims of Cairo, but also notes that *Mirror of the Body* was not an original work, rather a copy of a Viennese original. These small, drip-drip, ways of thinking infiltrated the Islamic world and, 'In this way, through innumerable small measures and advances, fudges and elisions, the modern principles of empiricism, observations and analysis began to spread' (Bellaigue 2017). Yes, Islam can, it seems, take on western ideas, albeit with some resistance and gradually, but what about original, 'Islamic', 'Enlightenment' thought? Perhaps the question of whether Islam can boast an 'internal enlightenment' may be steering us in the wrong direction and asking the wrong question. Ziauddin Sardar, in the *New Statesman*, was critical of journalistic accusations of Islam being bereft of an Enlightenment:

> Then there was this from Will Hutton in the *Observer*: Islam is "predominantly … pre-Enlightenment". This statement has several layers of ignorance. It projects Islam "predominantly" as monolithic. It suggests that being "pre-Enlightenment" is inferior to being post-Enlightenment. It assumes that "Islam" and "Enlightenment" have nothing to do with each other—as if the European Enlightenment emerged out of nothing, without

appropriating Islamic thought and learning. It betrays an ignorance of post-modern critique that has exposed Enlightenment thought as Eurocentric hot air. And, of course, it frames Muslims as "pre-Enlightenment" irredeemable barbarians. (Sardar 2006)

There are some significant issues in this quote that are worth more consideration. As I have already asserted in this book, Islam is not 'monolithic'; it is said from Chap. 2 that there are 'many Islams', and that the accusations made against Islam by militant atheists, secular transhumanists, and so on point the finger at a particular expression of Islam in its reified, prescriptive form. This form of Islam does exist, but it is one expression of many varying forms for which, Islam and religion being what it is, are all able to be justified by its adherents. Also, Sardar states that, 'It suggests that being "pre-Enlightenment" is inferior to being post-Enlightenment' and, again, as this book aims to show, there are many Islamic thinkers who were alive before the European Enlightenment who have much to contribute to science, culture, art, philosophy, and so on to this day. Finally, Sardar rightly points out that the Enlightenment did not emerge 'out of nothing'. We need not get into the historical details here, but, again, I have stressed that no system of thought exists in a vacuum. Egyptian ideas influenced Greek thought, which in turn influenced Islamic thought, which in turn influenced western European thought. As I continually stress, we need to rid ourselves of the ridiculous and outdated 'clash of civilisations' thesis, and to recognise the dialogue between cultures that has always been present.

If one were to talk of an 'Islamic Enlightenment' at all, and personally I am highly reluctant to do so, then we can look back much further than the European Enlightenment, to eighth- and ninth-century Baghdad under the Abbasid dynasty. The House of Wisdom is an example of a collection of intellectuals who struggled valiantly to learn ancient wisdom and to apply it to their contemporary world. In fact, to a smaller extent we can go back to the very early days of Islam when, in the sixth century, the Arabs entered Alexandria. It has to be appreciated that this new encounter with ancient philosophy was not simply a matter of picking up a book by Plato or Aristotle and translating it into Arabic. There is a story that, when the Academy of Athens was closed, seven of its philosophers first fled to Ctesiphon in the Persian empire, where they lived for about one year, before some of them went to Alexandria. It was, therefore, the works of these philosophers, notably John Philoponus (c. 490–c. 570, aka John the

Grammarian or John of Alexandria) and Simplicius of Cilicia (c. 490–c. 560) in the sixth century, that the Muslims first came across when they entered Alexandria, as well as the works of the third-century Ammonius Saccas, and the seventh-century Stephanus of Alexandria. When the Arab Muslims entered the great Library of Alexandria and began to digest its contents, the 'Greek' philosophy that they were confronted with was a very different being from what has existed hundreds of years earlier in Athens or, for that matter, what students today study when they pick up, say, a copy of *Timaeus*. Rather, the works of Plato and Aristotle had been transformed into a rather eclectic collection of Neoplatonic, Christian, mystical, and Egyptian thought. The works were available in Greek, but also in Syriac. One can imagine how the Arabs had to not only struggle with philosophical concepts and cultural references that were alien to them but also find Arabic equivalents to foreign words. While the scholars under the Umayyad did their best in translating and understanding these works, it really came to fruition during the Abbasid reign of Caliphs al-Mansur, Harun, and his son al-Ma'mun in the eighth and ninth centuries. Caliph al-Mansur founded the new city of *Madinat al-Salam*, the 'City of Peace', which the locals continued to call 'Baghdad', the name of the original settlement. The city itself demonstrates the influence of the findings in Alexandria, especially that of Euclid (c. 300 BC). It was as close as a city could get to a perfect circle, a ringed city with two sets of walls. Al-Mansur intended this to be the new intellectual centre of the Islamic empire and, in fact, so it proved to be for some centuries. It became the centre for not only scientific and intellectual exchange but also commerce and could claim to be the largest city in the world, with a population of some one million, until that status was acquired by another Muslim city, Cordoba in Spain. The Muslim geographer al-Yaqubi (d. c. 897/8) wrote of Baghdad a hundred years after it was founded:

> I mention Baghdad first of all because it is the heart of Iraq, and, with no equal on earth either in the Orient or the Occident, it is the most extensive city in area, in importance, in prosperity, in abundance of water, and in healthful climate. … No one is better educated than their scholars, better informed than their authorities in tradition, more solid in their syntax than their grammarians, more supple then their singers, more certain than their Quran readers, more expert than their physicians, more competent than their calligraphers, more clear than their logicians, more zealous than their ascetics, better jurists than their magistrates, more eloquent than their preachers. (Yaqubi 1892, p. 17)

During this period, notable translators such as Yahya ibn al-Batriq (d. 835) brought Plato's *Timaeus* and Aristotle's *On the Soul* to the Arabic-speaking world, while Hunayn ibn Ishaq (d. 873), a Nestorian, who, together with his son and nephew, also is an important figure in the translation movement. Hunayn is responsible for the translation of Galen's medical texts, as well as his writings on logic and ethics. Caliph al-Mansur, according to what historical accounts we have, possessed a good knowledge of logic and law, and populated his court with philosophers, astronomers, and other experts. His *Bayt al-Hikma*, the 'House of Wisdom', was much more than a library, for it was a veritable translation bureau and university, and it is due to their efforts that we have such Arabic-derived words as 'algebra' and 'alchemy'.

Revival and Renewal

According to the religious philosopher Louis Karel Dupré, 'Islam never had to go through a prolonged period of critically examining the validity of its spiritual vision, as the West did during the 18th century. ... Islamic culture has, of course, known its own crisis ... yet it was never forced to question its traditional worldview' (Dupré 2005, Preface p. ix). Such blanket statements regarding the whole of Islamic history and thought will, I hope, be shown to be way off the mark. The translation movement in Baghdad certainly meant that scholars had to struggle to equate the ideas of Greek philosophers and Neoplatonism with that of Islamic thought, and these were not always easy bedfellows. Questioning its 'traditional worldview' has, in fact, been a preoccupation for Muslims since its very beginning and is, I would argue, an internal driving force.

The constant self-interrogation is embedded within the concepts of 'revival' (*ihya*) and 'renewal' (*tajdid*). According to various hadiths, at the 'head of each century' a renewer (*mujaddid*) would come, and many of the figures discussed in this book have been identified as such renewers; for example, Hassan al-Attar, referred to above, is considered as such, as indeed is Muhammad Abduh, Ibn Arabi, and Muhammad al-Ghazali (see Chap. 6). Whilst they are all considered initiators of renewal, the actual features of the renewal differ considerably. Whilst some may be proponents of western modernity, others are 'purifiers' who set out to rid Islam of what is perceived as alien influences. For example, the great founder of the science of Islamic jurisprudence, Abū 'Abdillāh Muhammad ibn Idrīs al-Shāfiʿī (768–820) moved to Cairo in 815 and he was welcomed there, being declared the next 'renewer', for 815 in the Muslim calendar is 199, and so al-Shāfiʿī was seen as the renewer for the third Muslim century that was about to begin.

The resistance against Islam in particular, by the proponents of secular science and enlightenment thought, is that it is a religion—like many other religions, but only more so—that has a 'problem' with modernity. This, it should be noted, is not a view restricted only to western, non-Muslim, thinkers, but numerous Islamic scholars today and in the past have struggled to equate the Islamic worldview with rapid developments in science and technology. As Wilfred Cantwell Smith states, 'the fundamental malaise of modern Islam is a sense that something has gone wrong with Islamic history. The fundamental problem of modern Muslims is how to rehabilitate that history: to set it going in full vigour, so that Islamic society may once again flourish as a divinely guided society should and must' (Smith 1957, p. 47). Various Islamic scholars have set out to tackle this psychological malaise and to 'revive' Islam in a way that is not a mere imitation of what is considered Western thought. In other words, it is believed that Islam can internally tackle issues of modernity and can offer an Islamic response to issues that may well be an alternative to non-Islamic responses. This is important in the debate on transhumanism if we are to show that Islam can in some unique way contribute to this debate, and to get away from the perceived resistance of Islam.

There are certainly examples of internal revival, with perhaps the most notorious and still hugely influential being Wahhabism. The founder of the Wahhabi movement, Muhammad ibn Abd al-Wahhab (1703–1792), was influenced by the Hanbali thinker Taqī ad-Dīn Ahmad ibn Taymiyyah (1263–1328) to the extent that they both reacted to what they considered to be 'innovations' (bid'ah) and idolatry (shirk), such, in the case of al-Wahhab, as the celebration of Prophet Muhammad's birthday and the visit to Sufi shrines. These were 'innovations' in the sense that they were not considered to be truly Islamic and, therefore, were infecting the purity of Islam. Although such innovations may come from outside Islam by definition, in this case it has nothing to do with western influence. Importantly, al-Wahhab, in line with the thought of Ibn Taymiyyah, believed that Islam had its own internal mechanisms that could click into place as reactions to such innovations. If it can indeed be shown that Islam has its own mechanisms in this sense, then it does not have to face one of two choices when confronted by issues that arise from science and technology: to either adopt western Enlightenment 'mechanisms' or to bury itself in reified dogmatism and simply ignore scientific advancement. By adopting the former, the accusation is that Islam has in itself nothing to offer to science, while adopting the latter leads to reinforcing the view that Islam as an ideology is stuck in the time warp and is incapable of change or development without incurring a breakdown in its belief system. Al-Wahhab and Ibn Taymiyyah did not, in principle, resort to either of these options, but rather looked to the mechanism of *ijtihad*: engaging in active reasoning and interpretation of hadith to ensure it is conducive with the message of the Qur'an.

Whilst al-Wahhab emphasised the importance of *sharia*, this was not the same as blind obedience to *sharia*. Rather, God's law needed to be interpreted correctly, which required the skills of *ijtihad*. Islam, therefore, is not corrupted because the Qur'an is still considered universal and eternal, yet it is also a realisation that human beings are *not* universal and eternal; they can err in their interpretation of the Qur'an and can fail to adapt its universality to the particular. The 'malaise' that Cantwell Smith referred to is Islam's reluctance to allow *ijtihad* and instead to depend upon the hefty works of the rulings of medieval legal scholars. Of course, such scholars would have nothing to say on radical life extension or mind uploading! Logically, that would mean that Islam could have nothing to say about these issues either. In theory, anyway, the outlook of al-Wahhab and Ibn Taymiyyah allow for incredible flexibility and adaptability to circumstance, although in *practice* the result has tended to be more militant, conservative, and, frankly, petty in many cases such as the banning, through force, of visits to the tombs of saints or the perceived superstitious practices of spitting in a particular way or wearing charms to ward off evil. This is perhaps the great shame of Islam, although also characteristic of many inspiring ideas that get hijacked and reified. I have already referred to Mawdudi as a prime example of Islamic reification, yet it is ironic that Mawdudi himself praised Ibn Taymiyyah and seems to believe also that Islam can engage with the modern world. It is worth quoting in length what Mawdudi has to say here:

> Ibn Taymiyya removed these dangers, revived Islam's spirit of idea and morals and accomplished the explorations of renewal. A little before him, no one had dared to invite the people to Islam out of the fear of being calumniated; the narrow-minded scholars had cooperated with the cruel rulers, and it was his lot to unfurl the flag of renewal against them. He was profound in interpretation of the Qur'an and a leader in the Hadith and he took Islam from where al-Ghazali had left it forward. He defended Islamic faith and found more beautiful proofs for Islamic spirit than al-Ghazali had. Al-Ghazali's

judgement had remained under the harmful influence of rational thoughts. Ibn Taymiyya was more effective and chose the way of reason, which was closer to spirit of the Qur'an and Sunnat. Thus, he won a wonderful success. Men of knowledge did not know the interpretation of the Qur'an. Those who were educated scholastically were not able to establish the connection between themselves and the Qur'an and Hadith. It has been only Ibn Taymiyya's lot to accomplish the real explanation of Islam. He made ijtihads by deriving his inspiration directly from the Holy Book, from the Sunnat, and from the way of living of the Prophet's companions. Ibn al-Qayyim, his disciple, studied over the divine causes, the meanings of which had not been solved, and put Islamic rules. By clearing out the evil effects that had leaked into Islamic system, he purified and refreshed it. He attacked the bad customs that had been accepted as parts of Islam and had been support for religious punishments and tolerated by scholars for centuries. This honest act turned the whole world against him. Those who came later raced with one another to calumniate him. (Mawdudi 1995, p. 12)

Ibn Taymiyyah likewise recognised a 'malaise' that faced Islam, although in this case we are talking of an Islam that existed in the thirteenth century and a different kind of malaise which, while not affected by western thought, he saw as a time of ignorance, injustice, and a general loss in faith and knowledge of true Islam. How this malaise was to be cured was, therefore, to look back to when Islam did not suffer from such symptoms of malaise. The 'revivalism', then, is a looking back to the beginnings of Islam and to 'revive' it as it existed at that time. One can see the tensions here between adapting to modern circumstance and the more conservative notion of looking back to the past, but the point is not to imitate the past, rather to consider what mechanisms existed that have become redundant. Essentially, Islam is addressing the question as to why it, for so many centuries, could take pride in its cultural, political, economic, and scientific achievements. What was it doing right and what is it now doing wrong? Ibn Taymiyyah was critical of groups that he considered un-Islamic, notably Shi'a and Sufi practices, which he blamed to some extent for diluting Islamic purity, but it was also important to not simply resort to the often-erroneous Sunni scholarship and legal rulings, but to struggle (the literal meaning of *ijtihad*) to determine what the original sources have to say.[1]

---

[1] It is worth pointing out that, whilst Ibn Taymiyyah is often cited in the modern era, he was perhaps something of a minority figure during his own time and for quite some centuries after (see Rapoport and Ahmed 2010, Introduction p. 6). All the more reason to not give the relatively recent prescriptive approach to Islam as much attention as it seems to get.

By ridding Islam of outside practices and training Muslims to critically engage with its own authoritative sources, then Islam would be able to react *in an Islamic way* to changing circumstance. Note the importance of educating Muslims to engage critically, rather than follow blindly (*taqlid*) in the ways of past scholars. In theory, although referring to the teaching and practices of seventh-century Islam, this need not result in Islam being closed and restrictive. In the case of situations and activities that are not clearly covered by the canonical sources, then the educated Muslim must exercise independent reasoning in coming to conclusions. The reason why such conclusions may well differ from that of, say, a non-Muslim, or an atheist, and so on, is that the Muslim, while being 'rational', is nonetheless operating within a framework imbued by Islamic ethical principles and a way of thinking. Now, it may well be that the Muslim may come to the exact same conclusion as the non-Muslim on a particular, but it may well also be that he or she may not, or at least see things from a different angle that is worth some consideration. In the same way we look to those trained in Western philosophy to help us to see things in a different light that we may have otherwise overlooked to our peril, can it not be similarly valuable to look to Muslims for such enlightenment? Granted, the answer should rightly be in the negative if we are confronted by a Muslim who relies blindly on outdated and irrelevant texts or who fails to find any inspiration or guidance from Islam whatsoever, but we can have a third option here: *the educated Muslim who engages in critical thought within a specific worldview that has proven valuable in the past.*

In this way, to talk of an 'Enlightenment' in Islam really makes no sense: it does not need an Enlightenment because it has its own regular series of 'mini-Enlightenments' through the internal process of revival and renewal. It is unfortunate that Muslim scholars are often fearful of engaging in *ijtihad*, and it is ironic that the great 'revivalist' that we have already mentioned, al-Shāfiʿī, is to some extent to blame for the closing of the gates of *ijtihad*, although the extent to which one individual can be blamed is often overexaggerated. To his credit, al-Shāfiʿī's intentions were honourable, for he had little trust in the abilities of the jurists of his day to have the necessary skills to interpret the Qur'an, and he was to a large degree correct to doubt them. It, therefore, made a great deal of sense at the time to develop a science of authentication and to deny authority to the somewhat haphazard collection of hadith, much of which was of debatable authentication. However, by giving *fiqh* (Islamic jurisprudence) a more 'scientific' basis, with its roots firmly in place, the consequence of this was to leave little room for *ijtihad*.

Deliberately or not, al-Shāfiʿī is reflecting a concern that has its origins at least with the ancient Greeks; the importance of knowledge in order to be moral, and by 'knowledge' here we mean the ability to engage with material in a critical manner. This is the paradox that results from al-Shāfiʿī: on the one hand, his emphasis on the importance of the intellect, whilst, on the other hand, the lack of trust in the Muslim of the time to be able to exercise their intellect, hence the need to take the tool of independent reasoning away from the human, and rest it upon the lap of science in terms of 'the science of *fiqh*'. The problem with this is that axiology is separated from epistemology. Value judgements become marginalised or separated entirely from the science of *fiqh*, in a similar way we look at science today, and the concern I have expressed as regards secular transhumanism. As considered in Chap. 3, Mawdudi likewise distrusted the Muslims to engage in independent reasoning, and while 'he endeavours to expound, by an idiosyncratic combination of ijtihad and literalist exegesis, the Islamic dogma as he sees it, covering every field of human activity from politics to the sexual life' (Ruthven 2000, p. 327) it is that 'idiosyncratic' aspect that highlights Mawdudi's reluctance to embrace *ijtihad* and instead comes across as possessing a schizophrenic *ijtihad-taqlid* split which he struggles, and ultimately fails, to accommodate within his own all-encompassing ideology. The result is very typical of the Islamic reification that leads to a suspicion and concern that Islam cannot respond in any positive or constructive way to the transhumanist debate, or *any* modern issue that science brings to the table for that matter. Whilst Mawdudi was not anti-science, his insistence, like all modes of thought, that science should be set within an Islamic framework, and therefore possess 'intellectual independence' as he called it, results in a fear that attempts at independent empirical reasoning might be 'faulty' and misapprehend divine law. Consequently, stagnation follows.

As Mawdudi's disciple Khurshīd Ahmad states, 'The approach of the Islamic movement is to … modernise without compromising on Islamic principles and values. … It says "yes" to modernisation but "no" to blind Westernisation' (Ahmad 1983, p. 224). For Mawdudi, science and technology are not necessarily dehumanising, and, in fact, they could be the opposite. The Internet in itself is just a technological tool, but it is the *content*, and how Muslims digest that content, that really matters. Mawdudi did not really blame the west for the malaise that existed in the

Islamic world, and he did not see western technological advances as the enemy. Rather, the enemy is from within: it is the Muslims themselves that are to blame for its decline:

> The future of the whole world of Islam will depend upon the attitude that the Muslims ultimately adopt towards Islam ... unfortunately, the present hypocritical attitudes ... persist, I am afraid that the newly liberated Muslim nations will not be able to preserve their freedom for a long time. (Mawdudi 1985, p. 7)

As Mawdudi saw it, the reason for western ascendency was because Muslims, or rather 'partial Muslims' allowed it to happen, for there is nothing inherent in Islam that should in theory prevent it from equalling or surpassing the achievements of the western world provided Muslims are sufficiently educated in true Islam. As Muslims are to blame, so it is Muslims who must reverse this decline. Mawdudi's *da'wah*, was to 'scientifically prove that Islam is eventually to emerge as the World-Religion to cure Man of all his maladies' (Mawdudi 1963, p. iii). Note here Mawdudi's appeal to scientific proof, for he regarded Islam as 'scientific' in the sense that it is divine, and nature is also divine. The logic, then, is by following the will of God, the Muslim is uncovering the laws of nature, which is really what science is all about. Mawdudi's *tajdid* was a logical process that begins with individual Muslims of a required intellect and ends ultimately with a universal Islamic order that would emerge. It is a paradigm shift, but not one that is an entirely new way of perceiving the world, but a renewal of the way that it once was at the time of the Prophet Muhammad.

In answering the question, then, of whether transhumanism is a 'transgression' of God's law, for Mawdudi this can only be answered when an Islamic society exists that is entirely subject to divine law. The problem, of course, is that presently such a society does not exist, and one wonders what Muslims are meant to do in the meantime when confronted by these ethical dilemmas. Mawdudi does, however, make a point that we also saw with al-Shāfiʿī regarding the importance of knowledge in order to be virtuous. Secular transhumanism, as I have argued, considers its primary concern to be how we are to gain the scientific knowledge so that we may transcend the human, and the ethical concerns are often side-lined. So, whereas the epistemological enquiry deals with what we can know in order to transcend the human, the axiological aspect is concerned with the goodness or rightness of something. One of the reasons that science in the western world has advanced so rapidly is that it does not always step back and consider the ethical implications of its actions, and it has been the role of religion to then step in and question some of these scientific enterprises. The questioning of religious institutions has not, consequently, always been welcomed by scientists, and this may be justified to some extent, as the arguments presented by religion are not always as rigorous as one might hope for. Nonetheless, the importance of ethical reflection, whether that comes from religion, from philosophy, from politicians, or from the scientists themselves, is vitally important, especially in addressing transhumanism given we are dealing with that most central of human concerns: what it means to be human.

What Mawdudi and other Muslim scholars were concerned with was to harmonise Islamic thought with the conceptual scientific scheme that was predominant in western thought; for Mawdudi and others, the conclusion was that there is nothing 'western' about this conceptual scheme at all. The difference was only that western scientists were better educated than their Muslim counterparts and seemed less concerned with fitting science into any ethical or ideological framework. Ziauddin Sardar has expressed this concern in the following way: 'How to get science and technology to solve the compelling needs and monumental problems of Muslim society without dislocating the values and cultures which essentially make these societies Muslim?' (Sardar 1986, p. 29).

Irrespective of whether someone is a Muslim or not, a religious believer or not, surely it is important to consider the 'human condition' before we start dismantling the human and putting it back together again like some Humpty-Dumpty. The possession of an axiology of values is an essential part of being human and brings to the fore this seeming conflict between *psychologia empirica* and metaphysics. Kant, in his *Critique of Pure Reason*, may well have attempted to rid our psyche from metaphysics altogether (Kant 1998), but it stubbornly remains for the simple reason that our phenomenological perspective will not 'go away': it keeps jumping in front of the camera lens every time you try to take a picture of the objective world. Whilst Kierkegaard informs us just how paradoxical and downright impossible the ethical life is, we cannot, and should not, escape it. As Max Scheler's (1874–1928) anthropological philosophy brings out, this existential antinomy between ideals and reality is what helps us to understand who we are and how we perceive the world (Lehmann and Klempe 2015, p. 479). In fact, Scheler's observations are interesting in how he sees this confrontation with such antinomy as a sign of our 'spirit': 'This is the spiritual aspect of human life, which is first of all to be regarded as a necessary and inevitable product of an existential being. There are some fundamental contradictions in life that cannot be solved, neither intellectually nor ethically' (ibid., p. 480). Scheler, perhaps less known in the philosophical world, has influenced the field of psychology in, for example, the thoughts of the Austrian neurologist and psychiatrist Viktor Frankl (1905–1997) whose logotherapy 'is the result of an application of Max Scheler's concepts to psychotherapy' (Frankl 1967, p. 141). This spiritual dimension is what leads humans to reflect upon their existence and to question its meaning. Importantly, Frankl states that he is actually antagonistic towards forms of reductionism that divide the human into the psychological, spiritual, or biological for the spirit: though the spirit express itself through our biological bodies and our psyche, it is something that also *transcends* them (Frankl 1987; Hańderek 2007; Liccioli 2008; Scheler 2004). If we are talking of a 'spiritual' aspect that transcends the psychological, then what happens to it when we, through technology, also transcend the biological? Does it come with us or is it left behind? Whilst secular transhumanists might wish to resist terminology such as 'spirit', as this certainly brings us back to the 'mysterious' for which many transhumanists would simply deny and need to be overcome, we do need to consider what this says in terms of the holistic nature of the human condition, whatever terms one might use for this and the consequent associations that may be made with religious notions of 'spirit', 'soul', and so on. In terms of our axiology of values, Frankl and Scheler provide us with invaluable insights as to the historical, social, and cultural significance of what makes us human. In answering the question what is Islam to do in the meantime while waiting for the Mawdudi revolution, the Algerian astrophysicist Nidhal Guessoum observes that,

> The seventies and eighties of the last century witnessed a vigorous, rich, fascinating, and at times entertaining debate on the relationship between Islam and modern science. The protagonists covered a wide spectrum of schools of thought, from perennialist philosophy (Seyyed Hossein Nasr) to secular modernism (Pervez Hoodbhoy), to Islamic ethical science (Ziauddin Sardar and the Ijmalis), universalist science (Muhammad Abdus Salam), and the Islamization of knowledge (Ismail R. al-Faruqi and Seyyed Naquib Al-Attas). The thinkers and the nodes of the debates spanned the globe, from Malaysia and Pakistan to the United Kingdom and the United States,

in an era before email and the Internet existed and mass media was not yet globalized. (Guessoum 2015, pp. 854–855)

In many ways, however, these debates echo those of such figures as Mawdudi, featuring a lament for days gone by, a call for the Islamisation of knowledge. This is still prominent in one thinker who has continued in the twenty-first century, Muzaffar Iqbal, mostly sounded out in his own journal *Islam and Science*. Alas, it is not a 'new' voice that comes through, but echoes of the traditionalist, perennial views of the past century. There is an interesting published conversation between Iqbal and Hossein Nasr which took place when Nasr was giving a keynote at the International Conference on Science in Islamic Polity in the Twenty-First Century in March 1995. The conference was organised by OIC Standing Committee on Scientific and Technological Cooperation (COMSTECH), an inter-governmental body established by the Organisation of Islamic Conference (OIC) in 1983; an indication of Islam's concern to address the burning question of the relation between Islam and science. At this conference was the aforementioned Ziauddin Sardar, whose lecture 'Islamic Science: The Way Ahead' is extremely relevant to the issues arising in this chapter, in particular in relation to Mawdudi. The conference, it should be pointed out, took place in Pakistan in front of that country's scientific elite, and Pakistan is, of course, the country that Mawdudi hoped would be at the forefront of the Islamic revolution, yet Nasr's scathing attack on the situation in Pakistan in the 1990s has echoes of the Mawdudi paradigm:

> Within an Islamic polity—that is, an idealized "Islamic state"—the principles and injunctions of Islam which are the basis of the state, it was argued, would automatically guide science in the direction of Islamic values ... [but] we do not know really what constitutes a contemporary Islamic polity. The examples before us of states that claim to be "Islamic" hardly provide us with confidence: Saudi Arabia, Iran, the Sudan and Pakistan. It seems that the label Islamic is being used here to justify authoritarianism, naked oppression, suppression of dissent and criticism and state violence against the people. How can science, any science, develop in such states? (Nasr and Muzaffar 2009, p. 10)

This certainly is the anxiety that has been raised by many concerning Mawdudi's Platonic state, which would indeed consist of an elite, and an ideology that would constrain rather than free up independent thought; at least, as pointed out, until that great day when all Muslims are regarded as suitably educated and qualified to be equally enfranchised. Sardar states that, 'There are no scientists in the Muslim world', and 'we only have technicians who are like taxi drivers, taking passengers from one place to another' (ibid., pp. 7–8). Sardar argues that science is not value-free, and that western science has dominated and monopolised under the pretence that it is free of values, that it presents an absolute, universal, and neutral truth. As I have argued in this book, science, despite its attempts to be otherwise, cannot be entirely objective, if only because it still operates through the human. This is the paradox faced by transhumanism, for in order to transcend the human, the scientists have to operate within human values, however much the secular transhumanist might prefer to brush such values under the carpet. Sardar, having declared that science is not value-free, looks to the Muslim world for an 'indigenous science' (ibid.) that reflects Islamic values. Sardar has highlighted a thorny issue here: we saw in Bellaigue's work on an Islamic Enlightenment that the names presented seems more 'imitators' of western thought, than originators, and, there are currently only three Muslim scientists who have received the Nobel Prize for the sciences: the theoretical physicist Abdus Salam (1926–1996) and the chemists Ahmed Zewail (1946–2016) and Aziz Sancar (b. 1946), of which only the latter is alive today. However, Salam received his PhD in the UK, Zewail and Sancar in the USA, and so the fertile ground for scientific thought remains in the western world. The sad fact is we need to go back much further in the past, to—as we have seen—the great centres of learning in the House of Wisdom and in Cordoba, to scientists such as Jabir ibn Hayyan (c. 721–c. 815), who laid the foundations for chemistry in the eighth century, and to ibn al-Haytham (c. 965–c. 1040) who made such original contributions to the science of optics in the tenth century, or the astronomer Nasir al-Din al-Tusi (1201–1274) whose model of the planetary systems was used until Copernicus.

Sardar has been writing about the relation between Islam and science since the early 1980s, and is considered a member of the small group which called themselves the Ijmalis, which is a term taken from Rumi's *Diwan-i Shams* and reflects the holistic nature of their methodology. 'The Ijmali position is similar to that of al-Ghazzali', Sardar wrote in *Explorations in Islamic Science* (1989), 'the essence of Ijmali thought is reconstruction, complexity and interconnection' (Sardar 1989, p. 155). Sardar, the most outspoken of this group, states that science, like all knowledge, is a social construct:

[The] "purpose" of science is not to discover some great objective truth; indeed, reality, whatever it may be and however one perceives it, is too complex, too interwoven, too multidimensional to be discovered as a single truth. The purpose of science, apart from advancing knowledge within ethical bounds, is to solve problems and relieve misery and hardship and improve the physical, material, cultural and spiritual lot of mankind. The altruistic pursuit of pure knowledge for the sake of "truth" is a con-trick. An associated assumption is that modern science is distinctively Western. All over the globe all significant science is Western in style and method, whatever the pigmentation or language of the scientist. (Sardar 1989, p. 6)

Sardar and the Ijmalis group have denied that their view of science is akin to Kuhnian relativism, or Feyerabendian epistemology, but rather it is a distinctly *Islamic* view, that is, 'which is derived solely from the ethical, value and conceptual parameters of Islam. The essence of Ijmali thought is *reconstruction, complexity* and *interconnection*, or what Riaz Kirmani has called complementarity' (ibid., p. 155). Whilst wonderfully ambitious in its scope and aims, as a group it has since disbanded and never really caught on. Sardar, for his part, was very critical of Nasr's 'sacred science'. Both Sardar and Nasr do agree that science is not value-free, and they also agree that science, being not free of values, can accord to Islamic values. The difference, however, is that the Ijmalis, so far as I can determine, appeal more to methodology, especially the exercise of *ijtihad*, whereas Nasr, as he states in his keynote address at the 1995 conference, focuses more on the 'in-depth study of the traditional Islamic sources, from the Noble Qur'an and Hadith to all the traditional works on the sciences, philosophy, theology, cosmology, Sufi metaphysics, and the like, to formulate the Islamic worldview and especially the Islamic concept of nature and the sciences of nature' (Nasr and Muzaffar 2009, p. 188). Much of the criticism levelled against Sardar and Nasr seem to be of a somewhat personal nature and a dislike of one another, but if we break through the fog of personality clashes, the fundamental differences seem to rest with which authorities we should look to for an Islamic science. For Nasr, as a product of a Sufi, Shi'a and Persian milieu, he looks to the Andalusian Ibn Arabi (1165–1240) and the Persian Shahāb ad-Dīn Yahya ibn Habash Suhrawardī (1154–1191, see Chap. 6) in Islamic thought, but also the aforementioned Frithjof Schuon and René Guénon in western thought. What perhaps unites these thinkers is a 'mystical' bent that Sardar, more Sunni in outlook, is more critical of, leaning more towards al-Ghazali. Perhaps it is clearer to see Nasr as looking to Islam as perennial teaching, and so always there in some way or other since the beginnings of Islam, whereas Sardar looks more to contemporary, modern debates.

I personally find such distinctions somewhat nit-picking, as if there is one Islamic, right, way that science can be approached. From my nominalist perspective, as I hope has become clear, there is no 'one Islam', no 'essence' to Islam in this sense. Rather, it is up to Muslims to give their religion meaning and value, hence the resulting subjectivity. To emphasise one tradition over another, whether it is labelled 'mystical', 'rational', to what-have-you does, in fact, seem to go against the Ijmali notion of consensus. I find it strange that Sardar is so critical of Nasr, given the Rumi-inspired origins here. For my part, the kinds of issues, questions (and, even, answers) that thinkers from a number of different approaches within the Islamic tradition can all offer up provide important ingredients in determining how we approach this supposed 'malaise' in the Islamic world. In terms of transhumanism and the issues Islam must face here, Nasr's notion of the 'theomorphic being', for example, is worthy of some consideration. The fact that the Ijmali has faded away suggests it had little in the way of strong foundations to begin with, and much of its literature was of a journalistic nature rather than rigorous academic scholarship. Nasr's work is more nuanced and better informed, as well as wide-ranging, allowing for the kind of 'connectivity' that Sardar spoke of between various traditions, not just Islamic, hence the appropriate perennial label.

Muzaffar Iqbal, as already stated, continues the 'traditionalist' debate, although he seems to have taken up Nasr's Perennialist mantle, coupled with cries for Muslims to return 'to their identity, roots, and tradition, in terms of knowledge, education, social-economic-political settings, and so on' (Guessoum 2015, p. 855). This looking back to some rose-tinted bygone era is still to be found, notably amongst the *i'jaz* adherents, that is, those who look especially to the Qur'an (and, to a lesser extent, the Sunna) for miraculous scientific content. A prominent figure here is Zaghloul El-Naggar who makes regular appearances on TV programmes throughout the world and whose writings and website look to demonstrate the scientific miracles that occur in the Qur'an. Whilst El-Naggar does have a PhD in Geology from the University of Wales, he nonetheless declares that evolution is false and that God created Adam, quoting a hadith as a 'scientific sign' which says, 'Allah created Adam, on Adam's own image, making him 60 cubits tall' (El-Naggar 2012). In explaining this hadith, El-Naggar states that:

For decades, people were fascinated by the "Organic Evolution Theory" (known as Darwinism) which led many to try to make a link between man and this long chain of creation, but without having any clear or sound evidence. The current fossils record is still deficient, having many gaps, as evidenced by the ancient record of life on earth (at least 3800 million years), which has been inhabited by several consecutive patterns of creation that increased in their number and complexity of structure as time went by. This correct observation has been used in making many wrong deductions, which try to negate "Creation", but the Glorious Qur'an assures that: "Allah is the Creator of all things". (El-Naggar 2012)

For a trained scientist it is worrying that because evolution lacks complete and concrete evidence, then we should resort to the Qur'an to fill in any gaps in certainty, including the view that Adam was 60 cubits (30 metres) tall. In a similar, troubling vein, Adnan Oktar—better known as Harun Yahya—is another creationist whose televangelism captures large audiences. Whilst it would be easy to dismiss El-Naggar and Harun Yahya as misguided, naive, pseudo-scientists, it is unfortunate that these figures continue to be hugely influential in certain parts of the Islamic world and, therefore, add support to the secular transhumanist suspicion of Islam.

By believing that the Qur'an proves the theories of modern science, Sardar accuses Nasr of 'Bucaillism'. Maurice Bucaille (1920–1998) was a French medical doctor who studied Islam deeply. He is the author of *The Bible, the Qur'an and Science*, which was originally published in French in 1976, but has since been translated into many languages and continues to be extremely popular in the Islamic world. In this work, Bucaille focuses on four topics: astronomy, the earth, the animal and vegetable kingdom, and human reproduction. For each of these he looks to the Qur'an to demonstrate that the scientific 'discoveries' for these areas are actually to be found in there, which proves the miraculous status of the divine text. As he states:

The Quran most definitely did not contain a single proposition at variance with the most firmly established modern knowledge, nor did it contain any of the ideas current at the time on the subjects it describes. Furthermore, however, a large number of facts are mentioned in the Quran which were not discovered until modern times. (Bucaille 2003, p. 8)

This 'Bucaillism' seems prevalent today, and many similar examples can be given. One worth noting occurred in April 1985 when the Bulletin of the Islamic Medical Association of South Africa published an article enti-tled 'Canadian Scholar Confirms Qur'an and Hadith on Human Embryology'. The scholar in question, Keith Moore, chairman of the Anatomy Department of the University of Toronto's School of Medicine, had, it seemed, 'discovered' that the Qur'an contains a modern under-standing of embryology (Kiyimba 2007, p. 14). Moore reads modern biology into Qu'ranic verses: for example, in the case of the well-known verse 76:2, 'We created man from a drop of mingled fluid to put him to the test', Moore sees this as a reference to the mixture of sperm with the oocyte and its associated follicular fluid which then results in the zygote and, following that, the embryo. In like manner, the verse 23:12–14:

> We created man from an essence of clay, then we placed him as a drop of fluid in a safe place, then we made that drop into a clinging form, and We made that form into a lump of flesh, and We made that lump into bones, and We clothed those bones with flesh, and later We made them into other forms—glory be to God, the best of creators!.

More argues that this is an account of the embryo at 28 days, which then forms bones by the sixth week, then by the seventh week it takes human shape, and so on. Such enterprises seem to me bizarre and misguided, and somewhat concerning that any academic institution is prepared to waste ink on it. Rather like attempts to find Noah's Ark, it seems to miss the point of what the religious texts are there for and, as Sardar rightly states, Moore's article, 'throws considerable light on the state of the Muslim mind: its acute inferiority complex; its obsession with science and by extension with moder-nity; and its pathological concern with seeing the Qur'an as the end of knowledge rather than as a text that provides an ethical framework for the pursuit of knowledge' (Sardar 1985). Sardar goes on to state:

> But, more importantly, by equating the Qur'an with science, Bucaillism ele-vates science to the realm of the sacred and makes Divine Revelation subject to the verification of western science. Apart from the fact that the Qur'an needs no justification from modern science, Bucaillism opens the Qur'an to the counter argument of Popper's criteria of refutation: would the Qur'an be proved false and written off just as Bucaille writes off the Bible, if a particular scientific fact does not tally with it or if a particular fact mentioned in the Qur'an is refuted by modern science? And what if a particular theory, which is "confirmed" by the Qur'an and is in vogue today is abandoned tomorrow for another theory that presents an opposite picture? Does that mean that the Qur'an is valid today but will not be valid tomorrow? (ibid.)

Aisha Musa has argued that Bucaille is important because of his influence on contemporary Islamic thought towards scientific advances, and therefore, when Musa looks to radical life extension (RLE), 'Bucaille's work can provide Muslims with the means to regard these biomedical advances as being in conformity to norms established in the Qur'an' (Musa 2009, p. 126). Therefore, there seems to be pros and cons. On the one hand, Bucaillism helps Muslims to see their religion as 'scientific', whilst, on the other hand, Sardar raises the concerns that seeing the Qu'ran this way can lead to the questioning of its veracity if a scientific theory is later to be proven false. One suspects, in the latter case, interpreters will simply 're-interpret' the Qur'an to be in line with the latest scientific discoveries, and herein lies the hermeneutical problem of fitting the Qur'an into modern ideas. Sardar, in the above quote, looks to the Qur'an to provide an ethical framework, rather than give scientific validation, but this too is problematic for ethics likewise changes over time. There has been considerable exegesis over the years that struggles to demonstrate the Qur'an's validation on such matters as homosexuality, women's rights, abortion, non-Muslims, and so on and, in the same way Sardar accuses Moore and Bucaille of 'apologetics' (ibid.), the same accusation can be made against other forms of exegesis. It is not the remit for this book to engage deeply in these debates and, in fact, I wish to avoid the approach of looking to the Qur'an and hadith for 'justification' for transhumanism for, to do so, opens up a curate's egg and, ultimately, I question what this would really prove. The fact is, you can be a Muslim without being a literalist, and perhaps this is what Sardar means by stating the Qur'an provides an ethical framework, with the emphasis on the word 'framework' here: it does not provide a 'list' of do's and don'ts, but an overarching vision of the human that acts as a scaffold to support the detail.

With a new millennium upon us, there is obviously a lengthy and variable tradition of debates on the relationship between science and Islam to tap into, but also a worry that we are really not getting anywhere. There are recurring themes, notably a recognition that Islam on the whole is way behind western science; that there are strong strands within the tradition that resist scientific advances, hence providing grist to the mill for secular transhumanists (although there are, course, a number of other reason, including socio-economic, linguistic, and so on, as to why Islam is behind); that science is not and cannot be as objective as many western scientists suppose; and that Islam needs to establish what we mean by an 'Islamic science', otherwise what is the point of Islam or Muslims having anything whatsoever to say on the matter from an 'Islamic' point of view? However, there is a fear that we are simply going in circles, whilst western scientists continue on their linear path. Can we approach this new millennium with a 'new generation' of Islamic scientists?

THE NEW GENERATION?

Much credit has to be given to Stefano Bigliardi who has devoted a number of years to examining the debates on Islam and science, and he claims that we can now look to a 'new generation' of thinkers, so what is it that distinguishes this new generation from the traditionalists that we have so far explored? Bigliardi engaged in a series of conversations (Bigliardi 2014) with scholars he considers to be the new harmonisers of Islam and science: Mehdi Golshani, Mohammed Basil Altaie, Bruno Guiderdoni, and Nidhal Guessoum. As a result, Bigliardi draws up certain distinct features that they share. They must be practicing scientists for a start but, much more than that, they should possess a well-rounded education in the sense that they are aware of different cultural viewpoints and can engage in interdisciplinary research. This education should allow these scholars to tap into various philosophical and religious traditions, not just Islamic. Of course, the traditionalists, while not always practising scientists, would nonetheless have at least some understanding and knowledge of other cultural, religious, and philosophical traditions. Nasr, for example, frequently makes reference to Hegel, Heidegger, and Kierkegaard. However, leaving aside the fact that Nasr would be 'disqualified' from Bigliardi's criteria because he is not scientifically trained, it is perhaps not the fact that Nasr does reference non-Islamic philosophers, but in the extent to which he is *selective* in his readings; a methodology for which all critical academics should be wary of doing. If we stick with the topic of evolution, given how important the views on this are when considering transhumanism, Nasr is a staunch rejectionist of evolution, although he, for the large part, tries to justify this through philosophical means rather than relying on the Qur'an as, for example, El-Naggar might. For example:

> [First,] the question of form and the finality of form. A triangle is a triangle, and nothing evolves into a triangle; until a triangle becomes a triangle, it is not a triangle. So if we have three loose lines that gradually meet, even if there is one micron of separation, that is not a triangle. Only a triangle is a triangle. And life forms also have a finality of their own … the human being has been a human being since the first arrival of human beings in the world.

They have not evolved from other beings whose bones bear similarities to theirs, [which] does not mean that the human body has evolved on the basis of purely material factors from the chimp. There is obviously a discontinuity that reveals the manifestation of a higher level of being. (Nasr 2006, p. 194)

Nasr further states that, 'Anyone who identifies paradise with some place in Africa where Adam gradually evolved is guilty of the worst kind of heresy theologically speaking. Such people are not serious Muslims anymore' (ibid., p. 196). How, then, on the matter of evolution, do the 'new generation' differ? I would refer the reader to Bigliardi's monograph here (Bigliardi 2014) on the views of each of his interviewees. However, as a summation, they generally accept evolution, while not necessarily concurring that such acceptance rules out the existence of God. What role God plays in the evolutionary process depends on which of the new generation Bigliardi talks to, but there is nonetheless a recurring theme here of a criticism of a form of scientific exploration that is purely materialistic. Here we come back to the criticism levelled against secular transhumanism, that of methodological naturalism. The differences between the traditionalists and the new generation may, at first sight, seem subtle, but they are in actual fact quite fundamental; whereas the former display a suspicion of modern science and resort to the Qur'an and Sunna, the latter are much more accepting of what science reveals, adopting a more pragmatic approach, while nonetheless leaving the door open for the possibility of the 'non-material', whatever that may entail.

BIBLIOGRAPHY[2]

BOOKS

de Bellaigue, Christopher. 2017. *The Islamic Enlightenment: The Modern Struggle Between Faith and Reason*. London: Bodley Head.

Bigliardi, Stefano. 2014. *Islam and the Quest for Modern Science: Conversations with Adnan Oktar, Mehdi Golshani, Mohammed Basil Altaie, Zaghloul El Naggar, Bruno Guiderdoni and Nidhal Guessoum*. Istanbul: Swedish Research Institute in Istanbul.

Bucaille, Maurice. 2003. *The Bible, the Qu'ran and Science: The Holy Scriptures Examined in the Light of Modern Knowledge*. Scotts Valley, CA: CreateSpace Independent Publishing Platform.

[2] *Note*: All quotes from the Qur'an are from the translation by M.A.S. Abdel Haleem, Oxford University Press, 2005.

Dupré, Louis. 2005. *The Enlightenment and the Intellectual Foundations of Modern Culture*. New Haven, CT: Yale University Press.

El-Naggar, Zaghlul. 2012. *Treasures in the Sunnah: A Scientific Approach: Part Two*. Rochdale, UK: Scribe Digital.

Frankl, Viktor E. 1987. *El Hombre Doliente, Fundamentos Antropológicos de la Psicoterapia*. Barcelona: Herder Editorial.

Kant, Immanuel. 1998. *Critique of Pure Reason*. Cambridge: Cambridge University Press.

Mawdudi, Abu Al'a. 1985. *Islam Today*. Beirut: International Islamic Federation of Student Organisations.

———. 1995. *Jihad fi Sabillah: Jihad in Islam*. Translated and Edited by Khurshid Ahmad. Birmingham: Huda Khattab, UK Islamic Mission Dawah Centre.

Mawdudi, Mawlana. 1963. *A Short History of the Revivalist Movement in Islam*. Lahore: Islamic Publications.

Nasr, Hossein, and Muzaffar Iqbal. 2009. *Islam, Science, Muslims and Technology*. Islamabad: Dost Publication.

Rapoport, Yossef, and Shahab Ahmed, eds. 2010. *Ibn Taymiyya and His Times*. Oxford: Oxford University Press.

Ruthven, Malise. 2000. *Islam in the World*. 2nd ed. London: Penguin.

Sagan, Carl. 1997. *Pale Blue Dot: A Vision of the Human Future in Space*. New York: Ballantine Books.

Sardar, Ziauddin. 1989. *Explorations in Islamic Science*. London: Mansell Publishing Limited.

Smith, Wilfred Cantwell. 1957. *Islam in Modern History*. Princeton: Princeton University Press.

Yaqubi, Ahmad ibn Abi Yaqub. 1892. *Kitab al-Buldan (Book of Lands)*. Edited by M.D. Goeje. Leiden: Leiden University Press.

JOURNAL ARTICLES AND BOOK CHAPTERS

Ahmad, Khurshid. 1983. The Nature of Islamic Resurgence. In *Voices of Resurgent Islam*, ed. John L. Esposito, 218–229. Oxford: Oxford University Press.

Frankl, Viktor. 1967. Logotherapy and Existentialism. *Psychotherapy: Theory, Research and Practice* 4 (3): 138–142.

Guessoum, Nidhal. 2015. Reviews on Religion and Science around the World. *Zygon* 50 (4): 854–876.

Hańderek, Joanna. 2007. The Positionalist Notion of Human Nature in Plessner's and Gehlen's Philosophy. *Analecta Husserliana* XCIV: 533–547.

Kiyimba, Abasi. 2007. Islam and Science: An Overview. In *Islamic Perspective on Science*, ed. Ali Ünal, 1–27. Clifton, NJ: The Light Inc.

Lehmann, Olga V., and Sven Hroar Klempe. 2015. Psychology and the Notion of the Spirit: Implications of Max Scheler's Anthropological Philosophy in Theory of Psychology. *Integrative Psychological and Behavioral Science* 49 (3): 478–484. Springer.

Liccioli, Stefano. 2008. Il problema dell'uomo nel pensiero di Max Scheler. *Humana Mente* 2 (7): 79–104.

Musa, Aisha Y. 2009. A Thousand Years, Less Fifty: Toward a Quranic View of Extreme Longevity. In *Religion and the Implications of Radical Life Extension*, ed. Derek F. Mhaer and Calvin Mercer, 123–131. New York: Palgrave Macmillan.

Nasr, Hossein. 2006. On the Question of Biological Origins. *Islam & Science* 4 (2): 181–197.

Sardar, Ziauddin. 1985. Between Two Masters: Qur'an or Science? *Inquiry: An Interdisciplinary Journal of Philosophy* 2 (8): 37–41.

———. 1986. Redirecting Science towards Islam: An Examination of Islamic and Western Approaches to Knowledge and Values. *Hamdard Islamicus* 9 (1): 23–34.

———. 2006. Ziauddin Sardar Confronts the Commentators. *New Statesman*, February 6.

Scheler, Max. 2004. *Das Ressentiment im Aufbau der Moralen*. Frankfurt am Main: Klostermann Seminar.

CHAPTER 6

Beyond the Empirical Agent

The 'tension' that is often prevalent in the debate between the religious view of the human and the secular transhumanist 'Renaissance' human revolves around our epistemological outlook. Within western philosophy, this has been expressed through, for example, a Cartesian concept of mankind as possessing innate knowledge and able to go beyond mere sensual experiences, in contrast to a Humean understanding of humans as essentially empirical agents. Secular transhumanism veers towards the latter understanding: the human can be reduced like any other material object, though, admittedly, considerably more complex. The Cartesian notion of the human, however, is closer to the transhumanist view: the human is not to be 'reduced' to the mechanical, but to be 'expanded' to the God-like, to acquire God's point of view, or 'theomimesis' as Fuller calls it (Fuller 2008). Descartes' cogito ergo sum, therefore, can be regarded as 'the first modern secularization of the theomimetic moment' (Fuller and Lipinska 2014, Chap. 2), yet this follows in the footsteps of theologians such as John Duns Scotus' (1266–1308) univocal predication 'whereby divine attributes differ from human ones only by kind' (ibid.). As shall be demonstrated, such a notion of theomimesis, although under different names, is evident in Islam too.

Scouring the transhumanists literature, there are many articles that argue for the technological possibility of mind uploading. In fact, this is an important stage towards the quest for immortality, for if your mind is not necessarily attached to your brain, then the mind can be uploaded into a

© The Author(s) 2020
R. Jackson, *Muslim and Supermuslim*, Palgrave Studies
in the Future of Humanity and its Successors,
https://doi.org/10.1007/978-3-030-37093-0_6

variety of different forms before the physical deterioration of the brain. 'Mind' and 'brain', therefore, are seen as separate substances. The brain is what constitutes the underlying mechanics that are required to engage our thoughts. The mind, then, are our thoughts: it is a Substrate-Independent Mind (SIM). In order for us to be 'us' requires our thoughts, our mind, but this can be housed in an alternative mechanical construction, or computational platforms, than that of our brain. Essentially, the secular transhumanist prescribes to that often-told science fiction story of 'you' waking up in another body, quite possibly a mechanical robot of some kind.

This does, of course, raise all kinds of questions within the realm of the philosophy of mind, particularly what constitutes personal identity. For example, if the mind is uploaded into a mechanical robot that does not require the same kind of sustenance as a human body—plugging it in for a few hours would be quite sufficient—then what makes you *you* is not some basic fact about the digestive system. Nor for that matter is your physical appearance necessary for personal identity; a robot could be any shape or size and does not require two legs, two arms, two eyes, and so on. How far ought we to go in converting humans into some sort of post-biological form? Would you 'upload' yourself into a computer or robot if the technology is available? Can human identity be 'reduced' in this way and, if so, do we then lose what it means to be human? If the brain is all that is required for human identity then we can look to science fiction to provide us with a rich vein of thought experiments here, such as Robert Sheckley's (1928–2005) *The Body* in which a scientist's brain is transferred to a pet dog, or William Gibson's *Neuromancer*, where the distinction between machine and human consciousness appears non-existent, or the Culture series of Iain M Banks (1954–2013) where characters switch easily from one gender to another, one species to another, or become part of a 'group mind'. Many of the basic physical facts that make up the human would no longer be evident, for we are not merely talking slight enhancements here, for example eyes that can see better, but perhaps having no eyes *at all* as we understand them.

What is considered to be necessary and sufficient to maintain personal identity is a much-discussed philosophical issue. To say it is our thoughts that matter depends on what we mean by 'thoughts', and how these are tied to consciousness, our emotions, sensory experiences, aesthetic sensibilities, memories, and so on. These may all be grouped together as 'psychological states' and John Locke (1632–1704) was an early adherent of the view that what mattered in terms of personal identity is psychological continuity:

For, it being the same consciousness that makes a man be himself to himself, personal identity depends on that only, whether it be annexed only to one individual substance, or can be continued in a succession of substances. ... For it is by the consciousness it has of its present actions that it is self to itself now, and so will be the same self as far as the same consciousness can extend to actions past or to come, and would be by distance of time no more than two persons than a man be two men by wearing other clothes today than he did yesterday—with a long or short sleep in between: the same consciousness uniting these distant actions into the same person, whatever substances contributed to their production. (Locke 1975, chap. XXVIII, S.10)

The actual physical substance, therefore, is irrelevant. What matters for the survival of the self is equivalent to one's psychological states. An opposing view is given by the somaticist who would argue that a particular body is essential for personal identity. By way of illustration, Derek Parfit's (1942–2017) well-known thought experiment can help us here:

I enter the Teletransporter. I have been to Mars before, but only by the old method, a space-ship journey taking several weeks. This machine will send me at the speed of light. I merely have to press the green button. Like others, I am nervous. Will it work? I remind myself what I have been told to expect. When I press the button, I shall lose consciousness, and then wake up at what seems a moment later. In fact I shall have been unconscious for about an hour. The Scanner here on Earth will destroy my brain and body, while recording the exact states of all of my cells. It will then transmit this information by radio. Travelling at the speed of light, the message will take three minutes to reach the Replicator on Mars. This will then create, out of new matter, a brain and body exactly like mine. It will be in this body that I shall wake up. (Parfit 1987, p. 199)

For the defender of psychological continuity, or SIM, then Parfit does indeed wake up in this new body on Mars, but for the somaticist, the fact that the body on Earth has been destroyed means that the body on Mars is no longer Parfit. It is another person that nonetheless has Parfit's memories and personality but, in some sense—a sense that is not altogether clear—is not Parfit. Somaticism denies the possibility of SIM, and Parfit himself has found that in somewhat informal surveys, most would be unwilling to engage in this thought experiment, believing that it is effectively suicide (Parfit 1987, p. 279). There is, therefore, a certain intuitive sense that the mind and the body are in some way connected and that the transference of the mind only leaves something 'behind' that is necessary for personal identity. However, such intuition or, perhaps, emotional attachment does not make this concern any more veridical than, say, a fear of flying.

Even if you do not offer up a somatic defence, you may still be doubtful that our mind can be duplicated without 'something' missing. This 'something' may not be the physical body, but rather something that simply cannot be reduced to physics, at least not as we currently understand the physical world. This comes back to the hard problem in the philosophy of mind, for *qualia*, my experience, is not something that can be observed in a third-person way and, therefore, how can it be 'copied' if we cannot even detect what it is we wish to copy? Hence, an advocate of what is referred to as *weak AI* would argue that computers can be 'intelligent' in the sense that they can beat me at chess or do maths quicker than I can, but they cannot actually *think* or have consciousness in any human sense of the term. The defence of weak AI is illustrated by another famous philosophical thought experiment, John Searle's Chinese Room. In this example, Searle imagines being locked in a room where a piece of paper with incomprehensible 'squiggles' (actually, Chinese symbols) are passed to him. As Searle does not read Chinese, the symbols make no sense to him, but, fortunately, he has a rule book written in English which instructs him how to combine a set of squiggles and then write up a different set of squiggles which he passes over to people outside the room. What Searle is doing is 'computing' by providing intelligent answers, in Chinese, to questions that are also in Chinese. To any outsider, the person in the room, the 'intelligence' if you will, is engaging in a conversation in Chinese, yet Searle, in actual fact, has no idea what is going on! He is just following rules, but not thinking or understanding (Searle 1980).

The best, therefore, that artificial intelligence can achieve is to manipulate symbols according to set rules, or programmes. Coming back to the Parfit example, the Mars Parfit may well *appear* intelligent and 'be Parfit' in its behaviour, but that is deceptive. Parfit actually died when the body was destroyed on Earth. Secular transhumanists, on the other hand, propose that, with increasing advances in computational processing, there will be a time in the future when the mind can be uploaded onto a computer in its entirely, with nothing 'missing'. The term now more frequently used for this is Whole Brain Emulation (WBE), which was coined by Randal A. Koene back in 2000 on a 'mind uploading research group' (MURG) mailing list (Koene 2013, p. 147). It is not within the remit (or my competence) to get into the technical details, but suffice to say that the possibilities of WBE, of the belief in *strong AI*, are no longer considered by a number of transhumanists to be within the realm of science fiction, but as a very real possibility in the not-too-distant future, perhaps within the lifespan of the majority of the human population that are alive today.

Reading various articles of rather technical journals that, I must admit, at times leave me perplexed, there is nonetheless certain language used when describing the human being. The language that is *not* used, or extremely rarely (and then more often than not in a pejorative sense) is 'soul', 'spirit', 'feelings', 'moral sense', 'aesthetic awareness', or even 'emotion'. Instead, words such as 'data', 'software', 'neurons', 'synapses', 'functions', and so on are prevalent. It is, of course, inevitable that in reading technical journals you will be confronted by technical language. Those in the field of neural engineering and nanotechnology will be laughed out of the conference room if they start talking about their *feelings*! Yet, we do seem to be confronted by this duality of realities once more which was considered in Chap. 2. 'Soul', 'spirit', and so on are our 'imagined realities', whereas 'neurons', 'software', and so on are our 'objective realities'. The concern here, however, is that the imagined realities—some of them anyway—are often regarded as entirely unnecessary in what constitutes the human when it comes to WBE.

By Whole Brain Emulation, we mean what it says: the one-off event of 'uploading' the *whole* brain, our entire psychology, into a computer of some kind. The important question here is whether by making the decision to 'upload' you are indeed becoming a 'new and better you' or is this just a novel way of committing suicide? If it is the latter, then we need to address the question of what, then, does it mean to be human if it cannot be reduced to an 'objective reality'? Before we consider this from the perspective of Islamic thought, it should be pointed out that what we are talking about here is not the same thing as living forever. The gerontologist Aubrey de Grey believes that, with the continuing advances in technology, we may be able to regularly 'fix' faulty parts as we go along through life to the extent that we will be ageless, rather like a car you constantly replace with new parts. When a car ceases to be the *same* car is, of course, another one of those philosophical conundrums that has an intellectual history much longer than cars have existed, but the point here is that this constant fixing does not require mind uploading. There are some associative problems, especially if we are talking about the need to gradually replace the neurons in our brains with silicon chips, for at what point does such a gradual transformation result in the loss of self, if at all? Let us see if it is worth at least considering the possibility that we are something more than our empirical senses can determine.

Are Humans a 'Mystery'?

It is important to understand what we mean by humankind as something 'more than' an empirical agent. My reference point here is perhaps the greatest empiricist of them all, David Hume, who famously stated that 'no truth appears to be more evident, than that beasts are endow'd with thought and reason as well as men' (Hume 1978, p. 176). When Hume uses the term 'thought' he means by this 'belief', which he defined as a 'lively idea' or 'image' caused by (or associated with) a prior sensory experience (ibid., p. 94). For Hume, to exercise reason is actually a mere disposition or an instinct to form associations between these ideas on the basis of past experience. This is what empirical agents do: they experience the world and draw conclusions from it in order to act in the world and predict events, and it is, of course, how scientific method, on the whole, operates. Scientific studies rely upon the accurate analysis of data using standardised statistical methods, so animals do not *do* science, but they are, like humans, empirical in their reasoning. In the section of *A Treatise of Human Nature* entitled, 'Of the Reason of Animals', Hume argued that animals, certain animals at least, resemble in their behaviour that of human beings and, by analogy, there is good reason to believe (in fact, he stated that the proof is 'incontestable') that animals reason in a similar way to humans.

There are many problems with Hume's theories of mind and the epistemological conclusions he draws from these, and it is well beyond the remit of this modest work to engage directly in these philosophical responses to Hume to any great extent here, although it is relevant to mention the well-known problem that Hume's definition of 'belief' as vivid ideas presented to consciousness seems highly inadequate. The prevalent view in modern philosophy is that beliefs, as human beings experience them, have propositional content. That is to say, to have a thought or a belief about an object always correlates with a fact, or proposition, about that object. The perceiver does not just perceive 'blue' but, for example, *that* blue is the colour of the sky. Certainly, the perceiver can entertain an image of 'red', but that is not a *belief*. Belief is a propositional attitude, a mental state that has some opinion, stance, and so on, about the potential state of affairs in which that proposition is true. This is canonically expressed in the form 'S A that P', in which S signifies the subject possessing the mental state, A is the attitude of the subject, and P is the sentence that expresses the proposition. For example, Simon [S] hopes [A] that the sun will shine tomorrow [P].

In addition, beliefs, unlike ideas, have *intention*: they aim towards the truth and represent states of affairs as being the case. For example, you can have an extremely vivid idea that the Sun revolves around the Earth but that is different from your *belief* that the Earth actually revolves around the Sun. Further, Hume's inadequate definition of 'belief' as vivid ideas presented to consciousness is compounded by his narrow definition of 'reason' as the disposition to form associations among such ideas. Again, much ink has been spilt on Hume, and continues to do so, and I am wary of being too dismissive of the complexity of Hume's analysis of belief, but there is nonetheless a general consensus amongst Hume scholars that, at best, Dispositional Analysis might be *suggested* in his works (notably in Sections 9 and 10 of *Treatise*, Book I, Part iii), but certainly not developed and, generally, he is considered a traditional supporter of Occurrence Theory (Price 1969, Lecture 7). As said, the intention here is not to attack Hume, but to cite his empirical views as an example of the limitations of the 'empirical man' as something more akin to the beasts than of angels. This is hugely important in terms of secular transhumanism which, in its literature, often seems ridiculously casual and almost arrogant in its beliefs that the human can, in the relatively near future, be reduced to a set of data that can then be in some way 'uploaded'. Independent of Hume's understanding of 'reason' and 'belief' is his analogical reasoning based in the behaviour of certain animals vis-à-vis that of human beings. In what sense, for example, does a dog 'believe' the cat is up a tree? The human 'belief' in such a statement seems to bear little analogy with that of a dog. Similarly, you may be able to get a robotic vacuum to clean your floor for you, but that is vastly different from saying that the robot *believes* it is vacuuming a floor for you. Whilst we seem very easy in using terms such as 'intelligence' when applied to robots even today, the fact is they can't so much as cross a road by themselves safely.

Secular humanism, to some degree, with its relation to a form of militant atheism is, in turn, a legacy of the harsh empiricism of David Hume, but the extent to which Hume successfully committed to the flames the 'sophistry and illusion' of 'divinity and school metaphysics' (Hume 1978, S165) may well be overly optimistic; not only in Hume's time, but in the present day. Granted, much metaphysical speculation quite possibly does deserve to burn, yet much also deserves to remain and to be open to further reflection and consideration. Hume seems to have often had Descartes in mind in his attacks on such metaphysical speculation, yet Descartes' assertion that animals do not possess thought is something worth some rumination, for he does make some valuable contributions in the two independent arguments he puts forward to support the view that animals do not have thought or reason. These two arguments have since become known as the 'language-test argument' and the 'action-test argument'.

As regards the language-test argument, Descartes defines 'thought' as occurrent, that is thoughts that are entertained, or brought to mind, or a thought that suddenly occurs to you (Malcolm 1973). Human beings express their occurrent thoughts through speech which have propositional content. Occurrent thought can also be stimulus independent, for example I can suddenly start talking about what I had for breakfast even though this has no relation to what I may be talking about previous to this. Similarly, thoughts and speech can be action independent: my enthusiasm to share my breakfast details with my colleagues that express itself while driving my car, for example. Descartes had observed that animals produce calls, cries, and songs, as well as assorted gestures to express their wants and desires, but, he argued, they cannot 'use words, or put together other signs, as we do in order to declare our thoughts to others' (Descartes 1988, p. 45). This was not simply a matter of lacking the necessary speech organs, for Descartes argued that humans born deaf or dumb can use sign language, whereas those animals—such as parrots—that do have the necessary speech organs cannot produce declarative speech as expressions of occurrent thought. For Descartes, then, animals are no different from automata, completely incapable of 'thought' in the human sense. Now we have, of course, learned a great deal about animal behaviour since the seventeenth century. Green monkeys, for example, we now know use different calls to communicate warnings such as 'lion coming' which is distinguished from 'eagle coming' (Harari 2011, p. 24), and recent research on whales and elephants reveal an ability to produce a variety of distinct sounds. Having said that, Descartes is right to distance human thought and speech from the animal in terms of our complexity and suppleness. Neither animals nor the most complex forms of artificial intelligence that exist today can engage with their surrounding world to the extent of creating narratives as humans do. Of course, it may well be the case that artificial intelligence may turn out to be a different form of intelligence, rather than a copy of human intelligence but, if this is to be the case, then what are the implications for the transhuman prepared to 'upload' into a machine? Would the human cease to have those aspects of humanity that we consider makes us distinctively human, such as our ability to create 'imagined realities' and, let's face it, our seemingly unique ability to gossip, as Harari points out, 'the vast majority of human communication—whether in the form of emails, phone calls or newspaper columns—is gossip' (Harari 2011, p. 26).

Descartes' action-test argument sets out to prove that animals lack reason, as distinct from thought. By 'reason', Descartes defines this as 'a universal instrument which can be used in all kinds of situations' (Descartes 1988, p. 44). In other words, humans have the ability to act on general principles despite being confronted by often very different circumstances. This is not the forum to get too bogged down in the controversies regarding the extent to which animals can or cannot engage in reason in the way Descartes understands it, although suffice to say that there is considerable research in animal behaviour to suggest that other creatures aside from humans can transfer their general knowledge to quite a wide range of new situations. For that matter, there is some disagreement as to whether Descartes' definition of 'reason' is adequate, preferring Fodor's modularity of mind thesis (Fodor 1983). It may well be that animals do not have the 'modules' in the mind required to solve problems in various domains but, equally, humans may also not have certain 'modules' that animals possess; for example, the ability to navigate vast distances without any mechanical aid. The transhuman, however, will presumably break down such boundaries between what humans are 'naturally' capable of reasoning through, and what mechanical tools are required to solve problems. However, again, we must wonder whether this is all that there is to reason as being able to solve problems in a mechanical manner. Artificial intelligence is currently making great leaps in terms of adapting to different situations, although still at a ridiculously simplistic level, as well as hilariously awkward when compared to the human, but 'reasoning' at its peak anyway involves a degree of, for want of a better word, 'creativity' or 'inspiration'. There is a danger of using words such as 'inspiration' in a mysterious, nonphysical manner and, perhaps, such things can be reduced to a mechanical process, but it nonetheless remains to this day a feature of the human that defies such material reduction.

The extent to which the human is 'something more' than other animals or reducible to a mechanical structure needs to be seen within the context of the time Hume and Descartes were writing. Recall in Chap. 3 I spoke of the 'Universal Man', *Uomo Universale*, of the Renaissance. Descartes was writing in Paris in the seventeenth century, but it is worth considering what was happening in France the century before and the century after Descartes. Philip the Good (1396–1467) was the Duke of Burgundy from 1419 until his death and he was probably the most powerful and richest person in the whole of Christian Europe during his reign. He certainly liked to show off this wealth and power. He was a patron of the arts, populating his court with the greatest musicians and works of art and he held regular magnificent feasts in his various palaces in Brussels, Bruges, and Lille, but of particular interest here is Philip's renovation of the chateau at Hesdin in the north of France in the 1430s, which had fallen into considerable disrepair. In its better days, in the early fourteenth century, the castle was modelled on the Islamic gardens, which included the Islamic fondness for machines such as metal trees with artificial jewelled songbirds on its branches. The gardens at Hesdin boasted mechanical monkeys covered in badger skin to make them look more naturalistic, birds that sprang water from their beaks, elaborate mechanical fountains, moving statues, and even a mechanical king on a throne which was probably moved by water power (Truitt 2015, p. 124). The *engien* of Philip's Hesdin, however, takes us up another notch as a reflection of what fifteenth century technological engineering could now achieve. Philip seemed to have a fondness for practical jokes, especially involving water, flour, and soot. Alas, none of these mechanical wonders remain, except for the receipts, and the quote below gives you some idea of what the unsuspecting guests were in for:

> Item: There is a wooden figure that appears above a bench in the middle of the gallery, and it tricks people and can speak by a machine [*engien*] and make a cry on behalf of my lord the duke that everybody should go out of the gallery; and those who go because of that cry will be beaten by large figures like idiots … and they will fall into the water at the entrance to the bridge; and those who do not want to leave will be so completely soaked that they will not know where to go to escape from the water. A box is suspended in one window, and above the box is a figure that makes faces at people and replies to their questions, and one can both hear and see the voice in this box. (Ibid., p. 132)

Psychologically, the effect on the guests was inevitably to amuse but also to cause discomfort and unease, where the Hesdin constructs of the previous century were more edifying. This fear before the machine is an early example of a recurring theme to this day. Paris was the location a century after Descartes, in 1738 to be exact, for the next technological wonder that certainly raises the question of humankind's own nature. The story goes that Jacques de Vaucanson (1709–1782), who already had a considerable reputation for his building of automata, fell seriously ill and was bedridden for four months, during which he dreamt of a mechanical man that could play the flute that would be in the shape of the marble statue on display in the Tuileries Gardens. On recovery, Vaucanson got to work and the Automaton Flute Player was exhibited to the public on February 11, 1738. The cost to see this was three lires, which would have been a week's wages for the manual labourer, yet the queues were incredible. The figure itself was made of wood but painted white to resemble a marble statue. It was life size—five and a half feet tall—and stood upon a pedestal. The importance of this automaton is that it is not trickery, for it actually *breathed* into the flute: the lips opened and closed, moved forwards and backwards, and inside was a moveable metal tongue which governs the air-flow into the flute. The automaton could play 12 different melodies on an instrument that was regarded as one of the hardest to play in tune, yet the results were, largely, impressive according to most contemporary descriptions, although lacking the subtlety and softness that could be achieved by a human flute player. What the automata represents here in both time and place is that it was the centre of Enlightenment thinking, the Renaissance Man at His apex. The sound of the flute was not being mechanised here, rather it was the behaviour of the flute player, and this certainly raises question as to whether human movement is also simply mechanical. The idea that humans and machines might be the same began to become something of a plausible idea at least, rather than two very distinct phenomena. It brings into question, what Descartes declared 100 years earlier in his *Discourse on the Method*:

> For we can certainly conceive of a machine so constructed that it utters words, and even utters words which correspond to bodily actions causing a change in its organs (e.g., if you touch it in one spot it asks what you want of it, if you touch it in another it cries out that you are hurting it, and so on). But it is not conceivable that such a machine should produce different arrangements of words so as to give an appropriately meaningful answer to whatever is said in its presence, as even the dullest of men can do. (Descartes 1988, S.57, p. 44)

Here, Descartes maintains a machine can never be like a human, and yet, with the Flute Player, one commentator stated, 'What a shame the mechanician stopped so soon, when he could have gone ahead and given his machine a soul' (Wood 2002). The Enlightenment began to challenge the hegemony of the Church and, also, Vaucanson's automata did likewise. Although Vaucanson was taught by Jesuits and became a novice in the religious order of the Minimes in Lyon, this was not due to his religious inclinations, but rather it was the only door open at the time that would allow him to pursue his scientific studies and it was dangerous territory still for when one of the heads of the Minimes came to visit, Vaucanson chose this occasion to impress by having the meal served by machines. Yes, it did impress the visitor, but he also ordered Vaucanson's workshop to be destroyed as he considered it to be profane (Wood 2002).

Automatons motivated many to reflect upon ourselves as human beings and to consider the mechanics of what being a human involves. Vaucanson's motivation for building automatons was not, it should be stressed, to present an entertaining show, but he was primarily interested in anatomy, to build machines to show how humans function. The possibility was certainly being entertained that humans are no different ultimately than animals or machines. As Charles Darwin (1809–1882) points out concerning human and animal intelligence, he believed that the difference was by degree, not by kind. Therefore, human beings are more complex, but essentially there is nothing over and above the mechanical functions, and so the Cartesian distinction between body and mind was being brought into question. Charles Darwin's grandfather, Erasmus Darwin (1731–1802), wrote of the possibility of the human as merely functionalist with inputs and outputs. Erasmus Darwin himself built a speaking machine as he was fascinated by language, given his own speech impediment (Jackson 2005, p. 219). In his poem *The Temple of Nature*, Darwin provides this explanatory note for a passage:

> I contrived a wooden mouth with lips of soft leather, and with a vale back part of it for nostrils, both which could be quickly opened or closed by the pressure of the fingers, the vocality was given by a silk ribbon about an inch long and a quarter of an inch wide stretched between two bits of smooth wood a little hollowed; so that when a gentle current of air from bellows was blown on the edge of the ribbon, it gave an agreeable tone, as it vibrated between the wooden sides, much like a human voice. This head pronounced the p, b, m, and the vowel a, with so great nicety as to deceive all who heard it unseen, when it pronounced the words mama, papa, map, pam; and had a most plaintive tone, when the lips were gradually closed. (Darwin 1803/1973, pp. 119–20)

The productions by Vaucanson and the like influenced the development of machines during the Industrial Revolution, for example Edmund Cartwright's (1743–1823) revolutionary looms were the result of his observation of an automaton, but the limitations of machines in terms of 'being human' results in the irony that humans were made to be more like machines; the division of labour became blurred with humans behaving in a mechanical way. This image of man becoming machine is represented in Fritz Lang's 1927 film *Metropolis* and Charlie Chaplin's 1936 movie *Modern Times*. In literature, the concern that machines could replace humans was appearing in the eighteenth century. For example, the English novelist Samuel Butler's (1835–1902) satire *Erewhon* (1872) which is written in the manner of Swift's Gulliver adventures and anticipates in many ways the current debates in transhumanism. The chapter in *Erewhon*, 'The Book of the Machines' expresses the concern that humans will one day be replaced by machines, as described by the 'philosopher' in the novel:

> They have preyed upon man's groveling preference for his material over his spiritual interests, and have betrayed him into supplying that element of struggle and warfare without which no race can advance. The lower animals progress because they struggle with one another; the weaker die, the stronger breed and transmit their strength. The machines being of themselves unable to struggle, have got man to do their struggling for them: as long as he fulfils this function duly, all goes well with him—at least he thinks so; but the moment he fails to do his best for the advancement of machinery by encouraging good and destroying the bad, he is left behind in the race of competition; and this means he will be made uncomfortable in a variety of ways, and perhaps die. (Butler 1872/2003, p. 181)

Butler here expresses the concern for the 'preference for his material over his spiritual interests', which are sentiments and anxieties common amongst many of his contemporaries and can also be seen in the literature of William Wordsworth (notably his Preface to *Lyrical Ballads*) and, of course, Mary Shelley's *Frankenstein* (Page 2016, p. 135). As Herbert Sussman remarks in his work *Victorians and the Machine*, 'Butler's philosophical point here is that the mechanistic hypothesis necessarily implies complete philosophical determinism' (p. 153). Whilst the free will versus determinist debate is not something I will explicitly explore in this work, it is nonetheless implied throughout out that if humans are indeed complex machines then it *may* logically follow that we are subject to the same determined laws of cause and effect. This is something that troubled the empirical bent of Hume, hence his version of compatibilism. There are various philosophical attempts to explain how we experience freedom and choice whilst maintaining we are nothing more than the sum of our parts; for example, Daniel Dennett's 'Valerian' model of decision making:

> The model of decision making I am proposing, has the following feature: when we are faced with an important decision, a consideration-generator whose output is to some degree undetermined produces a series of considerations, some of which may of course be immediately rejected as irrelevant by the agent (consciously or unconsciously). Those considerations that are selected by the agent as having a more than negligible bearing on the decision then figure in a reasoning process, and if the agent is in the main reasonable, those considerations ultimately serve as predictors and explicators of the agent's final decision. (Dennett 1978, p. 295)

This very 'mechanical' language of describing our decision making, our hopes, dreams, desires, anxieties, and so on, with such terms as 'consideration-generator', 'output', 'agent', and so on, which are not that dissimilar from the language we have seen used by the secular transhumanists. It is this concern that the material aspects of the human are preferred over the spiritual or, rather, that there is really no such thing as the spiritual, it is a 'ghost in the machine' to quote Gilbert Ryle (1900–1976), that has been expressed over and over again by philosophers, artists, filmmakers, and so on. What the somewhat contrasting views of the human presented by Hume and Descartes show us is important in how we are to understand the human being and the extent to which the human can be 'transcended' without losing what it means to be human. Central to this argument is human beings are really not that 'easy', despite the confidence expressed in much transhumanist literature that we are not that far away in the future from transcending our limited bodies and entering a higher plane. The complexity and mystery of human beings is something to be celebrated and cherished, and crucially not to be ignored or so readily regarded as something that technology can 'copy' or 'upload'. Perhaps a hundred years from now, a future human may read this book and laugh at my naivety, but my concern is that this self-same human, or transhuman, will actually be incapable of such laughter and would consider talk of such things as 'inspiration', 'creativity', 'mystery', and so on as irrelevant, nonessential distractions from the more essential job of survival.

Within the scriptures of the world religions, the believer is confronted by many complexities, contradictions, ambiguity, and paradoxes. Attempts to 'rationalise' and reify these are destined to fail, because it is the very nature of belief that it does not allow itself to fit within the confines of strict rationality. This applies to any religious belief, hence the importance of story, of poetry, of mystical riddles, of art, of music. What often gets overlooked is this subtlety and complexity of religious belief, instead looking to the text in a literal way. As Lakoff and Johnson pointed out in their important study of metaphor, 'The most fundamental values in a culture will be coherent with the metaphorical structure of the most fundamental concepts in the culture' (Lakoff and Johnson 1980, p. 22). By ignoring metaphor, paradox, and so on, you are only grasping a small part of a belief. As Shahab Ahmed states, 'In the case of the Revelation of Islam, we have an instance where *metaphor itself is a fundamental value* cohering with the (metaphorical) structure of the fundamental concepts. *Metaphor and paradox are, in other words, of key semantic and existential significance to Muslims' modes meaning-making*' (Ahmed 2016, p. 392). For the transhuman to bear any resemblance at all to the human, what must be acknowledged is that we humans are filled with ambiguity and contradictions, and that religion plays an important role in striving to understand these fundamental characteristics of what it means to be human. Yes, certainly through the religious scriptures, but just as much—if not more so—through the rich diversity of its poetry, philosophy, and other creative expressions.

The fact that human beings are 'mysterious' is the reason why we create art, music, and other expressions of culture: we look to express what it is to be human in a way that factual data cannot. In the western tradition, philosophers such as Descartes and Hume may well reveal much of our nature, but we equally have much to learn from, for example, William Wordsworth, Mary Shelley, and Samuel Butler. We can look to history to give us human figures from the past, but it is often fiction that, somewhat paradoxically, makes humans more 'real'. Fictional characters can act as human archetypes, something that Nietzsche was only too aware of in the creation of his Zarathustra as a way of teaching the Übermensch. Islam, for its part, does also, of course, have important historical archetypes, most importantly the Prophet Muhammad as the Perfect Human, but also the Imam Ali b. Abu Talib as a symbol for chivalric youth (*futuwwah* in Arabic, or *javanmardi* in Persian), the Imam al Husayn b. Ali as the paradigm for martyrdom, or the Prophet's wives Khadija and Aisha as examples of women's power and influence (Ahmed 1993). However, outside of these historical figures, arguably the most influential is the fictional character of the love story *Majnun Layla* as an archetype, of which there are countless versions from poets such as Nizami, Amir Khusrow, Jami, and so on. Certainly, in attempting to understand that most slippery of human experiences, love, which is something that does not seem reducible to bits of data, the archetype of Majnun is 'the *personification of the ethos* of love' (Ahmed 2016, pp. 311–312) and, 'He has been invoked, proverbialized, metaphorized and sublimated into the image-vocabulary of the various languages spoken by Muslims to the point where he can be invoked without any need to name him at all' (Ahmed 2016, p. 312). Whilst I will not explore this love story here (although see next chapter), the point being made is just how important the creative arts are (let us not forget the many paintings and musical compositions that also portray this love story, as well as movies and theatre plays) as part of Islamic authority as *explorative*. Philosophy, art, poetry, and, indeed, religion can reveal much about these aspects of being human that are precious, and I want to demonstrate the limitations of Hume's 'empirical human' through the example of *Hayy ibn Yaqzan*; a work, whilst perhaps not as renowned as *Majnun Layla*, that nonetheless combines fiction, philosophy, and Islamic intellectual thought and, whereas *Majnun* can reveal much about love, *Hayy ibn Yaqzan* can reveal much about self-knowledge and what human beings are and can become.

Hayy ibn Yaqzan

The philosophical tale *Hayy ibn Yaqzan* is named after the protagonist. It is written by the Muslim philosopher Ibn Tufayl. It is regarded as the first Arabic novel, and considered by many to have anticipated the ideas expressed in Daniel Defoe's (1660–1731) *Robinson Crusoe* and Jean-Jacques Rousseau's (1712–1738) *Emile*. Ibn Tufayl tells the story of a remote and uninhabited island, located somewhere off the coast of India. This small island is near a much larger island which is populated and ruled over by a king who is very possessive over his sister, refusing her marriage without his permission. Despite this, she secretly married someone she loved called Yaqzan ('wide-awake') and she give birth to a son, Hayy ('Alive'), hence Hayy ibn Yaqzan ('Alive, son of Awake'). In fear that this baby will be discovered by the king, his sister casts her son into the sea upon a raft which washes ashore on the small neighbouring, uninhabited island. Hayy ibn Yaqzan is fortunately discovered by a doe, which provides milk for the baby and raises the child as her own. Hayy learns to walk when he is two years old and, as he lives amongst the deer, he naturally considers himself one of them, imitating their habits and mimicking the calls. When the child reaches the age of seven, his doe mother dies. However, Hayy, despite his young age, is able to survive on his own through his ability to engage in reasoned enquiry, which begins in an empirical manner by, for example, dissecting the doe in order to determine how she died. The point of this tale, however, is that Hayy, as he grows older, becomes more reflective and, unlike the other creatures that inhabit the island, he goes beyond the empirical agent that is firmly tied to the physical world as he begins to question the nature of existence and to speculate upon metaphysical issues. When Hayy reaches the age of 42 he has his first mystical experience and devotes the rest of his life in meditation and a retreat from the everyday concerns of the physical world as much as possible. However, the solitude is disturbed when Hayy is 50 years old by the arrival of Absal; a man who also has a spiritual yearning and has come to the island as a retreat. When Hayy and Absal meet, they are, at the level of common language, unable to understand each other, but there is an awareness between them that they share a common humanity in the spiritual beliefs that goes beyond declarative speech.

I wish to explore some of the themes in this novel in more detail, but first it needs to be put into its philosophical and religious perspective. Little is known about Ibn Tufayl. What we do know is that he was born in a small Spanish town by the name of Guadix (at that time it was called Wadi Ash), which is approximately 50 miles northeast of Granada. This was a time when Andalusia, or parts of it anyway, could boast a richness in many things, including its philosophical culture, and so Ibn Tufayl would have had access to the works of philosophers going back to the ancient Greeks. In terms of Islamic thought, he was influenced by, notably, al-Farabi (c.872–c.951, Latinised 'Alpharabius'), Ibn Sina, and Abu Hamid al-Ghazali (1058–1111, Latinised 'Algazel').

Al-Farabi is important as one of the first Muslim thinkers to engage in an attempt to harmonise Islam with Greek philosophical thought. Al-Farabi saw the prophets, Muhammad included, as first and foremost philosophers in the sense that their access to God was synonymous with the Neoplatonic concept of the Active Intellect. Undoubtedly, al-Farabi's attempts to blend Islamic theology with Plato, Aristotle, and Neoplatonism had a direct impact on Ibn Tufayl's own methodology and metaphysical understanding. Ibn Tufayl was also personally tutored by the Muslim philosopher and astronomer Ibn Bājja (1085–1138, Latinised 'Avempace'), and Ibn Tufayl was familiar with a work by Ibn Bājja called *The Hermit's Regime* or *Biography of a Solitary Being* (*Tadbir al-Mutawahhid*, although Ibn Bājja's book has also been translated as *The Conduct of the Solitary*, and *Governance of the Solitary*). This work, in fact, continues a discussion to be found in al-Farabi's work *On the Perfect State* (*Mabadi Ara Ahl Al-Madinat Al-Fadilah*) which explores the role of the philosopher in the political state and whether, in some political systems, it is better for the philosopher to retreat from state affairs and seek a life of solitude. One can see the Platonic influence here from *Republic* of course. Ibn Bājja explores the extent to which it is possible for a human being to live a life of solitude and yet still achieve spiritual and intellectual fulfilment. In other words, do human beings require society and, especially, the social interaction this involves, to acquire this spiritual awareness, or does it have the opposite effect of distracting from this goal? Plato's argument in *Republic* was that the state, if corrupt, would also corrupt the philosopher, which is a recognition of just how powerful the state apparatus can be.

From the transhumanist perspective this is interesting, for Ibn Bājja presents a Cartesian picture of human beings as 'god-like' to the extent that they are self-thinking intellects that can, intuitively, experience a knowledge of truth that seemingly bears no relation to the physical world, suggesting that human beings can, in a solitary state, attain self-awareness. Ibn Sina, for his part, wrote a, much shorter, allegorical tale also called *Hayy ibn Yaqzan* which, whilst considered less of a literary achievement than Ibn Tufayl's work, describes how Hayy is able to attain truth by being virtually self-taught. Interestingly, this is a topic that Ibn Sina explored as a philosophical thought experiment of the Floating Man where he conceives of a human being floating in mid-air and, therefore, deprived of any environmental influences other than the air itself. This Floating Man, with no objects to perceive, is also like a new-born baby with no past experience. Ibn Sina believes that such a creature will nonetheless be capable of accessing spiritual knowledge, for human beings, unlike other creatures, possess a soul. Once again, the links with Plato's and Descartes' epistemology are obvious here to any philosopher, regardless of the likelihood of such a human being really being capable of knowing *anything* with such extreme sensory deprivation and not even a past to tap into. Perhaps the point that the knowledge that the senses can provide us with is both limited and may even act as a distraction from other forms of knowledge is something that deserves some consideration and, indeed, it is what Ibn Tufayl sets out to explore in his novel.

As the character Hayy is an autodidact, the Latin title given to his work is *Philosophus Autodidactus*. This Latin translation was published in 1671, with the first English translation in 1708. Whilst in western scholarship today, Hayy seems to receive little attention, it was influential in Europe during the seventeenth and eighteenth centuries, including the aforementioned Daniel Defoe's *Robinson Crusoe* (Hassan 1980; Haque 2004). In terms of western philosophy, the empiricism of John Locke who, of course, proved in turn to influence Hume, has its roots with Ibn Tufayl, even though Locke himself does not refer to it. There are good reasons to believe in the connection, however, for it is known that Locke was a good friend and student of the Orientalist and biblical scholar Edward Pococke (1604–1691). Locke himself then became the personal tutor to Pococke' son Edward Pococke the Younger (1648–1727), who published the Latin edition of *Philosophus Autodidactus*. As pointed out by G.A. Russell:

> On the basis of all the evidence, the conclusion is inescapable that not only Locke must have known the work [*Philosophus Autodidactus*], but also that he must have been intimately acquainted with the progress of the whole project. Thus the period (1667–1671), during which Locke began to consider the 'problems' of the Essay [*An Essay Concerning Human Understanding*], and put them in writing for the first time, coincides precisely with that of the translation, publication and dissemination of *Philosophus autodidactus* by Edward and Dr. Pococke. (Russell 1994, p. 246)

Ibn Tufayl's work is relevant to the transhumanist debate for a number of reasons, for, to begin with, what we have is an example of a 'religious' work that does not fit within the secular transhumanist understanding of religion as closed and dogmatic. Like his fellow Andalusian Maimonides, Ibn Tufayl represents a strong philosophical and mystical (the two are not necessarily disparate) strands within religion that defies and denies its reification. In *Hayy*, we have a demonstration that Islam can be open to the ideas of other, 'non-Islamic', cultures and is able to reflect how this relates to Islam and what it means to be a Muslim which, let us remind ourselves, is considered as synonymous with what it means to be human. Hence, from an epistemological perspective, the fictional character of Hayy raises the question as to the extent to which 'being human' is akin to being firmly embedded in the physical world in the same way other creatures are.

If that is indeed the case, then the one goal of transhumanism for immortality of the self in some other physical form is theoretically possible. However, Ibn Tufayl does at least raise the possibility that human beings possess a uniqueness that is not easily 'copied' in this way; hence we have here an alternative view of the human as closer to angels than beasts.

Perhaps the central question of *Hayy* is: how are we to know God? Now, for the secular transhumanist, this may seem an entirely irrelevant question to be asking, since there is no God to know. However, the mistake here is, again, to buy into the militant atheist tradition of what we mean by 'God'. For example, to quote the high priest of atheism, Richard Dawkins:

> The God of the Old Testament is arguably the most unpleasant character in all fiction: jealous and proud of it; a petty, unjust, unforgiving control-freak; a vindictive, bloodthirsty ethnic cleanser; a misogynistic, homophobic, racist, infanticidal, genocidal, filicidal, pestilential, megalomaniacal, sadomasochistic, capriciously malevolent bully. (Dawkins 2007)

As previously pointed out, this may well be the God as understood by some believers and, in Islam too, its reification has likewise resulted in the image of an Old Testament God. However, this is not the 'God' of Ibn Tufayl or, for that matter, the majority of Muslims throughout Islamic history. For Ibn Tufayl the question 'how are we to know God?' is the same philosophical question that has preoccupied philosophers since at least the time of the ancient Greeks, if we are to understand the term 'God' not in the strict, orthodox, monotheistic sense that atheists often interpret it, but in the philosophical sense as the nature of 'Being', with all the epistemological, political, moral, and so on implications that arise from such vigorous intellectual speculation. Philosophy of religion has a long history of exploring the nature and existence of God, and how this relates to us as *human beings*; the awareness of something seemingly 'other', 'necessary', 'greater' in contrast to the human that is flawed, contingent, fragile, and so on. This intellectual quest tells us about *ourselves* with the disturbing realisation that our human intellect seems limited in what it can know in some respects, yet there are moments, or 'flashes', of inspiration when we seem to make that leap from the beast to the angel. The 'empirical human' sees knowledge in one sense only and looks at the world as 'sense-data' or interprets religious texts literally in the same way that religious fundamentalists do. Militant atheists do take great pains to argue that the world is nonetheless a magical and wonderful place and, granted, science and empirical method is indeed a fascinating way of knowing, but there is a danger of downplaying those other 'senses' or ways of knowing. It is a beautiful thing to be able to look through a powerful telescope and see distant stars, but it is even more beautiful when we can *appreciate* what we see from our own perspective as creative, philosophical, and, yes, 'religious' beings. Let it be stressed, by 'religious' here we mean an appreciation of the 'mysterious'; that which we are currently unable to translate into computational code and, perhaps, never will be able to. As already mentioned, it is difficult enough trying to express this through the limitations of language, hence Ibn Tufayl in his introduction to his work, describes the difficulty:

> Your request set off a stream of ideas in me—praise God—which lifted me to a state of sublimity I had never known before, a state so wonderful "the tongue cannot describe" or explain it, for it belongs to another order of being, a different world. But the joy, delight and bliss of this ecstasy are such that no one who has reached it or even come near it can keep the secret or conceal the mystery. The light-headedness, expansiveness, and joy which seize him force him to blurt it out in some sweeping generality, for to capture it precisely is impossible. (Ibn Tufayl 2009, 95:4)

The state of 'ecstasy', or *hal* in Arabic, reveals how difficult it is to describe that which is indescribable, with the best that one can do is to resort to emotional language, to talk of a sense of 'joy' and 'light-headedness'. Such states may be temporary, and this comes back to William James' account of such experiences as leaving the experiencer craving for more. Hayy, in the novel, craves to know God, but this is not the God that is reified, rationalised, anthropomorphised through the Kantian 'visible church', but the God of mystical experience which is the very foundation of Islam: the Prophet Muhammad's own mystical experience. While there can be no more prophets after Muhammad, so the Islamic tradition argues, it nonetheless opens up the question as to what us mere human beings can experience beyond the everyday sensual world, or do we decide that sense-data is sufficient, for that's all that there ultimately is that is allowed to us? Hayy is no prophet, but what we are presented with here is the *evolution* of one human being to a transhuman state and who struggles to communicate what this state implies. For example, when we read Hayy's account of his experience:

Passing through a deep trance to the complete death-of-self and real contact with the divine, he saw a being corresponding to the highest sphere, beyond which there is no body, a subject free of matter, and neither identical with the Truth and the One nor with the sphere itself, nor distinct from either—as the form of the sun appearing in a polished mirror is neither sun nor mirror, and yet distinct from neither. The splendor, perfection, and beauty he saw in the essence of that sphere were too magnificent to be described and too delicate to be clothed in written or spoken words. But he saw it to be the pinnacle of joy, delight, and rapture, in blissful vision of the being of the Truth, glorious be His Majesty. (Ibn Tufayl 2009, 152:157)

Like Maimonides and Wittgenstein that we looked at in Chap. 4, Ibn Tufayl is also aware that language has its limitations, and that Hayy's experience is 'too delicate to be clothed in written or spoken words'. It is significant that immediately preceding the above quote, Ibn Tufayl states that, 'a hint or a glimpse will be enough to give you some idea of the divine world, and if you can avoid conjuring my words in their ordinary sense' (152:157). This reminds one of Maimonides once more, but also of Socrates; the concern that words will cause the reader to misunderstand and that the best that can be proffered is a 'hint or glimpse'. In Chap. 3, I referred to '*marifa*', this 'intuitive knowledge', and how Kant expressed his concern with this as genuinely constituting a form of knowledge. Interestingly, in Gauthier's French translation of *Hayy* (Gauthier 1936, p. 91, note 3) he notes that Ibn Tufayl's concern with intuition predates Kant's by some 600 years. The Muslim philosopher and theologian Muhammad al-Ghazali was also wary of certain claims to philosophical truth in his *The Incoherence of the Philosophers (Tahafut al-Falasifah)* where he condemns the ancient Greek philosophers for their metaphysical inconsistencies. In turn, al-Ghazali is critical of Ibn Sina and his followers for following in the footsteps of the ancient Greeks and committing the same inconsistencies in logic. Yet al-Ghazali underwent an intellectual crisis of his own, which resulted in being paralysed by doubt and leaving the world of academia. As he describes in his short but fascinating work *Deliverance from Error (al-Munqidh min al-dalal)*:

I considered the circumstances of my life, and realised that I was caught in a veritable thicket of attachments. I also considered my activities, of which the best was my teaching and lecturing, and realised that in them I was dealing in sciences that were unimportant and contributed nothing to the attainment of eternal life. After that I examined my motive in my work of teaching, and realised that it was not a pure desire for the things of God, but that the impulse moving me ... was the desire for an influential position and public recognition. (al-Ghazali in Reid, 1995, p. 163)

What resulted from this was years of travel in the Islamic world by al-Ghazali, including pilgrimages to Mecca and Medina. Al-Ghazali engaged in Sufi practices, wearing the rough woollen clothing that would often typify the Muslim mystic, and leading the life of an ascetic through abstinence, self-discipline, prayer, and meditation. It is a result of this way of life and of attitude that led to al-Ghazali's own *marifa*; a recognition that book-reading and conventional study can only get you so far. The experience of Hayy, therefore, is by no means uncommon in the Islamic tradition and what both Hayy and al-Ghazali experienced is often named as 'Illumination' (*ishraq*) within Sufism. The 'Master of Illumination' ('*Shaykh al-Ishraq*') was Suhrawardi mentioned in the previous chapter. It is to Suhrawardi we must look to for introducing the language, ideas, and methodology of the Illuminationist school, which is also traditionally (though perhaps unhelpfully) known as the 'Oriental' school, and to which Ibn Tufayl is very much a subscriber of, as he states in his introduction to *Hayy ibn Yaqzan*:

Noble brother, my dear, kind friend, God grant you eternal life and everlasting happiness. You have asked me to unfold for you, as well as I am able, the secrets of the oriental philosophy mentioned by the prince of philosophers Avicenna. (95:4)

The importance of how this all relates to the transhumanist debate is, if this needs to be pointed out some more, that when we look to Islamic thought for what it can contribute to the debate, we must steer away from the presumed 'clash of civilisations' thesis: that Islam is simply too 'other' to have anything of value to offer. In addition, what transhumanism entails makes no sense unless we contextualise it in terms of what we understand by the 'human' and the extent to which the best (i.e., most knowledgeable or wisest) human beings are portrayed in some idealised (and blatantly false) 'western', 'empirical', 'rational', 'enlightened', 'scientific' animal that has its intellectual origins amongst the ancient Greeks and western Europe as a whole. Such dichotomies are both unhelpful and false. The boundaries are always blurred, and even secular transhumanists are open to, for example, Confucianism, but only to a form of Confucianism through western eyes; a

Hybrid Confucianism, or 'New Confucianism'. There is nothing essentially *wrong* with this, for religion is always changing, as it should do, but it is puzzling as to why Islam is seen as less open to hybridity, whereas, in reality, it always has been engaging in a process of 'revival and renewal' (see previous chapter). Suhrawardi and Ibn Tufayl are both Muslim, yet the former was writing in the twelfth century in Seljuk territories that were permeated with mystical, 'Oriental', thought, whereas Ibn Tufayl, whilst a contemporary of Suhrawardi, was a 'westerner', a European brought up in Andalusia in which, Ibn Tufayl felt (and another Andalusian, Maimonides), a large part of Islamic thought was being neglected:

> before the spread of philosophy and formal logic to the West all native Andalusians of any ability devoted their lives to mathematics. They achieved a high level in that field but could do no more. The next generation surpassed them in that they knew a little logic. But study logic as they may, they could not find in it the way to fulfilment ... our own contemporaries, are as yet at a developmental stage, or else their development has halted prematurely— unless there are some of whom I don't yet have a full report. (99:12–100:13)

Philosophy, '*falsafa*', is not just Plato and Aristotle, rich though that tradition is, but it is also 'peripatetic philosophy' or *hikmah-ul-mashriqiyya*. *Hikmah* is Semitic for 'wisdom', and *mashriqiyya*, with its root *sh-r-q* related to '*ishraqi*'; hence Suhrawardi's Illuminationism. Here 'east' and 'west' meet once more. Suhrawardi taps upon ancient traditions so that he would not regard Illumination as 'his' philosophy, but would see it as the perennial true philosophy that has been expressed in other cultures and times. In fact, Suhrawardi is fond of making reference to many ancient, especially Greek and Persian, thinkers as his predecessors in the 'Oriental' tradition, and the analogy of 'illumination' for Suhrawardi is influenced notably by Neoplatonism and emanation. Suhrawardi's epistemology divides knowledge into the more empirical and rational 'acquired' (*al-ʿilm al-husuli*), whereas Illuminationist knowledge is far more intuitive, that is knowledge 'by presence' (*al-ʿilm al-huduri al-ishraqi*). Suhrawardi, then, emphasises the importance of subjective experience, whether these be dreams, visions, 'flashes' of illumination, out of body experiences, and so on, as valuable in themselves and, for that matter, correlating with objective reality. Suhrawardi argued that the form of knowledge 'by presence' is higher than 'acquired' because the former consists of the most fundamental kind of knowledge, that of self-awareness. The question that may well be asked by the empirical sceptic concerning the veracity of such a subjective experience would result in the Illuminationist response of 'the self intuitively *knows*!' (Jackson 2014, pp. 64–67). For Suhrawardi, knowledge 'by presence' should not be simply dismissed as lacking any veracity and, therefore, in logical positivist terms, classed as 'meaningless' but, rather, should be explored, reflected upon and analysed. By way of illustration:

> provided we have all our senses, then all human beings are capable of having empirical experiences: we are all confronted by "sense data" which, on the whole, we are all share in common, e.g. if there is a blue car that drives by me, then anyone who is at that point will see the same blue car that I do. Therefore, we have all have a shared empirical experience. But the next stage is what is done with that empirical experience. In the case of the blue car, it is such a mundane everyday experience that it is promptly dismissed, but there are many other experiences that are subject to further study. For example, we may study newly-discovered planets circling a distant star through a telescope but not simply dismiss these as "mundane": the desire for humans to know more leads to us engaging in reasoning to find out more about these observations, and this is where the science of astronomy comes in. Similarly, the intuitive approach requires subsequent discursive analysis as a result of the visionary experience, and this requires the skills of the "science" of philosophy. Whereas the empirical is shared "sense-data" as the foundation for study, the acquired is subjective revelation—which differs from one person to the next—as its foundation for the science of illumination. Whilst these visions will differ from one subject to the next, for some may see visions of angels, or perhaps an historical figure—Suhrawardi himself often had visions of Aristotle—the end result, as in the knowledge acquired, will be the same for all. (Ibid., p. 67)

Suhrawardi's philosophy has been very influential in Islamic thought, especially amongst such Shi'a philosophers as al-Shirazi (aka Mulla Sadra, 1572–1640) and, as has been acknowledged, the philosophy has many of its roots in the 'western' philosophical tradition. But, in addition to that, and why this is able to inform the transhumanism debate, is not so much whether one subscribes to the epistemological belief that 'intuition' can count as 'knowledge' in any real, objective sense but, rather, Suhrawardi predates the philosophy of, for example, Nietzsche and the existential tradition in recognising the importance of myth, dreams, and fantasy in providing us with 'knowledge' of the world that is just as valuable as that provided by, say, physics, regardless of the issues of which is more 'true' than the other.

BIBLIOGRAPHY[1]

BOOKS

Ahmed, Leila. 1993. *Women and Gender in Islam: Historical Roots of a Modern Debate*. New Haven, CT: Yale University Press.

Ahmed, Shahab. 2016. *What Is Islam? The Importance of Being Islamic*. Princeton and Oxford: Princeton University Press.

Butler, Samuel. 2003. *Erewhon*. New York: Dover Publications.

Darwin, Erasmus. 1973. *The Temple of Nature*. London: Scolar Press.

Dawkins, Richard. 2007. *The God Delusion*. London: Black Swan.

Dennett, Daniel. 1978. *Brainstorms*. Cambridge, MA: MIT Press.

Descartes, René. 1988. Discourse on the Method. Translated by John Cottingham. In *Descartes: Selected Philosophical Writings*. Cambridge: Cambridge University Press.

Fodor, Jerry A. 1983. *Modularity of Mind: An Essay on Faculty Psychology*. Cambridge, MA: MIT Press.

Fuller, Steve, and Veronika Lipinska. 2014. *The Proactionary Imperative: A Foundation for Transhumanism*. Hampshire: Palgrave.

Gauthier, Leon, ed. 1936. *Hayy ben Yaqdhan: roman philosophique d'Ibn Thofail*. 2nd ed. Beirut: Imprimerie catholique. Reprinted Paris: Vrin, 1992.

Harari, Yuval Noah. 2011. *Sapiens: A Brief History of Humankind*. London: Penguin.

Hassan, Nawal Muhammad. 1980. *Hayy bin Yaqzan and Robinson Crusoe: A Study of an Early Arabic Impact on English Literature*. Republic of Iraq: Al-Rashid House for Publication.

Hume, David. 1978. *A Treatise of Human Nature*. 2nd ed. Edited by P.H. Nidditch. Oxford: Oxford University Press.

Ibn Tufayl. 2009. *Ibn Tufayl's Hayy Ibn Yaqzan: A Philosophical Tale*. Translated by L.E. Goodman. Chicago: University of Chicago Press.

Jackson, Roy. 2014. *What Is Islamic Philosophy?* Oxon: Routledge.

Lakoff, George, and Mark Johnson. 1980. *Metaphors We Live By*. Chicago: University of Chicago Press.

Locke, John. 1975. *An Essay Concerning Human Understanding*. Oxford: Oxford University Press.

Page, Michael R. 2016. *The Literary Imagination from Erasmus Darwin to H.G. Wells: Science, Evolution and Ecology*. Oxon: Routledge.

Parfit, Derek. 1987. *Reasons and Persons*. Oxford: Oxford University Press.

Price, H.H. 1969. *Beliefs*. New South Wales: Allen & Unwin.

---

[1] *Note*: All quotes from the Qur'an are from the translation by M.A.S. Abdel Haleem, Oxford University Press, 2005.

Russell, Gul A. 1994. *The 'Arabick' Interest of the Natural Philosophers in Seventeenth-Century England.* Leiden: Brill Publishers.
Truitt, E.R. 2015. *Medieval Robots: Mechanism, Magic, Nature, and Art.* Philadelphia: University of Pennsylvania Press.
Wood, Gaby. 2002. *Living Dolls: A Magical History of the Quest for Mechanical Life.* London: Faber & Faber.

JOURNAL ARTICLES AND BOOK CHAPTERS

Fuller, Steve. 2008. The Future Is Divine: A History of Human God-Playing. In *Human Futures,* ed. A. Miah, 6–19. Liverpool and Chicago: University of Liverpool Press and University of Chicago Press.
Al-Ghazali, Abū Ḥāmid Muḥammad ibn Muḥammad aṭ-Ṭūsī. 1995. That Which Delivers from Error. In *Readings in Western Religious Thought: The Middle Ages Through The Reformation,* ed. Patrick V. Reid, 154–168. Mahwah, NJ: Paulist Press.
Haque, Amber. 2004. Psychology from Islamic Perspective: Contributions of Early Muslim Scholars and Challenges to Contemporary Muslim Psychologists. *Journal of Religion and Health* 43 (4): 357–377.
Jackson, Philip J.B. 2005. Mama and Papa: The Ancestors of Modern-Day Speech Science. In *The Genius of Erasmus Darwin,* ed. Christopher Smith and Robert Arnott, 217–236. Aldershot: Ashgate.
Koene, Randal A. 2013. Uploading the Substrate-Independent Minds. In *The Transhumanist Reader,* ed. Max More and Natasha Vita-More, 146–156. Chichester: Wiley-Blackwell.
Malcolm, Norman. 1973. Thoughtless Brutes. *Proceedings and Addresses of the American Philosophical Association* 46 (September): 5–20.
Searle, John. 1980. Minds, Brains and Programs. *Behavioral and Brain Sciences* 3 (3): 417–457.

CHAPTER 7

Transcending the Human

VISIONS OF PERFECTIBILITY

Most of the expressions of concern by transhumanists towards religion are the belief that the latter is resistant to improvements in human beings because it is 'playing God'. John Hedley Brooke, in his paper 'Visions of Perfectibility', asks the question, 'Have not our visions of perfectibility been largely secular visions? Have not our religious values been lodged in the defence of a pristine nature or of a human nature with which we interfere at our peril?' (Brooke 2005, p. 1). However, Brooke rightly notes that, 'the story is not so simple' (ibid.). As, hopefully, this book has demonstrated, the lines between science and religion are often blurred, and the relationship between them much stronger and multifarious than many secular transhumanists assume, and here I would include Islam. Even one so strongly vocal concerning religious opposition to science, Francis Fukuyama, in his controversial work *Our Posthuman Future*, states:

> Religion often intuits moral truths that are shared by non-religious people, who fail to understand that their own secular views on ethical issues are as much a matter of faith as those of religious believers. Many hardheaded natural scientists, for example, have a rational materialist understanding of the world, and yet in their political and ethical views are firmly committed to a version of liberal equality that is not all that different from the Christian view of the universal dignity of humankind. (Fukuyama 2002, p. 90)

© The Author(s) 2020
R. Jackson, *Muslim and Supermuslim*, Palgrave Studies
in the Future of Humanity and its Successors,
https://doi.org/10.1007/978-3-030-37093-0_7

Interestingly, the 'supernatural' is not necessarily ruled out by transhumanists, although that understanding of the supernatural may not be akin to the current religious understanding. For example:

> If we live in a synthetic reality, then in a certain sense we cannot even rule out the supernatural, or miracles. The simulators, the system admins, cannot violate their laws of physics, but they can violate our laws of physics if they want. It seems that the supernatural, which we have kicked out of the back door of superstition, may come back through the main door of science. (Prisco 2013, pp. 237–238)

In other words, Prisco is presenting a transhumanist vision of human resurrection in which we are living in a synthetic world created by God-like 'simulators' who can change the way we understand the laws of nature and make a back-up copy of our synthetic world. While Prisco is keen to steer clear of traditional religion, I find it interesting that so many transhumanists make use of religious language. As Julian Huxley notes, he often found himself 'inevitably drawn to use the language of religion' (Huxley 1963, p. 157) when envisaging the future human. Whilst the transhumanist may at one level reject the God of the Bible or the Qur'an, they seem more willing to buy into the possibility that they are part of a computer game run by Geek-Gods. Leaving aside the extent to which one view is more or less credulous than the other, it must be acknowledged how the language and ideals of religions interact and intertwine with transhumanism. Even if the secular transhumanist rejects religious claims, they aspire to many of its ideals.

Undoubtedly, visions of the Perfect Human have been presented in religion and philosophy for thousands of years, but the important objection raised by some transhumanists is that this is not transhumanism as understood in the modern, technological sense of the term, but has more to do with, for example, spiritual growth. And so, while the ideals and language used by religion and transhumanism are similar or the same, the practical reality of what is being said is very different. This is a very important point and, I believe, a valid one: the secular vision of the perfect being is not by any means the same as the religious vision. *However, what I can, more modestly, propose is that religion and science are not as divergent as supposed and nor is it the case that with the rapid developments in science there is a parallel decline in religious values.* If anything, one borrows from the other: there is, and should be, continuous and useful dialogue, not two enemies battling it out for supremacy.

THE TELEOLOGICAL NARRATIVE

Transhumanist philosophy borrows more from religion than it is aware, perhaps no more so than in providing the 'disciple' with its own teleological narrative. In the Abrahamic faiths, for which Islam belongs of course, there is a linear cosmology consisting of various periods in history, culminating in the ends of times: the Day of Judgement. Islam has its own historical narrative that begins with the creation of the Universe by God, then in Earthly terms we have Adam and Eve, the prophets, and the final revelation given to the Prophet Muhammad. Mankind is given purpose by God, and is therefore duty-bound to seek out this purpose by following God's will, which is acknowledged to be no easy task but a 'struggle' (*jihad*). In fact, it is much easier to be led astray and lead a life that lacks such faith and discipline, but the consequences of this path in life go beyond *this* physical, Earthly life. God is a merciful but also strict judge of human actions; hence the Day of Judgement (*Yawm al-din*) is also the Day of Reckoning (*Yawm al-Hisab*) and the Day of Separation (*Yawm al-Fasl*). The Qur'an presents us with a theology of promise and threat (*wa'd wa-wa 'id*) regarding mankind's reward or punishment on the Last Day, with descriptions of the Day of Paradise (*jannah*) and the Day of Hell (*jahannam*) being frequently and often luridly described in the Qur'an. For example, the early Meccan suras 81 to 84 present us with vivid portrayals of *jahannam*, which is indicative of the titles of these suras: 'Shrouded in Darkness' (*Al-Takwir*), 'Torn Apart' (*Al-Infitar*), 'Those who Give Short Measure' (*Al-Mutaffifin*), and 'Ripped Apart' (*Al-Inshiqaq*). An often-quoted sura is 55, 'The Lord of Mercy' (*Al-Rahman*), which describes both Hell and Heaven. In the case of Hell:

The guilty will be known by their mark and will be seized by their foreheads and their feet. Which, then, of your Lord's blessings do you both deny? This is the Hell the guilty deny, but they will go round between its flames and scalding water. (Qur'an 55:41–44)

Whereas for Heaven:

For those who fear [the time when they will] stand before their Lord there are two gardens. ... With shading branches. ... With a pair of flowing springs. ... With every kind of fruit in pairs. ... They will sit on couches upholstered with brocade, the fruit of both gardens within easy reach. ... There will be maidens restraining their glances, untouched beforehand by man or jinn. ... Like rubies and brilliant pearls. (Qur'an 55: 46–58)

The passages themselves do raise the kind of hermeneutical approaches that have been explored in this book, with some looking to such texts in the literal, prescriptive sense as an example of 'the coarse and sensual materialism of the paradise depicted in the Koran' (Palacios 2008, p. 136), whilst others adopt a more 'modernist', explorative view of the text as mythic, and expressed in a language that people of the time could relate to. This latter interpretation of the text may seem counter-intuitive for many, and also raises concerns from, for example, the Indian Sufi reformer and self-declared *mujaddid* Ahmad Sirhindi (1564–1624) that the move away from literalism 'might lead common, initiated people to heresy and neglect of the *shari'ah*' (Friedmann 1971, p. 67). Sirhindi's concern was targeted at Ibn Arabi who, though he 'speaks of Hell and Heaven with utmost interest and in accordance with the sensual explication of traditional eschatology, he finds a number of occasions to introduce a spiritual explanation for them' (Diyab 2000, pp. 40–41).

This, therefore, brings us back to the justified concern of transhumanists for the more literalist approach to religious belief, for which I also am equally concerned. Nonetheless, the more 'spiritual' understanding of Islamic cosmology, teleology, and eschatology brings us much more within the same working arena as much of the transhumanist philosophy. Ray Kurzweil's *The Singularity is Near* also has its own historical narrative in which he divides evolution into a series of successive epochs, six in all as a countdown to singularity:

Epoch 1. Physics and Chemistry
At the beginning of the universe, all information existed at the sub-atomic level.
Epoch 2. Biology and DNA
With the beginning of life on Earth, genetic information was stored in DNA molecules, and yet organisms take thousands of years to evolve.
Epoch 3. Brains
Evolution produced increasingly complex organisms. The birth of the brain allowed organisms to change their behaviour and learn from past experiences.
Epoch 4. Technology
Humans evolved into organisms with the ability to create technology. We are right now in the final stages of this epoch.
Epoch 5. The Merger of Human Technology with Human Intelligence

Biology and technology will begin to merge in order to create higher forms of life and intelligence.
Epoch 6. The Universe Wakes Up
This epoch will see the birth of super-intelligence, and with it, humans/machines expanding into the Universe.

These epochs, then, are seen within the context of the history of information with a kind of universal will at work within technology that is leaning towards extropy and the 'waking up' of the universe when surviving intelligences are, to all intents and purposes, gods. We are presently in Epoch 5, of course, and Kurzweil, amongst others, may well be overly optimistic in their time projection of when Epoch 6 is likely to occur; that is the point of Singularity when we transfer our minds onto supercomputers and become what he calls 'Spiritual Machines'. Nonetheless, the teleology and eschatology are there as much as you will find it in any religion, with the primary difference that this vision of the future of the human is supported by scientific advancements, regardless of their present theoretical nature. The very title of Kurzweil's book is reminiscent of religious exclamations that the Day of Judgement is *near*, and it may well be that this 'near-ness' is not quite as near as we might suppose. Yet the *belief* that it is near, whether we are talking of Singularity or Day of Judgement, nonetheless informs the psyche of the present. The apostle Paul, for example, believed that the Day of Judgement would occur in his own lifetime and he describes the Day of Resurrection as the moment when God 'will transform our lowly bodies so that they will be like his glorious body' (Philippians 3:21). This certainly sees the human body as something to be overcome. Later on, St Augustine writes that the resurrected man will possess a 'universal knowledge':

> Think how great, how beautiful, how certain, how unerring, how easily acquired this knowledge then will be. And what a body, too, we shall have, a body utterly subject to our spirit and one kept so alive by spirit that there will be no need of any other food. For it will be a spiritual body, no longer merely animal, one composed, indeed, of flesh but free from every corruption of the flesh. (Augustine 1953, Vol. 24: 503–5)

These views of the resurrection by Christian theologians is echoed by Islamic thinkers, as well as many poetic passages in the Qur'an, for example in the analogy of the universe as a book unfolded which, at the end of time, can be rolled up by God and then recreate the universe and mankind in a much better and different form:

> On that Day [Resurrection], We shall roll up the skies as a writer rolls up [his] scrolls. We shall reproduce creation just as We produced it the first time: this is Our binding promise. We shall certainly do all these things. (21:104)

For God, bringing the dead back to life is not a problem of course:

> Do the disbelievers not understand that God, who created the heavens and earth and did not tire in doing so, has the power to bring the dead back to life? Yes indeed! He has power over everything. (46:33)

The Quran likens the Resurrection to the rejuvenation of the earth in springtime, following the death in winter:

> Another of His signs in this: you see the earth lying resolute, but when We send water down to it, it stirs and grows. He who gives it life will certainly give life to the dead. He has power over everything. (41:39)

What Has Athens to Do with Mecca?

Very beautiful and picturesque passages abound in the Qur'an on death and resurrection, but the mistake of many transhumanists is to see an Islamic 'blind faith' as interpreting these texts literally, and that a supernatural resurrection has no relation to the material resurrection subscribed to by transhumanists. Again, there *is* a literal tradition, but this is not the only way of interpreting resurrection. The *hikmah* tradition reveals to us the complex discourse engaged in by philosophers and theologians as what awaits us in the next life and what this entails in terms of the material and the non-material. The Christian writer Tertullian (c.160–225 AD) famously exclaimed, 'What has Athens to do with Jerusalem?' which reflects an unease at the time over the influence of philosophy—more from Alexandria than Athens by then—over Christian thought. A similar expression along the lines of, 'What has Athens to do with Mecca?' may equally be a thought for many Muslims theologians over the years. Indeed, the primary aim of al-Ghazali's first two books of his *Incoherence of the Philosophers (Tahafut al-Falasifah)* was to attack the perceived Aristotelianism of the Muslim philosophers al-Farabi and Ibn Sina. We have seen in the previous chapter that al-Ghazali recognised the limitations of a literal understanding of scripture, and so it might seem curious that he is critical of the some of his philosophical predecessors, yet it must be stressed that the *Incoherence* is not a refutation of philosophy at all, or even Aristotelianism for that matter. Rather, his criticism was that the likes of al-Farabi and Ibn Sina were doing *bad* (i.e. poorly reasoned) philosophy that, while perhaps true in their conclusions, lacked the critical engagement and demonstrative techniques that good philosophy demands to reach those conclusions (Griffel 2005). In other words, these philosophers were merely 'imitating' (*taqlid*) the conclusions reached by other figures from history; not just philosophers, but prophets.

Nonetheless, there are some views of the past philosophers that al-Ghazali declares to be wrong in that they are in conflict with *shari'a*, which can be narrowed down to three specific issues: on God's knowledge of universals, but not of particulars; the philosophers' teachings on the eternity of the world; and the denial of the resurrection of the body. In this third criticism of the philosophers, al-Ghazali states that the *falasifah* are:

> opposed to all Muslims in their affirming that men's bodies will not be assembled on the Last Day, but only disembodied spirits will be rewarded and punished, and the rewards and punishments will be spiritual, not corporal. They were indeed right in affirming the spiritual rewards and punishments, for these also are certain; but they falsely denied the corporal rewards and punishments and blasphemed the revealed Law in their stated views. (Al-Ghazali 1980, p. 76)

It is perhaps such attack against the philosophers that has resulted in the historically erroneous accusations that al-Ghazali was in some way single-handedly responsible for the decline of explorative thought in Islam. Al-Ghazali, like so many of his ilk, was not only a philosopher in his own right, but also a religious scholar, and so his challenge (through the use of logical and philosophical principles) is against those philosophers who incorrectly (in his view) interpret religious belief, rather than an attack on philosophy as such. Indeed, as he points out:

> Regarding mathematical sciences, there is no sense in denying them or disagreeing with them. For these reduce in the final analysis to arithmetic and geometry. As regards to logical sciences, these are concerned with examining the instrument of thought in intelligible things. There is no significant disagreement encountered in these. (Al-Ghazali 2000, p. 11)

Yet not all agree with al-Ghazali's criticism of these philosophers, hence the work in response by Ibn Rushd amusingly titled *The Incoherence of the Incoherence* (*Tahāfut al-Tahāfut*). Although, chronologically, the philosopher Ibn Rushd comes after al-Ghazali, there is a danger that his philosophy could also be treated with some suspicion and, indeed, he was often accused of being an infidel; after his death, his books were banned or, in some cases, burnt. The tension between what the Qur'an may declare and what the Islamic philosopher may explore may always be there, yet Ibn Rushd is also proudly declared to be one of Islam's greatest thinkers. As Ibn Rushd states in *On the Harmony of Religion and Philosophy* (aka *The Decisive Treatise*) he made a point of arguing that philosophy and religion are compatible:

> Philosophy is the friend and milk-sister of religion; thus injuries from people related to philosophy are the severest injuries [to religion] apart from the enmity, hatred and quarrels which such [injuries] stir up between the two, which are companions by nature and lovers by essence and instinct. (Ibn Rushd 1961, p. 70)

Given this, what's the problem? The problem is in the detail: while it is admirable that Ibn Rushd seeks to create harmony between philosophy and faith, and that they express the same truths (although in different ways), the detail may suggest otherwise. For example, when one reads what Ibn Rushd says about the soul, coupled as it is with his Aristotelian outlook, his claim that there is no essential difference between his views on the afterlife and that of 'normative' Islamic theological teaching seems somewhat fragile. In fact, it may seem that Ibn Rushd is in an even tighter straitjacket than the predecessors that al-Ghazali criticised, as both al-Farabi and Ibn Sina adopt a less Aristotelian concept of the afterlife than does Ibn Rushd. Ibn Rushd's predecessor al-Farabi was, in the words of the philosopher of history Ibn Khaldun (1332–1406), regarded as the 'second teacher', second only to Aristotle himself. For al-Farabi, his views are a mix of Plato and Aristotle: the Platonic (and, indeed, Neoplatonic) influence is evident in his belief that the soul ultimately desires to be free from the material body and join the intelligible world.[1] He does, however,

---

[1] Although al-Farabi does not consider this possibility for all souls. Only those rational souls which acquire the knowledge of eternal aspects of the universe can survive the death of the body. Other rational souls will be destroyed with the destruction of the body.

agree with Aristotle that the soul also requires the body in order to achieve what Aristotle called *eudaimonia*, for it is only through interaction with other bodies, other people as part of a community, that the soul can achieve this state of bliss. Whereas al-Farabi seems to reject the possibility of the resurrection of the body with the soul, he is at least open to the belief that there is an afterlife, with the soul as a separate substance. As Ibn Rushd is much stricter in adhering to Aristotelian principles, then the very idea that there is any kind of afterlife *at all* is open to question. In the case of Ibn Sina, incidentally, he follows to a certain extent in the footsteps of al-Farabi although he maintains that all rational souls, by virtue of being simple, survive the death of the body. Although Ibn Sina is probably more Neoplatonic, generally the somewhat mystical Platonic elements are very much there when he talks of the soul as achieving a state of apprehending universals and ultimately joining with the Active Intellect.

Importantly, any literal reading of the Qur'an will provide the believer with a very close, personal relationship between the individual believer and God, whilst Ibn Rushd *does not*. Ibn Rushd's views on scriptural interpretation are elaborated in his *Treatise*, although to appreciate this we also need to place it into the context of the influence of al-Farabi, who wrote extensively on logic and philosophy of language and which includes commentaries on Aristotle's works in logic, but he goes beyond a mere summary and explication by developing his own personal interpretations of Aristotelian logic. A concern of his was to mark out precisely the relationship between philosophical logic and the grammar of ordinary language. For al-Farabi, philosophical logic was not a foreign import, external to the Islamic worldview and therefore 'apostasy', but actually an expression of universal truths that provides the ground rules for rational thought. As reason is universal, then philosophical logic, which is nothing more than an expression of reason, is not particular to the Greeks only. However, reason still needs to be expressed through *language*, and it is this that particularises the universal.

Therefore, grammar and logic are distinct sciences, one universal and one particular. Al-Farabi was aware that any understanding of philosophical logic was dependent upon how it is interpreted thorough the medium of one's chosen language. Logic is an important tool that helps us to distinguish truth from error and, indeed, philosophers are duty-bound with the task of utilising their philosophical skills to communicate to the non-philosopher through the arts of rhetoric, poetics, and dialectic, which, though not universal in the way logic is, are nonetheless a conduit for communication to those unfamiliar with logic. This is important in terms of our understanding of what the Islamic explorative tradition can contribute to the transhumanist debate, and is reminiscent of certain western philosophers—for example Wittgenstein that we looked at in Chap. 4—that language such as poetry, myth, and so on is important in our understanding of who we are and the world we live in. In other words, the world of logic and science is not separate from the philosophical, religious, and artistic. They all complement and feed off each other.

Al-Farabi believed that the Prophets, including Muhammad, were first and foremost *philosophers*, for it was true philosophers—as opposed to those with faith—who have access to 'revelation' in the sense of knowledge of God. Following the Neoplatonic tradition of so many of the Islamic philosophers, al-Farabi equated God with Aristotle's Active Intellect. Al-Farabi presents a Neoplatonic conception of a God that is the Perfect Being who, being all-good, 'emanates' this goodness which results in creation, including that of human beings who, though somewhat low in this hierarchical process of emanation, nonetheless possess a 'spark' of the Divine within them due to the possession of a soul which ultimately rests with the Active Intellect but is bound by the material body. Al-Farabi equates happiness with the soul's rejoining with the intelligible world and, in line again with Aristotle, this is achieved through engagement with society (man is a political animal) rather than seclusion and asceticism.

What al-Farabi also shares with Ibn Rushd is the view that philosophy is a superior science. Farabi's political philosophy is very Platonic in arguing that, given there is such a thing as universal truth, and that the best method of attaining this truth is through philosophy, then philosophers should be rulers of the state. Al-Farabi made a clear distinction between those few who were capable of philosophy and the majority who needed religion. The 'common people' do not have the mental capacity to understand the inner meaning of revelation and, therefore, God's true commands, for they can only understand the Qur'an at a literal level, rather than its symbolic, metaphorical meaning. The elite, being expert not only in the tools of philosophy but also in their knowledge of the Islamic sciences of jurisprudence (*fiqh*), theology (*kalam*), and mysticism are closer to a knowledge of God and, to some extent, 'partake' in God's will.

Ibn Rushd likewise emphasises the importance of the philosophy of language in the understanding of the message of the Qur'an and he also is akin to al-Farabi in the exclusivity of a philosophical interpretation (i.e. the demonstrative method) as restricted to those 'well-grounded in knowledge' (*al-rasikkhun fi al-'ilm*), whereas the non-philosopher (obviously the majority of believers) interprets the Qur'an at the dialectical or rhetorical level. In his *Treatise*, Ibn Rushd divides scripture into three classes: in the first class, its meaning is to be understood in the same way by the rhetorical, the dialectical, and the demonstrative classes. That is to say, that philosophers and non-philosophers alike are to accept these Qur'anic verses literally. In the second class we have those verses that are considered ambiguous: Ibn Rushd believes that these are the sole reserve of the philosopher as they are likely to be misinterpreted by the non-philosopher. The third and final class is those for which it is uncertain whether they are literal or ambiguous in their nature, as opinion is divided amongst scholars. In these cases, it is again the philosopher who should solely determine whether or not in fact they should be regarded as either literal or allegorical.

Ibn Rushd's and al-Farabi's view that the majority cannot grasp the intellectual subtleties of philosophy may seem worryingly elitist, but no more so than any of the 'sciences', including the natural sciences. There are many 'popular science' books today, and I admit my own dependence on many of these, not being a scientist myself, but the very nature of populism is that something does get lost in translation. Hopefully, this will encourage the reader to dig deeper, but it can also have the effect of taking that populist understanding literally and naively. From my own perspective, I suspect that I am also in danger of treating the writings of scientists on transhumanism in a naive way, and so I admit my own scientific ignorance and instead consider the *implications* of this technology from a philosophical perspective (my own discipline), rather than hark on too much as to the technological possibilities: that is, if the human can indeed be uploaded onto a machine one day, what are the implications of what this means to be human? I am certainly in no position to argue for the technological possibility of such an achievement, only that, in my view, it does fly against what I understand what it means to be human as a non-reductive, non-empirical agent. I may, of course, be proved to be wrong one day, but my philosophical understanding of human nature presently leads me to believe that I am not.

Nonetheless, the complexity of philosophical and theological discourse can lead to confusion and downright aggression from the reader, for which Richard Dawkins probably wins the prize for the most forthright of attacks, for example:

Perhaps there are some genuinely profound and meaningful questions that are forever beyond the reach of science. Maybe quantum theory is already knocking on the door of the unfathomable. But if science cannot answer some ultimate question, what makes anybody think that religion can? I suspect that neither the Cambridge nor the Oxford astronomer really believed that theologians have any expertise that enables them to answer questions that are too deep for science. I suspect that both astronomers were, yet again, bending over backwards to be polite: theologians have nothing worthwhile to say about anything else; let's throw them a sop and let them worry away at a couple of questions that nobody can answer and maybe never will. Unlike my astronomer friends, I don't think we should even throw them a sop. I have yet to see any good reason to suppose that theology (as opposed to biblical history, literature, etc.) is a subject at all. (Dawkins 2007, p. 80)

I could cite many such examples from Dawkins' works that mirror this naive and narrow-minded view of theology, as well as the misguided notion that religion is in some way even *trying* to answer scientific questions. Again, yes, there are the literalists who do claim that Islam has the scientific answers, but do not put them in front of stage and declare that this is what Islam, or religion generally, *is*. What I hope is demonstrated in this book is that Islam is deeply philosophical and rational, and that the Qur'an, for its part, has not always been taken literally but that it is subordinated to the supremacy of reason and, more than that, in the words of Shahab Ahmed, 'the concept of the Qur'an as the text of divine revelation is constructed and read subject to the demands of a total Truth-matrix elaborated by reason in which reason/philosophy is the higher truth and the text of revelation the lower' (Ahmed 2016, p. 97).

MUHAMMAD AS THE PERFECT BEING: IQBAL AND NIETZSCHE

In Chap. 4 I referred briefly to Mawdudi's narrow, more political understanding of Iqbal's concept of *khudi* (selfhood). Mawdudi represents a school within Islam that tends to take sacred text in a literal manner and to reify scripture. The result is the expression of Islam that militant atheists and secular transhumanists find distasteful and in opposition to their ideals. However, I also have considered that Islamic authority can be read in a different way which is more in sympathy with the approach of, for example, Wittgenstein, Nietzsche, Derrida, or Maimonides. Such a reading may also make the ideas of forms of transhumanism a bedfellow, while I cannot go so far as to suggest that militant atheism would also want to jump in this bed (a less militant, more Nietzschean 'atheism' is a different matter). I concluded Chap. 4 with what I see as *a problem of communication*; of struggling to use everyday language to express ideas that defy such factual narrative. In attempts to define what it means to be human, and hence how we can or should transcend the human, what Islam can contribute here is the fact that the human is complex and likewise defies all attempts to be reduced to a series of parts and nothing more. In this understanding of Islam, I do not propose we look to the literal reading of the Qur'an or hadith, which simply leads to falling into that reification trap, but to see Islam as a holistic narrative, imbued with story, myth, ideals, our fears and hopes, and so on. This 'narrative' certainly includes the Qur'an and hadith, but not exclusively or literally. Beyond the authoritative texts we have Islamic history, culture, and philosophy. We have Islamic poetry, Islamic works of art and architecture. We have Islamic gardens that can generate meaning that is not readily articulated through the written or spoken word.

In Chap. 6 I considered the importance of the creative arts in Islam with reference, very briefly, to the love poem *Majnun Layla*: in the case of Muhammad Iqbal we have a modern poet who not only portrays himself as poet-lover like Majnun, but in the poem below, *Bal-i Jibril*, he alludes to the story of Majnun in personifying God as Lover:

> On the Day of Gathering, my passion will not rest purposeless:Either my collar will be torn—or the shirt of God will be torn! (Iqbal 1990, p. 375)

The story of Majnun (which literally means 'possessed by a *jinn*') is based on the life of a poet from the first century of Islam called Says who fell madly in love with an unobtainable woman called Layla to the extent that his love drove him to madness as he traversed the desert seeking out her caravan. Qays/Majnun rented open his shirt in an expression of torment over his passion. The 'torn shirt' has come to mean the struggle and torment of being a Muslim, of being human, and so here the simple image of a torn shirt has a much more powerful expression of the human condition than a thousand words of descriptive narrative could possibly hope to portray. Hence, in Iqbal's poem, come the Day of Judgement the torn collar of the poet or the torn shirt of God symbolises Truth laid bare.

In the struggle to understand what it means to be human, Iqbal's elaboration of the notion of *khudi* has to be seen with this context of the vagaries of language. In the same way Ibn Tufayl resorted to fictional narrative through the protagonist Hayy ibn Yaqzan for his *bildungsroman* (see Chap. 6), Iqbal uses poetry primarily to express his conception of selfhood. This method is a mirror of a strand in western philosophical thought, often referred to as 'Continental philosophy'—though I personally find that such a term can confuse as much as it can clarify—which appreciates the need for ambiguity and embracing the paradoxical when dealing with the nature of being and the self. It is less concerned with providing 'proofs' or engaging in the kind of philosophical arguments you find in the analytic tradition, and more in considering our psychological states and the phenomenology of our experiences. Iqbal, likewise, stresses that his main work that explores *khudi*, *Mysteries of the Self* (*Asrar-e Khudi*, 1915) is not a philosophical argument, but rather 'poetic proofs' (*shairana sabut*) that cannot be examined from a logical point of view (Iqbal 1973, pp. 3–78). As noted by Javed Majeed, 'It is mainly through poetic conceits, metaphors and images that Iqbal articulates his notion of selfhood in his metrically measured verse' (Majeed 2009, p. 19). Iqbal, in some senses, may be seen as part of the mystical tradition in Islam, and, for that matter, in religion generally, but to describe Iqbal as a 'mystic' is not overly helpful given the incredible diversity that exists within the mystical tradition, especially in terms of the concept of the self. While some mystics believe that personal identity remains in the presence of the divine, others seek self-annihilation (*fana*). Iqbal subscribes more to the former than the latter, seeing the mystical tradition that emphasises *fana* as at least partly to blame for the decadence of Islam; Iqbal—like Mawdudi—was especially concerned for the Muslims in India and the effect that the spread of Sufism had in the subcontinent (Majeed 2009, p. 22). Iqbal's self, or ego (sticking, as Iqbal does, to the strict Persian term of *khudi*), is not annihilation, but greater individuation. This has interesting parallels with the distinctions made in Chap. 2 between transhumanism and posthumanism: the former in which the self remains but is 'enhanced' so as to be God-like, whilst in the latter, human identity is effectively 'annihilated' like *fana*.

As Iqbal asserts in *The Reconstruction of Religious Thought in Islam*, 'the end of the ego's quest is not emancipation from the limitations of individuality; it is, on the other hand, a more precise definition of it' (Iqbal 1989, pp. 156–57). Whilst some religious adherents oppose transhumanism because it is seen as 'playing God', or as a form of hubris, of wanting to *be* God, Iqbal's concept of the self is a form of self-divination: a free individual who 'shares in the life and freedom of the Ultimate Ego' that is 'consciously participating in the creative life of his Maker' (ibid., pp. 86–87). Here, then, there is no hesitancy in striving to be God-like, and this is the ultimate concept of the self as *insan al-Kamil*, the Perfect Human. As RA Nicholson describes this term:

> every man is potentially a microcosm, and ... when he has become spiritually perfect, all the Divine attributes are displayed by him, so that as saint or prophet he is the God-man, the representative and vice-regent of God on earth. (Nicholson 1983 [1920], p. 79)

Note 'all the Divine attributes are displayed by him'; if God possesses the attributes of immortality, perfection, and so on, *then so can the human*.

Yes, we look to our scientists to tell us what is technically possible for the human to become, but we—and by 'we' I mean scientists too—look to our visionaries, our philosophers, religious thinkers, poets, and so on, for what it means to become something other than what we are or how we perceive ourselves. Islamic thought has its visionaries too, and Iqbal presents a paradigm that resonates with the vision of transhumanism. Section 9 of *Secrets of the Self*, entitled 'Mysteries of the Self' is where we are presented with the vision of the three stages of the self, and this is especially where Iqbal's Perfect Human, Nietzsche's *Übermensch* or 'Overhuman', and the Transhuman meet. In fact, Iqbal's thought has been described as, 'an integrated concept of the Self, fusing together the Sufi's passion for union with God, the idea of dynamism expounded by Bergson, the groping for self-assertion which was the philosophy of Nietzsche, and the Sharia of Islam' (Mujeeb 1967, p. 454).

Nietzsche's most 'religious work' is *Thus Spoke Zarathustra*, and this work, more specifically the character of Zarathustra, has been seen as the paradigm for the transhumanist movement. Zarathustra, when talking of the spirit of man, says there are three 'metamorphoses of the spirit'—first the camel, second the lion, third the child—and these are in line with Iqbal's three stages of *khudi*, obedience to the law, self-control, and the third stage, Divine Regency; this latter being Iqbal's interpretation of the Perfect Human. In fact, Iqbal, when describing the first stage of obedience to the law (*sharia*) likens this to the experience of the camel in the sense that this creature is obedient, but also useful and hardy. In the case of Nietzsche, the camel represents the heroic spirit or the 'weight-bearing spirit' that the human requires in order to be strong enough to move to the second stage in human development. Whilst the camel may suggest to us a creature that is homely, domesticated and, once trained, obedient to a large extent, it is also for a reason they are referred to as beasts of burden, for they are—in the Nietzschean sense—able to carry the burden of the spirit.

It is worth pausing for a moment to consider Nietzsche's terminology here. As already stated, the boundaries between what is science and what is religion are often blurred, if only because our language is imbued with religiosity and, in turn, our language informs our ideas. Nietzsche, as a skilled philologist, was only too aware of the power of language. Therefore, in his use of the term 'spirit' the reader may think of this in the traditional religious sense of a metaphysical soul of some kind, but Nietzsche was no metaphysician. The German word here is *Geist*, which can be translated as 'mind', or 'spirit', 'consciousness', or even 'wit'. How one translates the term into English creates its own problems. Using the word 'spirit' is understandable given Nietzsche's own all-inclusive meaning of *Geist*; hence the word 'consciousness' or 'wit' would not really capture it. At the same time, 'spirit' does lead the English reader to link this in a religious manner. Perhaps the term 'esprit' is more appropriate as suggesting a liveliness of intellect, although I am aware of the irony that we are now reverting to a French term! When Nietzsche is read in context with his other works, the understanding of *Geist* is linked with his own admiration for the ancient 'Greek spirit'; as that which defines the character of a people or nation. While Nietzsche had his own 'positivist' phase, he also believed that scientific reductionism 'leaves out' what it means to be human, hence *Geist* can be seen in the context of the German term *Geisteswissenschaften*, the 'science of spirit' or the Humanities, as distinct from *Naturwissenschaft*, the 'science of nature', or the Physical Sciences. In this way, the three metamorphoses can be seen as a spiritual transformation.

In Chap. 6 I referred to Ray Kurzweil's bestselling book, *The Age of Spiritual Machines*, yet it is intriguing that he used the term 'spiritual' here, for his vision of the human as a machine actually seems to declare the opposite; there is no 'spirit', even in the sense Nietzsche understood it. While Nietzsche would wish to avoid a duality of 'body' and 'spirit', he also denies that we are merely body in the way Kurzweil sees us. The best of humanity can be paraded before us; our 'heroes', whether they be political or, so far as Nietzsche was more concerned, artistic. There is a scene from an episode of *Star Trek: The Next Generation* where the android Data plays the violin in a technically perfect way, yet something is 'missing'; his performance lacks *spirit*. Kurzweil talks of computers that can currently compose music and produce paintings but, really, what *awful* music and painting! We know that computers can now beat grandmasters at chess, but does the computer appreciate the meaning and the artistry of chess? Kurzweil predicts that by the end of this century, we will be able to download our consciousness into a machine and live forever, but in his understanding of our consciousness as 'data' I worry that, like Data of *Star Trek*, something is 'missing'.

Nietzsche's camel, then, from a human perspective is analogous to someone who is prepared to quest for knowledge, but also prepared to accept the burden that comes with such heavy wisdom. The person is eager to embrace knowledge and understanding and not shy away from it, despite the dangers that knowledge can bring. 'What is heavy? Thus asks the weight-bearing spirit. That I may take it upon me and become well pleased with my strength' (Nietzsche 1974, Part 1, S1). It is a psychological awareness that the burden of understanding can, over time, be poisoned by despair, bitterness, and resentment (*ressentiment*) unless the spirit can move to the next stage. Ultimately, we are talking here of a process of self-discovery and actualisation. The character of Zarathustra represents a *spirit* that is able to take on what is the hardest, engage in difficult tasks, and be willing to move to the next stage. However, this transformation from the camel to the next stage, the lion, is not something that can be taught. The individual must possess the qualities within—the psychological state—to make the journey towards the *Übermensch*. For Iqbal, the journey to the Perfect Human requires also an inner bravery involving submission to God, but it is a submission not unlike Kierkegaard's leap of faith which equally results in a psychological 'fear and trembling' before the existential realisation of one's individual responsibility.

Importantly, to become the *Übermensch* you must revere the *Übermensch*. Thus, to become the Perfect Muslim you must revere the Perfect Muslim. Again, notice the use of religious imagery in *Zarathustra*, to renounce and to revere, to carry the load of commandments and obligations, and then to the next stage:

> But in the loneliest desert the second transformation occurs: the spirit here becomes a lion; it will seize freedom for itself and become lord in its own desert. Its ultimate lord it seeks out here: his enemy it will become and enemy of his ultimate god; it will wrestle for victory with the great dragon. What is the great dragon that the spirit no longer likes to call Lord or God? "Thou shalt" is the name of the great dragon. But the spirit of the lion says "I will". (Ibid.)

The need to move to the stage of the lion, to the king of the beasts, is so that one can break traditional values and create one's own values. The dragon here is not Nick Bostrom's 'death', but societal norms, which, at the time Nietzsche was writing, included religious commandments (and, some might argue, still does today). One must destroy what one reveres and, for Iqbal, writing at the time of the rise of western modernity and capitalism which corresponded with Islamic decline and decadence, the destruction and rejection of values were materialism and atheism. The words *Faqir* (or its synonym 'qalandar') and '*Faqr*' (or '*istighna*') appear often in Iqbal's works. Iqbal uses '*Faqr*' to denote an inner attitude of detachment and superiority to material possessions. 'It is a kind of intellectual and emotional asceticism which does not turn away from the world as a source of evil and corruption but uses it for the pursuit of good and worthy ends' (Saiyidain 2012, pp. 187–88). Here, Iqbal is recognising that a materialist conception of the universe does not provide us with a full or healthy account of the human, of our Nietzschean *Geist* but in rejecting past values there is also a danger of nihilism. This is where the third transformation, or metamorphosis, comes in: that of the child. 'The child is innocence and forgetfulness, a new beginning, a sport, a self-propelling wheel, a first motion, a sacred Yes. Yes, a sacred Yes is needed, my brothers, for the sport of creation: the spirit now wills its own will, the spirit sundered from the world now wins its own world' (Nietzsche 1974, Part 1, S1). The child is the beginning of what it will become, which is the *Übermensch*. For Iqbal, this will become the Perfect Human, of which the finest example is the Prophet Muhammad. Speaking of the Prophet, he says:

> He is the preface to the book of two worlds,
> All the people of the world are slaves and he is the master.
> Mankind is the cornfield and thou the harvest,
> Thou art the goal of life's caravan. (Kashyap 1955, p. 183)

This is all-important in respect of the transhumanist debate because Iqbal's Perfect Human or *insan al-Kamil* and Nietzsche's *Übermensch* are paradigms of human transformation towards a 'better human'. In addition, both Nietzsche and Iqbal recognise the 'religiosity' of being human and of how our language and understanding of our world are driven and frame-worked by religious ideals. By 'religion' and 'religiosity' here I mean it in the manner so far described; that is in its, for want of a better term, anti-realist sense, or the 'spiritual' or 'mystical' sense that the transhumanist writer Prisco hopes for (see Chap. 2).

Importantly it is a trope that can be found in other Islamic thought, notably that of the poet Rumi's *Mard-e-Haqq*, as Riffat Hassan notes:

> The resemblance between Rumi's "Mard-e-Haqq" and Iqbal's "Mard-e-Mo'min" is quite unmistakable. In both cases the Ideal Person is a combination of a person of contemplation and a person of action. Iqbal places more stress on action than Rumi does but this hardly constitutes a fundamental difference. (Hassan 1972, p. 75)

The Perfect Human, or the 'Ideal Person' as Hassan translates it, is seen by both Iqbal and Rumi as part of the human evolutionary process, for:

> He is the final cause of creation and, therefore, though having appeared last in point of time, he was really the first mover. Chronologically, the tree is the cause of the fruit but, teleologically, the fruit is the cause of the tree. (Hakim 1959, p. 110)

Am I pushing the analogies with Nietzsche, Iqbal, and Rumi too far in relation to the transhumanist debate? In the case of Nietzsche's *Übermensch*, for example, Nick Bostrom states that:

> What Nietzsche had in mind … was not technological transformation but rather a kind of soaring personal growth and cultural refinement in exceptional individuals (who he thought would have to overcome the life-sapping "slave-morality" of Christianity). Despite some surface-level similarities with the Nietzschean vision, transhumanism—with its Enlightenment roots, its emphasis on individual liberties, and its humanistic concern for the welfare of all humans (and other sentient beings)—probably has as much or more in common with Nietzsche's contemporary J.S. Mill, the English liberal thinker and utilitarian. (Bostrom 2005b, p. 4)

However, I am in strong agreement to a response to Bostrom by Stefan Lorenz Sorgner, which I want to outline here. Sorgner quotes Bostrom when he says that, 'Transhumanists view human nature as a work-in-progress' (Bostrom 2005b, p. 1) and, Sorgner argues, so does Nietzsche when referring to his central concept of the will to power, 'which implies that all things are permanently undergoing some change' (Sorgner 2009, p. 30). Now there is considerable literature on what Nietzsche actually meant by the will to power, and I do not agree with Sorgner when he refers to it as a metaphysics. In Nietzsche's more mature works, in particular in his 'trilogy' of *Thus Spoke Zarathustra, Beyond Good and Evil* and *The Genealogy of Morals*, he has seemingly dismissed any association of the will to power with Arthur Schopenhauer's (1788–1860) metaphysical doctrine of the Will and, in fact, by this time in his writings Nietzsche is more explicit in his rejection of any kind of metaphysical speculation. For example, in his Preface of *Beyond Good and Evil* he considers such 'philosophical dogmatism' to be 'some folk superstition from time immemorial … some play on words perhaps, some seductive aspect of grammar, or a daring generalization from very limited, very personal, very human, all-too-human facts' and then, in Section One, he considers a belief in metaphysical truths as the 'prejudice' of philosophers. My own reading of Nietzsche is that the will to power is an 'imagined reality' to the extent that no proof can be found for it, but it has immense phenomenological force as a psychological awareness of how we as humans do interact with others and constantly undergo change. Again, it is important to recognise the limits of our language, hence Nietzsche resorting to metaphor and ambiguity, riddles, humour, and irony, rather than demonstrating objective truths. It is from Nietzsche's own perspective but, as no one can step outside one's own perspective— including scientists—then what else is one to do? Of course, such a reading of Nietzsche raises the problem why should anyone take him seriously if he is being 'metaphorical'. Nietzsche would on occasion say that he was addressing a small audience, a 'select few', although he was not so lacking in vanity as to not wish that more people bought his books, and so, provided they found something appealing in his writings, then he has succeeded. His writings, therefore, should be approached as you might approach a good novel which can reveal something about the world and about what it means to be human. The same can, of course, be said of religious texts. You can read the Qur'an literally and look for scientific proofs within the text, but this seems to be missing the purpose of the work as revealing 'truths' about human beings, their motives, drives, and so on. This is why Nietzsche writes in a poetical and literary way and, in the case of *Thus Spoke Zarathustra*, we have a work that reads more like scripture than a standard work of philosophy, remembering also that Zarathustra was a prophet. It frequently resorts to parables as a way of revealing 'truths' about ourselves. Similarly, as mentioned already, Iqbal prefers the medium of poetry to express his philosophical ideas.

In the case of both Nietzsche and Iqbal, the self is seen in this fluctuating, fluid, and changing manner. There is an existential quality to the extent that the self is always in a process of becoming, for to 'be' is to cease to be creative and cease to challenge and create. At the same, both

Nietzsche and Iqbal recognise that creativity is not an anarchic process but requires discipline. For Nietzsche, what is required is, 'Critical discipline and such habits as leads to neatness and rigour in matters of the spirit' (Nietzsche 1998, S.210). For Iqbal, the ninth section of *Mysteries of the Self* stresses the importance of religious duty and, by using garden imagery (a not uncommon practice with Nietzsche too), how selfhood must be restrained while being restructured:

> Imprisonment in the flower-bud makes the fire fragrant
> Confinement in the navel of the musk-deer makes the perfume become musk. (Iqbal 1973, couplet 416)

The self, then, in Iqbal's terms, is not a fixed essence, but 'an interplay between khudi and be-khudi' (Majeed 2009, p. 53). This image of the human presented by Iqbal, and Rumi, is in a fluctuating state of evolution and change, not an 'essence' for which transhumanism would 'destroy'. To transcend our 'selves' is what it means to be human, but it is a *constrained* transcendence to the extent that it brings out what is best in our nature, like the perfume of the musk. The concern with transhumanism is that we lose what is best in our nature, our spirit, and become mere automatons. Like Nietzsche's concept of the will to power, Iqbal shares Rumi's notion that evolution is a vital life force that manifests itself in many forms. This notion of a vital force in evolution, together with an attack on the hegemony of reductionist materialism has many parallels with the writing of the French Jewish philosopher Henri Bergson (1859–1941), and this is no coincidence. In Chap. 5, it was stressed that science is a human construct and, like certain expressions of Islam, has become reified. Bergson sees science as contingent in its selection of variable as well as the order in which it presents its problems (Bergson 1983, p. 219). In the case of evolutionary theory, the whole idea of 'evolving' can only be comprehended within a framework of particular time-scales, but, as Bergson wrote to William James in 1908, 'I realised to my great astonishment that scientific time has no duration, that there would be no change in our scientific knowledge of things if the totality of the real were posited straightaway in an instant' (Howard 2011, p. 53). Bergson's concept of *durée* (duration) is when time is experienced as indivisible, fluid, and dynamic, whereas the scientific worldview sees time as homogenised, spatialised states in the external world that are seen, 'under the form of a discrete multiplicity, which amounts to setting them out in line, in the space in which each of them existed separately' (Bergson 1910, p. 121). This is the fundamental *bias* of science that Nietzsche was so critical of; it does not see the world as it really *is*, but what we can *do* with it in terms of manipulation for the benefit of the human. In a Kantian way, the human mind processes world it sees and divides it up in various categories, but this also, incidentally, implies that we can break away from the free will versus determinism dichotomy by experiencing time as *durée* which then makes us realise that we are, for the most part, free. There are two levels of the self: the everyday, superficial, material self, and a deeper self that breaks through these artificial boundaries. We come back here to the problems we have encountered with language because it explains the world through its categorisation of the world, so to experience *durée* requires liberation from the strictures of language, hence the need to resort to poetry, metaphor, aphorism, and so on.

The implications of this are immense and radical and have direct relevance for transhumanism which looks to its roots in Enlightenment thought. The transhumanist criticism that religious and philosophical views of the posthuman are not the same thing as modern transhumanism relies upon the superficial and material understanding of the evolution of the human to what is now seen as its technology stage, or the 'silicon age'. Transhumanism, it is argued, is fundamentally about a *technological* transformation of the human, and not a *spiritual* one. Yet, stemming from Bergson's writings, Deleuze and Guattari declare that, 'There is no biosphere or noosphere, but everywhere the same Mechanosphere' (Deleuze and Guattari 1988, p. 69). In other words, quoting Ansell Pearson, 'All systems from the "biological" to the "social" and economic are made up of machine assemblages, complex foldings, and movements of deterritorialisation that serve to cut across and derange their stratification' (Ansell Pearson 1997, p. 125). Human beings are both bios and technos and, indeed, 'metallurgy has an ancient prehuman history, with human metalworking following the bacterial use of magnetite for internal compasses by almost three thousand million years' (ibid., p. 124). Secular transhumanism, therefore, creates false boundaries; an antinomy that by its nature splits reason from religion when they can actually learn from each other and, more than that, we can go *beyond* science and religion in the Nietzschean sense.

Bergson, in his work *Creative Evolution* (1983), is highly critical of Darwinian natural selection due to its lack of a teleology. Instead he puts forward his *élan vital* which does have direction to the extent that it follows its own nature, although this is not as fatalistic or Aristotelian as it may at first seem, for the *élan* is a fluid process that continuously embodies itself in matter and expresses itself in life forms. Hence it is rather a self-organising principle, rather than a Darwinian, random process. While Bergson himself seemed less concerned with God in a direct sense, he does present a cosmological dualism that has important implications for how we understand religion. This is a dualism of, at one level, the *élan* which can intuit *durée* and, therefore, remain rooted in its nature and liberated from the strictures of the empirical human, while the other is that very empirical human that identifies its being with the material world of cause and effect. Bergson, in *The Two Sources of Morality and Religion* (1977), relates the latter to 'static religion' that is conservative and rule-bound, whereas the former, the *élan*, is the kind of dynamic religion we find amongst the mystics. While Bergson was thinking of Christianity, we can apply this to the *shari'a* of Islam as opposed to the mysticism of the likes of Iqbal and Rumi. Again, however, we must be careful in always seeing these as opposites, for the three metamorphoses presented by both Nietzsche and Iqbal emphasise the interdependence of the 'khudi and be-khudi', of the fluid and the disciplined. Iqbal's aim, in fact, was to repair this split of the two selves presented by Bergson. Undoubtedly, Iqbal was influenced by Bergson's writings, but the former would also look to the Islamic tradition (Iqbal 1995) stating, for example, that Bergson's ideas are anticipated by the Sufi poet Mirza Abdul Qadir Bedil (1641–1720) and that the Bergsonian vision of an open and fluid cosmos can be found in the works of the Persian philosophers Ibn Miskawayh (932–1030) and Al-Bīrūnī (973–c.1050), as well as Ibn Khaldun (Iqbal 1989). In addition, though Iqbal certainly read some Bergson, he was less concerned with the biological detail and did not agree with Bergson entirely. Rather, Iqbal's views need to be seen as a synthesis of philosophies, both 'east' and 'west', resulting in his own original thought.

Whilst consciousness in some sense or other may one day be technologically possible, the question needs to be asked what this posthuman will actually *be*. As Ansell Pearson states (paraphrasing Pierre-Felix Guattari), 'within the machine universe beings have only the status of virtual entities; that is, they are sites of becoming in which what becomes is always something alien' (Ansell Pearson 1997, p. 6). There is this tension between the existential need to creatively be in a state of becoming, and that drive to take us beyond the human into 'something alien'. As Ansell Pearson goes on to say:

In its conceptions of the will-to-power and the eternal return, through which it endeavours to articulate an alternative biological model of selection to prevailing Darwinian ones, Nietzsche's thinking reveals itself to be ensnared as anthropomorphism as any philosophy of life of the modern epoch. It is not simply a question of critiquing Nietzsche for replacing the prejudices of morality with prejudices of his own; rather, the task is to show how his attempt to go beyond the human is implicated in the becoming of the human. (Ibid., p. 8)

This is insightful, and Ansell Pearson admits that his own relationship with Nietzsche is 'complex' (ibid.), which would apply equally to myself, for Nietzsche's philosophy is both complex and subtle. Whilst his thinking may well offer support for transhumanism, which Sorgner at least recognises, it is always with reference to the human. This may well be a 'prejudice', but some prejudices are justifiable: to determine what we are as human beings and to desire to maintain what we are should not be something we are ashamed of, otherwise the existential question for becoming can, somewhat paradoxically, result in alienation from our selves. When Nietzsche declares that man has, 'an interest, a tension, a hope, almost a certainty, as if with him something were announcing and preparing itself, as if man were not a goal but only a way, an episode, a bridge, a great promise' (Nietzsche 1966, S.16), this is not to see the human as an ugly thing that needs to be discarded, but as rather continuing within the person a spirit that needs to be released. Michael Hauskeller wrote an article to counter Sorgner's view of Nietzsche's Overhuman, in which he saw Nietzsche as disparaging humanity and that he 'had nothing but contempt for those who sought to improve the human condition' (Hauskeller 2010, p. 5) but this is a serious and naive misreading of Nietzsche (alas, a frequent occurrence to this day) and ignores Nietzsche's emphasis on a particular *kind* of humanity that he is less than enthusiastic about. This 'kind' would, interestingly, include those scientists who believe hubristically they have exclusive access to the 'one truth' that transcends historical perspectivism.

Concluding Remarks

Nietzsche's prescience here serves as a concluding observation, as well as a warning to us all: we should look to the goals of transhumanism with, at the very least, eagerness and interest and, more urgently, recognise the responsibility humans have to future generations and the planet as whole which may well require us to evolve to survive. At the same time, the reason Mary Shelley's *Frankenstein* continues to have relevance is because of the message it provides regarding the responsibility of the scientific community. Transhumanism as a school of thought considers itself as interdisciplinary, which is encouraging, but there is nonetheless a suspicion or antagonism towards certain religious traditions. As has been demonstrated, to some extent this is understandable, and religion for its part must shoulder some of the blame. Islam, especially, has in more recent years presented an image to the world as intolerant and literalist. Yet it is a crying shame if the rich philosophical and cultural tradition that Islam possesses is ignored by the transhumanist school in the belief that it has nothing to offer. It is hoped that this modest work has shown that, in fact, it can offer much, that it is not as alien to other 'western' disciplines as some might suppose and that, ultimately, it can help to steer transhumanism in a direction that is fully aware of its moral responsibility towards the future human, whatever that may be.

In the introduction to this book I referred to the call for a new epoch, the Anthropocene and I wish, by way of conclusion, return to this call for a new epoch that, in fact, leaves the Anthropocene behind before it has, perhaps, even properly begun! Some may consider it hubris, given how brief the human race has been on this earth, yet in a recent work, James Lovelock has championed the importance of the human as a 'chosen people' which comes with a heavy moral responsibility and 'gives us cause to be proud, but not to be full of hubris' (Lovelock 2019, pp. 27, 28). As he states:

> Where the new atheists and their secular fellow travelers have gone wrong, I think, is that they have thrown the baby of truth out with the bathwater of myth. In their dislike of religion, they have failed to see its inner core of truth. I think we are a chosen people, but not chosen directly by God or some individual agency; instead we are a species that was selected naturally—selected for intelligence. (Lovelock 2019, p. 27)

The notion that religion possesses an 'inner core of truth', in the sense that any of us can really know what is true, is where religion—and Islam is a major religion—has a key role to play in the transhumanist debate. Lovelock, for his part, looks to the cosmic anthropological principle to suggest that intelligence on this Earth may be unique in the Universe. Whilst I personally would not go quite so far to say we are the *only* intelligence in the universe, it may well be that intelligence and self-awareness is extremely *rare* and, regardless, the point Lovelock makes that we are 'chosen' and, by implication, have a *natural* purpose is something that, philosophically and theologically, can inform the transhumanism debate. Never mind the call for the Anthropocene epoch, for Lovelock that's old hat: we now need a new epoch, the Novacene:

> This is the age I call the Novacene. I'm sure that one day a more appropriate name will be chosen, something more imaginative, but for now I'm using 'Novacene' to describe what could be one of the most crucial periods in the history of our planet and perhaps even the cosmos. (Lovelock 2019, p. 30)

Lovelock outlines two key historical events; firstly, was when the first photosynthetic bacteria first appeared, some 3.4 billion years ago. Secondly, Lovelock pinpoints the year 1712 when Thomas Newcomen invented the steam engine, effectively the start of the Anthropocene. However, we are now entering the third epoch of the Novacene: a new age marked by the rise of the cyborg which will, in time, become the dominant species. The term 'cyborg' was coined by Nathan Kline and Manfred Clynes in 1960 with reference to a cybernetic organism that is as self-sufficient as a human. More recently, the term is specific to an entity that is part machine and part flesh. With the rise of the cyborg, humans, for their part, would consequently lose their status as the dominant intelligent species on the planet, but Lovelock does not see this as a detrimental thing at all, but rather a necessity if the planet earth, or Gaia, is to survive as a liveable planet: 'The world of the future will be determined by the need to ensure Gaia's survival, not the selfish needs of humans or other intelligent species' (Lovelock 2019, p. 103). Lovelock envisages a possible collaboration between humans and cyborgs, at least for a time, for who can predict what the cyborg will do in the future?

Lovelock is, overall, optimistic for the future of Earth, although not perhaps so much for the human race. His vision of two separate species—the human and the cyborg—living side by side is not, for me, the only possibility. Rather, the human will *become* the cyborg and, in time, the posthuman. There may well be some humans who are 'left behind' or, indeed, prefer to reject this intentional evolution in the same way people today would rather live 'off-grid', but I suspect these numbers will be small because they will be effectively signing their death warrant, whether due to death by natural old age, or because the earth's environment has been altered so much that it is impossible for humans to survive, or that their offspring would prefer to live, quite possibly, forever. This may all seem science fiction, but much of this genre in the past has now become a reality, and we would be intellectually blind to not seriously consider the implications of these technological advances for future generations.

Islam, for its part, can and should be playing a key role in engaging and helping to determine this future. After all, the number of Muslims globally is moving towards the two billion, and, if it is the case that humans will evolve into another species, then the issue of whether these posthumans will be 'Muslims' or not is an important one for, if the answer is that they will not be Muslims, a view I reject, then Islam may well cease to exist as humans in their present form likewise cease. There is a Mormon Transhumanist Association (MTA) and a Christian Transhumanist Association (CTA). The MTA website looks to transhumanism as an opportunity and in accordance with their theological belief that 'scientific knowledge and technological power are among the means ordained of God to enable such exaltation, including realization of diverse prophetic visions of transfiguration, immortality, resurrection, renewal of this world, and the discovery and creation of worlds without end' (MTA website, 'Mormon Transhumanist Affirmation' accessed 11/07/19). The CTA also has a similar Affirmation which includes the statement: 'We believe that the intentional use of technology, coupled with following Christ, will empower us to become more human across the scope of what it means to be creatures in the image of God' (CTA website, 'The Christian Transhumanist Affirmation, accessed 11/07/19). In time, it is hoped, I see no reason why there cannot be a Muslim Transhumanist Association with its own set of Affirmations that would contain within them the same aspirations as the MTA and CTA, but specific to Islamic belief and practice.

I, therefore, in the spirit of these existing Associations (and, I admit, I have wantonly cribbed and adapted their Affirmations) I wish to end this book with some suggested Affirmations for a future Muslim Transhumanist Association:

1. We believe that the purpose of Islam involves the revival (*ihya*) and renewal (*tajdid*) of creation, including humanity, and that we should work towards the elimination of pain and suffering, poverty, injustice, and death.
2. We seek growth and progress along every dimension of our humanity, whether this is spiritual, physical, emotional, mental, and at all levels; individual, communal, social, and global

3. We understand that the Islamic tradition is compatible with and complementary to many cultures, religions, and philosophies that likewise seek transformation and renewal of creation

4. We believe that the intentional use of technology will empower us to transcend our current state and move towards perfectibility, guided by the example of the Prophet Muhammad as the Perfect Human (*insan al-Kamil*).

BIBLIOGRAPHY[2]

BOOKS

Ahmed, Shahab. 2016. *What Is Islam? The Importance of Being Islamic.* Princeton and Oxford: Princeton University Press.

Ansell Pearson, Keith. 1997. *Viroid Life: Perspective on Nietzsche and the Transhuman Condition.* Oxon: Routledge.

Bergson, Henri. 1910. *Time and Free Will: An Essay on the Immediate Data of Consciousness.* Translated by F.L. Pogson. London: George Allen and Unwin.

———. 1977. *The Two Sources of Morality and Religion.* Translated by R.A. Audra and C. Brereton. Notre Dame: University of Notre Dame Press.

———. 1983. *Creative Evolution.* Translated by F.L. Pogson. New York: Harper Torchbooks.

Dawkins, Richard. 2007. *The God Delusion.* London: Black Swan.

Deleuze, Gilles, and Felix Guattari. 1988. *A Thousand Plateaus.* Translated by B. Massumi. London: Athlone Press.

Friedmann, Yohanon. 1971. *Shaykh Ahmad Sirhindi: An Outline of His Thought and a Study of His Image in the Eyes of Posterity.* Montreal: McGill-Queen's University Press.

Fukuyama, Francis. 2002. *Our Posthuman Future: Consequences of the Biotechnology Revolution.* London: Profile Books.

Al-Ghazali, Abū Ḥāmid Muḥammad ibn Muḥammad aṭ-Ṭūsī. 1980. *Freedom and Fulfillment, An Annotated Translation of Al-Ghazali's al-Munqidh min al-dalal and Other Relevant Works of Al-Ghazali.* Translated by Richard Joseph McCarthy. Boston: Twayne.

———. 2000. *The Incoherence of the Philosophers.* Translated by Michael Marmura. Utah: Brigham Young University Press.

---

[2] *Note*: All quotes from the Qur'an are from the translation by M.A.S. Abdel Haleem, Oxford University Press, 2005.

Hakim, Khalifa Hakim. 1959. *The Metaphysics of Rumi: A Critical and Historical Sketch*. Lahore: Institute of Islamic Culture.

Howard, Damian A. 2011. *Being Human in Islam*. Oxfordshire: Routledge.

Huxley, Julian. 1963. *Evolution in Action*. Harmondsworth: Pelican.

Ibn Rushd, Abūl-Walīd Muḥammad Ibn ʾAḥmad. 1961. On the Harmony of Religion and Philosophy. In *Averroes: On the Harmony of Religion and Philosophy*. Translated by George F. Hourani. London: Gibb Memorial Trust.

Iqbal, Muhammad. 1920. *Muhammad Iqbal's The Secrets of the Self*. Translated by R.A. Nicholson. Lahore: Ashraf Press.

———. 1973. *Kulliyat-e Iqbal Farsi*. Lahore: Sheikh Ghulam Ali and Sons.

———. 1989. *The Reconstruction of Religious Thought in Islam*. Lahore: Institute of Islamic Culture.

———. 1990. *Kulliyat-i Iqbal*. Lahore: Iqbal Academy Pakistan.

———. 1995. *Bedil in the Light of Bergson*. Lahore: Iqbal Academy Pakistan.

Lovelock, James. 2019. *Novacene: The Coming Age of Hyperintelligence*. London: Allen Lane.

Majeed, Javed. 2009. *Muhammad Iqbal: Islam, Aesthetics and Postcolonialism*. Oxon: Routledge.

Mujeeb, Mohammad. 1967. *The Indian Muslims*. London: Allen & Unwin.

Nietzsche, Friedrich. 1966. *On the Genealogy of Morals*. Translated by Walter Kaufmann. New York: Vintage Books.

———. 1974. *Thus Spoke Zarathustra*. Translated by R.J. Hollingdale. London: Penguin.

———. 1998. *Beyond Good and Evil*. Translated by Marion Faber. Oxford: Oxford University Press.

Palacios, Miguel Asin. 2008. *Islam and the Divine Comedy*. Oxon: Routledge.

Saiyidain, K.G. 2012. *Iqbal's Educational Philosophy*. Lahore: Shubhi Publications.

St. Augustine. 1953. *The City of God, Books XVII–XXII (The Fathers of the Church, a New Translation, Volume 24)*. Translated by Gerald W. Walsh and Daniel J. Honan. Washington, DC: The Catholic University of America Press.

JOURNAL ARTICLES AND BOOK CHAPTERS

Bostrom, Nick. 2005b. A History of Transhumanist Thought. *Journal of Evolution and Technology* 14: 1–25.

Brooke, John Hedley. 2005. Visions of Perfectibility. *Journal of Evolution and Technology* 14 (2): 1–12.

Diyab, Adib Nayif. 2000. Ibn Arabi on Human Freedom, Destiny and the Problem of Evil. *al-Shajarah* 5: 25–43.

Griffel, Frank. 2005. Taqlîd of the Philosophers. Al-Ghazâlî's Initial Accusation in the *Tahâfut*. In *Ideas, Images, and Methods of Portrayal. Insights into Arabic Literature and Islam*, ed. Sebastian Günther, 273–297. Leiden: Brill.

Hassan, Riffat. 1972. Iqbal's Concept of *Mard-e-Momin* and Rumi's Influence. *Journal of the Regional Cultural Institute* V (2&3): 61–83.

Hauskeller, Michael. 2010. Nietzsche, the Overhuman and the Posthuman: A Reply to Stefan Sorgner. *Journal of Evolution and Technology* 21 (1): 5–8.

Kashyap, Subhash. 1955. Sir Muhammad Iqbal and Friedrich Nietzsche. *Islamic Quarterly* 2: 175–186.

Prisco, Giulio. 2013. Transcendent Engineering. In *The Transhumanist Reader*, ed. Max More and Natasha Vita-More, 234–240. Chichester: Wiley-Blackwell.

Sorgner, Stefan Lorenz. 2009. Nietzsche, The Overhuman, and Transhumanism. *Journal of Evolution and Technology* 20 (1): 29–42.

Bibliography[1]

Books

al-Afghānī, Jamāl al-Dīn. 2002. *Khatirat Jamal al-Din al-Afghani.* Cairo: Maktabat al-Shuruq.

Ahmed, Leila. 1993. *Women and Gender in Islam: Historical Roots of a Modern Debate.* New Haven, CT: Yale University Press.

Ahmed, Safdar. 2013. *Reform and Modernity in Islam: The Philosophical, Cultural and Political Discourses Among Muslim Reformers.* London: Tauris Academic Studies.

Ahmed, Shahab. 2016. *What Is Islam? The Importance of Being Islamic.* Princeton and Oxford: Princeton University Press.

———. 2017. *Before Orthodoxy: The Satanic Verses in Early Islam.* Cambridge, MA: Harvard University Press.

Akhtar, Shabbir. 1990. *A Faith for All Seasons: Islam and the Challenge of the Modern World (And Behavioral Science).* Chicago: Ivan R. Dee.

Almond, Ian. 2010. *A History of Islam in German Thought: From Leibniz to Nietzsche.* Oxon: Routledge.

Ansell Pearson, Keith. 1997. *Viroid Life: Perspective on Nietzsche and the Transhuman Condition.* Oxon: Routledge.

Arberry, A.J. 1956. *Revelation and Reason in Islam.* London: George Allen & Unwin.

---

[1] *Note:* All quotes from the Qur'an are from the translation by M.A.S. Abdel Haleem, Oxford University Press, 2005.

© The Author(s) 2020
R. Jackson, *Muslim and Supermuslim,* Palgrave Studies
in the Future of Humanity and its Successors,
https://doi.org/10.1007/978-3-030-37093-0

Aristotle. 1986. *De Anima (On the Soul)*. Translated by Hugh Lawson-Tancred. London: Penguin.

St. Augustine. 1953. *The City of God, Books XVII–XXII (The Fathers of the Church, a New Translation, Volume 24)*. Translated by Gerald W. Walsh and Daniel J. Honan. Washington, DC: The Catholic University of America Press.

Bauman, Zygmunt. 2000. *Liquid Modernity*. London: Polity Press.

de Bellaigue, Christopher. 2017. *The Islamic Enlightenment: The Modern Struggle Between Faith and Reason*. London: Bodley Head.

Bergson, Henri. 1910. *Time and Free Will: An Essay on the Immediate Data of Consciousness*. Translated by F.L. Pogson. London: George Allen and Unwin.

———. 1977. *The Two Sources of Morality and Religion*. Translated by R.A. Audra and C. Brereton. Notre Dame: University of Notre Dame Press.

———. 1983. *Creative Evolution*. Translated by F.L. Pogson. New York: Harper Torchbooks.

Bigliardi, Stefano. 2014. *Islam and the Quest for Modern Science: Conversations with Adnan Oktar, Mehdi Golshani, Mohammed Basil Altaie, Zaghloul El Naggar, Bruno Guiderdoni and Nidhal Guessoum*. Istanbul: Swedish Research Institute in Istanbul.

Blackburn, Simon. 1996. *The Oxford Dictionary of Philosophy*. Oxford: Oxford University Press.

Bucaille, Maurice. 2003. *The Bible, the Qu'ran and Science: The Holy Scriptures Examined in the Light of Modern Knowledge*. Scotts Valley, CA: CreateSpace Independent Publishing Platform.

Butler, Samuel. 2003. *Erewhon*. New York: Dover Publications.

Calvino, Italo. 1988. *Six Memos for the Next Millennium*. Cambridge: Harvard University Press.

Cromer, Evelyn Baring. 1908. *Modern Egypt*, Vols. 1 & 2. London: Macmillan.

Dabashi, Hamid. 2013. *Being a Muslim in the World*. New York: Palgrave Macmillan.

Darwin, Erasmus. 1973. *The Temple of Nature*. London: Scolar Press.

Davies, Merryl Wyn. 1988. *Knowing One Another: Shaping an Islamic Anthropology*. London and New York: Mansell Publishing.

Dawkins, Richard. 2007. *The God Delusion*. London: Black Swan.

Deleuze, Gilles, and Felix Guattari. 1988. *A Thousand Plateaus*. Translated by B. Massumi. London: Athlone Press.

Dennett, Daniel. 1978. *Brainstorms*. Cambridge, MA: MIT Press.

Derrida, Jacques. 1973. *Speech and Phenomena*. Evanston, IL: Northwestern University Press.

Descartes, René. 1988. Discourse on the Method. Translated by John Cottingham. In *Descartes: Selected Philosophical Writings*. Cambridge: Cambridge University Press.

Dummett, Michael. 2010. *The Nature and Future of Philosophy*. New York: Columbia University Press.

Dupré, Louis. 2005. *The Enlightenment and the Intellectual Foundations of Modern Culture*. New Haven, CT: Yale University Press.

El-Naggar, Zaghlul. 2012. *Treasures in the Sunnah: A Scientific Approach: Part Two*. Rochdale, UK: Scribe Digital.

Eldredge, Niles. 1982. *The Monkey Business: A Scientist Looks at Creationism*. New York: Washington Square Press.

Engelmann, Paul. 1968. *Letters from Ludwig Wittgenstein, with a Memoir*. Translated by L. Furtmüller. Oxford: Wiley-Blackwell.

Esposito, John L., and John Voll. 2001. *Makers of Contemporary Islam*. Oxford: Oxford University Press.

Fodor, Jerry A. 1983. *Modularity of Mind: An Essay on Faculty Psychology*. Cambridge, MA: MIT Press.

Frank, Richard M. 1996. *Al-Ghazali and the Asharite School*. Durham, NC: Duke University Press.

Frankl, Viktor E. 1987. *El Hombre Doliente, Fundamentos Antropológicos de la Psicoterapia*. Barcelona: Herder Editorial.

Friedmann, Yohanon. 1971. *Shaykh Ahmad Sirhindi: An Outline of His Thought and a Study of His Image in the Eyes of Posterity*. Montreal: McGill-Queen's University Press.

Fukuyama, Francis. 2002. *Our Posthuman Future: Consequences of the Biotechnology Revolution*. London: Profile Books.

Fuller, Steve, and Veronika Lipinska. 2014. *The Proactionary Imperative: A Foundation for Transhumanism*. Hampshire: Palgrave.

Gauthier, Leon, ed. 1936. *Hayy ben Yaqdhan: roman philosophique d'Ibn Thofail*. 2nd ed. Beirut: Imprimerie catholique. Reprinted Paris: Vrin, 1992.

Al-Ghazali, Abū Ḥāmid Muḥammad ibn Muḥammad aṭ-Ṭūsī. 1964. *Mizan al-'amal (Balance of Action)*. Edited by Sulayman Dunya. Cairo: Dar al-Ma'arif.

———. 1980. *Freedom and Fulfillment, An Annotated Translation of Al-Ghazali's al-Munqidh min al-dalal and Other Relevant Works of Al-Ghazali*. Translated by Richard Joseph McCarthy. Boston: Twayne.

———. 1982. *Divine Predicates and Their Properties: Al-Iqtisad fil-Itiqad*. Translated by A.R. Zayd. Apex Books Concern (Open Library).

———. 2000. *The Incoherence of the Philosophers*. Translated by Michael Marmura. Utah: Brigham Young University Press.

Goetz, Stewart, and Charles Taliaferro. 2008. *Naturalism*. Grand Rapids, MI: William B. Eerdmans Publishing Co.

Gould, Stephen Jay. 1998. *Leonardo's Mountain of Clams and the Diet of Worms*. London: Jonathan Cape.

———. 2002. *Rocks of Ages*. New York: Vintage.

Guarente, Lenny. 2003. *Ageless Quest*. New York: Cold Spring Harbor Laboratory Press.

Hadot, Pierre. 1995. *Philosophy as a Way of Life: Spiritual Exercises from Socrates to Foucault*. Oxford: Wiley-Blackwell.

Hakim, Khalifa Hakim. 1959. *The Metaphysics of Rumi: A Critical and Historical Sketch*. Lahore: Institute of Islamic Culture.

Harari, Yuval Noah. 2011. *Sapiens: A Brief History of Humankind*. London: Penguin.

———. 2017. *Homo Deus: A Brief History of Tomorrow*. London: Penguin.

Harris, Sam. 2010. *The Moral Landscape: How Science Can Determine Human Values*. London: Transworld.

Hassan, Nawal Muhammad. 1980. *Hayy bin Yaqzan and Robinson Crusoe: A Study of an Early Arabic Impact on English Literature*. Republic of Iraq: Al-Rashid House for Publication.

Heidegger, Martin. 1982. *The Basic Problems of Phenomenology*. Translated by Albert Hofstadter. Bloomington, IN: Indiana University Press.

Howard, Damian A. 2011. *Being Human in Islam*. Oxfordshire: Routledge.

Hughes, Bettany. 2010. *The Hemlock Cup: Socrates, Athens and the Search for the Good Life*. London: Jonathan Cape.

Hume, David. 1975. *Enquiries Concerning Human Understanding and Concerning the Principles of Morals*. 3rd ed. Edited by L.A. Selby-Bigge. Revised by P.H. Nidditch. Oxford: Oxford University Press.

———. 1978. *A Treatise of Human Nature*. 2nd ed. Edited by P.H. Nidditch. Oxford: Oxford University Press.

Hunter, Shireen T. 1998. *The Future of Islam and the West*. Washington, DC: The Centre for Strategic and International Studies.

Husserl, Edmund. 1997. *Psychological and Transcendental Phenomenology and the Confrontation with Heidegger (1927–1931)*. Translated and Edited by Thomas Sheehan and Richard E. Palmer. Dordrecht: Kluwer Academic Publishers.

Huxley, Julian. 1963. *Evolution in Action*. Harmondsworth: Pelican.

Ibn Rushd, Abūl-Walīd Muḥammad Ibn ʾAḥmad. 1921. *The Book of the Exposition of the Methods of Proofs Regarding the Beliefs of the Religion in the Philosophy and Theology of Averroes' Tractacta*. Translated by Mohammad Jamil-Ub-Behman Barod. Baroda: Manibhai Mathurbhal Gupta.

———. 1961. On the Harmony of Religion and Philosophy. In *Averroes: On the Harmony of Religion and Philosophy*. Translated by George F. Hourani. London: Gibb Memorial Trust.

Ibn Sina. 2005. *The Metaphysics of the Healing*. 2nd ed. Translated by Michael E. Marmura. Chicago: University of Chicago Press.

Ibn Tufayl. 2009. *Ibn Tufayl's Hayy Ibn Yaqzan: A Philosophical Tale*. Translated by L.E. Goodman. Chicago: University of Chicago Press.

Iqbal, Muhammad. 1920. *Muhammad Iqbal's The Secrets of the Self*. Translated by R.A. Nicholson. Lahore: Ashraf Press.

———. 1973. *Kulliyat-e Iqbal Farsi*. Lahore: Sheikh Ghulam Ali and Sons.

———. 1989. *The Reconstruction of Religious Thought in Islam*. Lahore: Institute of Islamic Culture.

————. 1990. *Kulliyat-i Iqbal.* Lahore: Iqbal Academy Pakistan.

————. 1995. *Bedil in the Light of Bergson.* Lahore: Iqbal Academy Pakistan.

Istvan, Zoltan. 2013. *The Transhumanist Wager.* Nevada: Futurity Imagine Media LLC.

Jackson, Roy. 2006. *Fifty Key Figures in Islam.* Oxon: Routledge.

————. 2007. *Nietzsche and Islam.* Oxon: Routledge.

————. 2011. *Mawdudi and Political Islam.* Oxon: Routledge.

————. 2014. *What Is Islamic Philosophy?* Oxon: Routledge.

Johnson, Boris. 2007. *The Dream of Rome.* London: Harper Perennial.

Kant, Immanuel. 1900. *Dreams of a Spirit-Seer.* Translated by Emanuel F. Goerwitz. London: Swan Sonnenschein and Co.

————. 1981. *Universal Natural History and Theory of the Heavens.* Translated by Ian Johnston. Arlington, VA: Richer Resources Publications.

————. 1998. *Critique of Pure Reason.* Cambridge: Cambridge University Press.

Khan, Syed Ahmad. 1891. *Essay on the Question Whether Islam Has Been Beneficial or Injurious to Human Society in General.* Lahore: Mohammadan Tract and Book Department.

Kurtz, Paul. 2012. *Meaning and Value in a Secular Age: Why Eupraxsophy Matters – The Writings of Paul Kurtz.* Edited by Nathan Bupp. London: Prometheus Books.

Kurzweil, Ray. 1999. *The Age of Spiritual Machines.* London: Penguin.

————. 2006. *The Singularity Is Near: When Humans Transcend Biology.* London: Penguin.

Lakoff, George, and Mark Johnson. 1980. *Metaphors We Live By.* Chicago: University of Chicago Press.

Lebor, Adam. 1997. *A Heart Turned East: Among the Muslims of Europe and America.* New York: Warner Books.

Lindholm, Charles. 1996. *The Islamic Middle East: An Historical Anthropology.* Chichester: Wiley-Blackwell.

Locke, John. 1975. *An Essay Concerning Human Understanding.* Oxford: Oxford University Press.

Lovelock, James. 2019. *Novacene: The Coming Age of Hyperintelligence.* London: Allen Lane.

Lyons, Jonathan. 2010. *The House of Wisdom: How the Arabs Transformed Western Civilization.* London: Bloomsbury.

Mabey, Richard. 2015. *Cabaret of Plants: Botany and Imagination.* London: Profile Books Ltd.

MacLeod, Roy, ed. 2004. *The Library of Alexandria: Centre of Learning in the Ancient World.* London: I.B. Tauris.

Maher, Derek F., and Calvin Mercer, eds. 2009. *Religion and the Implications of Radical Life Extension.* New York: Palgrave Macmillan.

Maimonides, Moses. 1963. *The Guide of the Perplexed.* Translated by Schlomo Pines. Chicago: University of Chicago Press.

Majeed, Javed. 2009. *Muhammad Iqbal: Islam, Aesthetics and Postcolonialism.* Oxon: Routledge.

Marrakushi, 'Abd al-Wāḥid. 1881. *Al-Mujib fi Talkhis Akhbar al-Maghrib (The Pleasant Book in Summarizing the History of the Maghreb).* 2nd ed. Edited by R. Dozy. Leiden: University of Leiden.

Mawdudi, Abu Al'a. 1969. *Islami Riyasat.* Lahore: Islamic Publications Ltd.

———. 1985. *Islam Today.* Beirut: International Islamic Federation of Student Organisations.

———. 1995. *Jihad fi Sabillah: Jihad in Islam.* Translated and Edited by Khurshid Ahmad. Birmingham: Huda Khattab, UK Islamic Mission Dawah Centre.

Mawdudi, Mawlana. 1963. *A Short History of the Revivalist Movement in Islam.* Lahore: Islamic Publications.

Mercer, Calvin, and Derek F. Maher, eds. 2014. *Transhumanism and the Body: The World Religions Speak.* New York: Palgrave Macmillan.

Mercer, Calvin, and Tracy Trothen, eds. 2014. *Religion and Transhumanism: The Unknown Future of Human Enhancement.* Santa Barbara, CA: Praeger.

Merleau-Ponty, Mauric. 1968. *The Visible and the Invisible.* Translated by Alphonso Lingis. Evanston: Northwestern University Press.

Minault, Gail. 1982. *The Khilafat Movement: Religious Symbolisms and Political Mobilization in India.* New York: Columbia University Press.

Mujeeb, Mohammad. 1967. *The Indian Muslims.* London: Allen & Unwin.

Murnane, Ben. 2018. *Ayn Rand and the Posthuman: The Mind-Made Future.* New York: Palgrave Macmillan.

Nagel, Thomas. 1986. *The View from Nowhere.* Oxford: Oxford University Press.

———. 2012. *Mind and Cosmos: Why the Materialist Neo-Darwinian Conception of Nature Is Almost Certainly False.* Oxford: Oxford University Press.

Nasr, Hossein, and Muzaffar Iqbal. 2009. *Islam, Science, Muslims and Technology.* Islamabad: Dost Publication.

Nasr, Seyyed Vali Rez. 1994. *The Vanguard of the Islamic Revolution: The Jam'at-i Islami of Pakistan.* Berkeley: University of California Press.

Nietzsche, Friedrich. 1966. *On the Genealogy of Morals.* Translated by Walter Kaufmann. New York: Vintage Books.

———. 1974. *Thus Spoke Zarathustra.* Translated by R.J. Hollingdale. London: Penguin.

———. 1998. *Beyond Good and Evil.* Translated by Marion Faber. Oxford: Oxford University Press.

O'Connell, Mark. 2018. *To Be a Machine: Adventures Among Cyborgs, Utopians, Hackers, and the Futurists Solving the Modest Problem of Death.* London: Granta.

Ouspensky, P.D. 2012. *Strange Life of Ivan Osokin.* Eastford, CT: Martino Fine Books.

Page, Michael R. 2016. *The Literary Imagination from Erasmus Darwin to H.G. Wells: Science, Evolution and Ecology*. Oxon: Routledge.

Palacios, Miguel Asin. 2008. *Islam and the Divine Comedy*. Oxon: Routledge.

Parfit, Derek. 1987. *Reasons and Persons*. Oxford: Oxford University Press.

Parvez, G.A. 2008. *Islam: A Challenge to Religion*. Lahore: Talou-e-Islam Trust.

Pigliucci, Massimo. 2010. *Nonsense on Stilts: How to Tell Science from Bunk*. Chicago: University of Chicago Press.

Plantinga, Alvin. 2011. *Where the Conflict Really Lies: Science, Religion, and Naturalism*. Oxford: Oxford University Press.

Plato. 2012. *Republic*. Translated by Christopher Rowe. London: Penguin.

Price, H.H. 1969. *Beliefs*. New South Wales: Allen & Unwin.

Quine, W.V. 1981. *Theories and Things*. Cambridge: Harvard University Press.

al-Qurtubi, Abu 'Abdullah Muhammad. 2003. *Tafsir al-Qurtubi*. Vol. 1. London: Dar al-Taqwa.

Rapoport, Yossef, and Shahab Ahmed, eds. 2010. *Ibn Taymiyya and His Times*. Oxford: Oxford University Press.

Remes, Paulina. 2008. *Neoplatonism (Ancient Philosophies)*. Durham: Acumen.

Rippin, Andrew. 2018. *Muslims: Their Religious Beliefs and Practices*. 5th ed. Oxon: Routledge.

Russell, Gul A. 1994. *The 'Arabick' Interest of the Natural Philosophers in Seventeenth-Century England*. Leiden: Brill Publishers.

Russell, Matheson. 2006. *Husserl: A Guide for the Perplexed*. London: Continuum.

Ruthven, Malise. 2000. *Islam in the World*. 2nd ed. London: Penguin.

Sagan, Carl. 1997. *Pale Blue Dot: A Vision of the Human Future in Space*. New York: Ballantine Books.

Said, Edward. 1978. *Orientalism*. London: Penguin.

Saiyidain, K.G. 2012. *Iqbal's Educational Philosophy*. Lahore: Shubhi Publications.

Sardar, Ziauddin. 1989. *Explorations in Islamic Science*. London: Mansell Publishing Limited.

———. 2016. *Science, Technology and Development in the Muslim World*. Oxon: Routledge.

Scheler, Max. 2004. *El puesto del Hombre en el Cosmos*. Buenos Aires: Losada.

Shaw, George Bernard. 1970. *Bodley Head Bernard Shaw: Collected Plays with Their Prefaces*. Edited by Dan H. Laurence. London: Bodley Head Ltd.

———. 1987. *Back to Methuselah: A Metabiological Pentateuch*. London: Penguin.

———. 2000. *Man and Superman: A Comedy and a Philosophy*. London: Penguin.

Sheldrake, Rupert. 2012. *The Science Delusion: Feeling the Spirit of Enquiry*. London: Hodder & Stoughton.

Smith, Wilfred Cantwell. 1957. *Islam in Modern History*. Princeton: Princeton University Press.

———. 1959. *The Meaning and End of Religion*. Minneapolis, MN: Augsburg Fortress.

———. 1981. *On Understanding Islam: Selected Studies.* The Hague: Mouton.

Steiner, George. 1989. *Martin Heidegger.* Chicago: University of Chicago Press.

Swanwick, Helena Maria Lucy. 1935. *I Have Been Young.* London: Gollancz.

Swedenborg, Emanuel. 2009. *Arcana Coelestia.* Vols. 1–12. Translated by John Clowes. West Chester, PA: Swedenborg Foundation.

Swinburne, Richard. 2004. *The Existence of God.* Oxford: Oxford University Press.

Taliaferro, Charles. 1994. *Consciousness and the Mind of God.* Cambridge: Cambridge University Press.

Truitt, E.R. 2015. *Medieval Robots: Mechanism, Magic, Nature, and Art.* Philadelphia: University of Pennsylvania Press.

Waardenburg, Jacques. 2002. *Islam: Historical, Social and Political Perspectives.* Berlin: Walter de Gruyter.

Ward, Keith. 2008. *Why There Almost Certain Is a God.* Oxford: Lion Book.

Waters, C.N., et al., eds. 2014. *A Strategical Basis for the Anthropocene.* London: Geological Society Publication (GSL).

Williams, Bernard. 2006. *Philosophy as a Humanistic Discipline.* Princeton: Princeton University Press.

Wittgenstein, Ludwig. 1961a. *Notebooks 1914–1916.* Oxford: Basil Blackwell.

———. 1961b. *Tractatus Logico-Philosophicus.* London: Routledge.

Wood, Gaby. 2002. *Living Dolls: A Magical History of the Quest for Mechanical Life.* London: Faber & Faber.

Yaqubi, Ahmad ibn Abi Yaqub. 1892. *Kitab al-Buldan (Book of Lands).* Edited by M.D. Goeje. Leiden: Leiden University Press.

Young, Simon S. 2005. *Designer Evolution: A Transhumanist Manifesto.* New York: Prometheus Books.

Journal Articles and Book Chapters

Ahmad, Khurshid. 1983. The Nature of Islamic Resurgence. In *Voices of Resurgent Islam,* ed. John L. Esposito, 218–229. Oxford: Oxford University Press.

Ahmed, Shahab. 2013. Progressive Islam and Quranic Hermeneutics: The Reification of Religion and Theories of Religious Experience. In *Muslim Secular Democracy: Voices from Within,* ed. Lily Zubaidah Rahim, 77–92. New York: Palgrave Macmillan.

Bostrom, Nick. 2005a. The Fable of the Dragon-Tyrant. *Journal of Medical Ethics* 31 (5): 273–277.

———. 2005b. A History of Transhumanist Thought. *Journal of Evolution and Technology* 14: 1–25.

Boudry, Maarten, Stefaan Blancke, and Johan Braeckman. 2010. How Not to Attack Intelligent Design Creationism: Philosophical Misconceptions About Methodological Naturalism. *Foundations of Science* 15 (3): 227–244.

———. 2012. Grist to the Mill of Anti-Evolutionism: The Failed Strategy of Ruling the Supernatural Out of Science by Philosophical Fiat. *Science and Education* 21: 1151–1165.

BouJaoude, Saouma, et al. 2011a. Biology Professors' and Teachers' Positions Regarding Biological Evolution and Evolution Education in a Middle Eastern Society. *International Journal of Science Education* 33 (7): 979–1000.

———. 2011b. Muslim Egyptian and Lebanese Students' Conceptions of Biological Evolution. *Science and Education* 20 (9): 895–915.

Brooke, John Hedley. 2005. Visions of Perfectibility. *Journal of Evolution and Technology* 14 (2): 1–12.

Campbell, Heidi, and Mark Walker. 2005. Religion and Transhumanism: Introducing a Conversation. *Journal of Evolution and Technology* 14 (2): i–xiv.

Cellucci, Carlo. 2015. Is Philosophy a Humanistic Discipline? *Philosophia* 43: 259–269.

Cerullo, Michael A. 2016. The Ethics of Exponential Life Extension Through Brain Preservation. *Journal of Evolution and Technology* 26 (1): 94–105.

Chalmers, David. 1995. Facing Up to the Problem of Consciousness. *Journal of Consciousness Studies* 2 (3): 200–219.

Crutzen, Paul, and Eugene F. Stoermer. 2000. The 'Anthropocene'? *IGBP Newsletter*, no. 41.

Dembski, William. 2002. Kurzweil's Impoverished Spirituality. In *Are We Spiritual Machines? Ray Kurzweil vs. The Critics of Strong AI*, ed. J.W. Richards, 98–114. Seattle: The Discovery Institute.

Diyab, Adib Nayif. 2000. Ibn Arabi on Human Freedom, Destiny and the Problem of Evil. *al-Shajarah* 5: 25–43.

Drees, Willem B. 2013. Islam and Bioethics in the Context of 'Religion and Science'. *Zygon* 48 (3): 732–744.

Fishman, Yonatan I., and Maarten Boudry. 2013. Does Science Presuppose Naturalism (or Anything at All)? *Science and Education* 22 (5): 921–949.

Forrest, Barbara. 2000. Methodological Naturalism and Philosophical Naturalism: Clarifying the Connection. *Philo* 3: 7–29.

Frankl, Viktor. 1967. Logotherapy and Existentialism. *Psychotherapy: Theory, Research and Practice* 4 (3): 138–142.

Fuller, Steve. 2008. The Future Is Divine: A History of Human God-Playing. In *Human Futures*, ed. A. Miah, 6–19. Liverpool and Chicago: University of Liverpool Press and University of Chicago Press.

Gardet, Louis. 1970. Religion and Culture. In *The Cambridge History of Islam, Volume 2B: Islamic Society and Civilisation*, ed. P.M. Holt, Ann K.S. Lambton, and Bernard Lewis, 569–603. Cambridge: Cambridge University Press.

Al-Ghazali, Abū Ḥāmid Muḥammad ibn Muḥammad aṭ-Ṭūsī. 1995. That Which Delivers from Error. In *Readings in Western Religious Thought: The Middle Ages Through the Reformation*, ed. Patrick V. Reid, 154–168. Mahwah, NJ: Paulist Press.

Gibbs, A.M. 1976. Comedy and Philosophy in Man and Superman. *Modern Drama* 19 (2): 161–175.

de Grey, A.D.N.J. 2005. Life Extension, Human Rights, and the Rational Refinement of Repugnance. *Journal of Medical Ethics* 31: 659–663.

de Grey, Aubrey. 2009. Radical Life Extension: Technological Aspect. In *Religion and the Implications of Radical Life Extension*, ed. Derek F. Maher and Calvin Mercer, 13–24. New York: Palgrave Macmillan.

Griffel, Frank. 2005. Taqlîd of the Philosophers. Al-Ghazâlî's Initial Accusation in the *Tahâfut*. In *Ideas, Images, and Methods of Portrayal. Insights into Arabic Literature and Islam*, ed. Sebastian Günther, 273–297. Leiden: Brill.

Guessoum, Nidhal. 2015. Reviews on Religion and Science around the World. *Zygon* 50 (4): 854–876.

Hameed, Salman. 2008. Bracing for Islamic Creationism. *Science* 322 (12 December): 1637–1638.

Hańderek, Joanna. 2007. The Positionalist Notion of Human Nature in Plessner's and Gehlen's Philosophy. *Analecta Husserliana* XCIV: 533–547.

Hanson, Jim. 2012. Ontos and Theos: A Case for Neo-Ontotheology. *Theology Today* 69 (2): 213–224.

Haque, Amber. 2004. Psychology from Islamic Perspective: Contributions of Early Muslim Scholars and Challenges to Contemporary Muslim Psychologists. *Journal of Religion and Health* 43 (4): 357–377.

Hassan, Riffat. 1972. Iqbal's Concept of *Mard-e-Momin* and Rumi's Influence. *Journal of the Regional Cultural Institute* V (2&3): 61–83.

Hauskeller, Michael. 2010. Nietzsche, the Overhuman and the Posthuman: A Reply to Stefan Sorgner. *Journal of Evolution and Technology* 21 (1): 5–8.

Hourani, George F. 1970. The Early Growth of the Secular Sciences in Andalusia. *Studia Islamica* 32: 143–156.

Jackson, Philip J.B. 2005. Mama and Papa: The Ancestors of Modern-Day Speech Science. In *The Genius of Erasmus Darwin*, ed. Christopher Smith and Robert Arnott, 217–236. Aldershot: Ashgate.

Kashyap, Subhash. 1955. Sir Muhammad Iqbal and Friedrich Nietzsche. *Islamic Quarterly* 2: 175–186.

Kass, Leon R. 1997. The Wisdom of Repugnance. *New Republic* 216 (22): 17–26.

Kiyimba, Abasi. 2007. Islam and Science: An Overview. In *Islamic Perspective on Science*, ed. Ali Ünal, 1–27. Clifton, NJ: The Light Inc.

Koene, Randal A. 2013. Uploading the Substrate-Independent Minds. In *The Transhumanist Reader*, ed. Max More and Natasha Vita-More, 146–156. Chichester: Wiley-Blackwell.

Latif, Amer. 2009. *Qur'anic Narratives and Sufi Hermeneutics: Rumi's Interpretation of Pharaoh's Character*. PhD Dissertation. New York: Stony Brook University.

Law, Stephen. 2017. Scientism! In *Science Unlimited? The Challenge of Scientism*, ed. Maarten Boudry and Massimo Pigliucci, 121–144. Chicago and London: The University of Chicago Press.

Leach, Antonia. 2018. Iain M. Banks – Human, Posthuman and Beyond Human. *ELOPE: English Language Overseas Perspectives and Enquiries* 15 (1): 69–81.

Lehmann, Olga V., and Sven Hroar Klempe. 2015. Psychology and the Notion of the Spirit: Implications of Max Scheler's Anthropological Philosophy in Theory of Psychology. *Integrative Psychological and Behavioral Science* 49 (3): 478–484. Springer.

Liccioli, Stefano. 2008. Il problema dell'uomo nel pensiero di Max Scheler. *Humana Mente* 2 (7): 79–104.

Majeed, Javed. 2003. Modernity. In *Encyclopedia of Islam and the Muslim World*, ed. S.A. Arjomand et al. (3 vols., 2: 456–458). London: Macmillan Reference.

Malcolm, Norman. 1973. Thoughtless Brutes. *Proceedings and Addresses of the American Philosophical Association* 46 (September): 5–20.

Mavani, Hamid. 2014. God's Deputy: Islam and Transhumanism. In *Transhumanism and the Body: The World Religions Speak*, ed. Calvin Mercer and Derek F. Maher, 67–84. New York: Palgrave Macmillan.

McCann, J. 2001. Wanna Bet? *Scientist* 15: 8.

Minsky, Marvin. 2013. Why Freud Was the First Good AI Theorist. In *The Transhumanist Reader*, ed. Max More and Natasha Vita-More, 167–176. Chichester: Wiley-Blackwell.

More, Max. 2013. The Philosophy of Transhumanism. In *The Transhumanist Reader*, ed. M. More and N. Vita-More. Chichester, West Sussex: Wiley-Blackwell.

More, Max, and Natasha Vita-More. 2013. Roots and Core Themes. In *The Transhumanist Reader*, ed. Max More and Natasha Vita-More. Vols. 1–2. Chichester: Wiley-Blackwell.

Muller, H.J. 1959. One Hundred Years Without Darwinism Are Enough. *School Science and Mathematics* 59 (4): 304–305.

Musa, Aisha Y. 2009. A Thousand Years, Less Fifty: Toward a Quranic View of Extreme Longevity. In *Religion and the Implications of Radical Life Extension*, ed. Derek F. Mhaer and Calvin Mercer, 123–131. New York: Palgrave Macmillan.

Nagel, Thomas. 1974. What Is It Like to Be a Bat? *The Philosophical Review* 83 (4): 435–450.

Nasr, Hossein. 2006. On the Question of Biological Origins. *Islam & Science* 4 (2): 181–197.

Peters, Ted. 2011. Transhumanism and the Posthuman Future: Will Technological Progress Get Us There? In *H+/−: Transhumanism and Its Critics*, ed. Gregory R. Hansell and William Grassie, 147–175. Philadelphia, PA: Metanexus Institute.

Plantinga, Alvin. 1996. Science: Augustinian or Duhemian? *Faith and Philosophy* 13: 369–394.

———. 1997. Methodological Naturalism. *Perspectives on Science and Christian Faith* 49: 143–154.

Prisco, Giulio. 2013. Transcendent Engineering. In *The Transhumanist Reader*, ed. Max More and Natasha Vita-More, 234–240. Chichester: Wiley-Blackwell.

Roy, Rustum. 2005. Scientism and Technology as Religions. *Zygon* 40 (4): 835–844.

Sardar, Ziauddin. 1985. Between Two Masters: Qur'an or Science? *Inquiry: An Interdisciplinary Journal of Philosophy* 2 (8): 37–41.

———. 1986. Redirecting Science towards Islam: An Examination of Islamic and Western Approaches to Knowledge and Values. *Hamdard Islamicus* 9 (1): 23–34.

———. 2006. Ziauddin Sardar Confronts the Commentators. *New Statesman*, February 6.

Scheler, Max. 2004. *Das Ressentiment im Aufbau der Moralen*. Frankfurt am Main: Klostermann Seminar.

Searle, John. 1980. Minds, Brains and Programs. *Behavioral and Brain Sciences* 3 (3): 417–457.

Sheckley, Robert. 1956. The Body. *Galaxy Magazine*, January, Vol. 11 (3). New York: Galaxy Publishing.

Sorgner, Stefan Lorenz. 2009. Nietzsche, The Overhuman, and Transhumanism. *Journal of Evolution and Technology* 20 (1): 29–42.

Stilwell, Phil. 2009. The Status of Methodological Naturalism as Justified by Precedent. *Studies in Liberal Arts and Sciences* 41: 229–247.

Stroumsa, Sarah. 2003. Saadya and Jewish Kalam. In *The Cambridge Companion to Medieval Jewish Philosophy*, ed. Daniel H. Frank and Oliver Leaman, 71–90. Cambridge: Cambridge University Press.

Vita-More, Natasha. 2013. Aesthetics: Bringing the Arts & Design into the Discussion of Transhumanism. In *The Transhumanist Reader*, ed. Max More and Natasha Vita-More, 18–27. Chichester: Wiley-Blackwell.

Wisenthal, J.L. 1971. The Cosmology of Man and Superman. *Modern Drama* 14 (3): 298–306.

Wittgenstein, Ludwig. 1965. A Lecture on Ethics. *Philosophical Review* 74 (1): 3–12.

Websites

Amsterdam Declaration, International Humanist and Ethical Union. Accessed July 26, 2019. https://iheu.org/about/humanism/the-amsterdam-declaration/.

Bostrom, Nick. 2002. Transhumanist Values. Accessed July 26, 2019. http://www.nickbostrom.com/ethics/values.html.

Christian Transhumanist Association (CTA). Accessed July 26, 2019. https://www.christiantranshumanism.org.

Coffey, John. 2006. *The Abolition of the Slave Trade: Christian Conscience and Political Action*. Jubilee Centre. Accessed July 26, 2019. http://www.jubilee-centre.org/the-abolition-of-the-slave-trade-christian-conscience-and-political-action-by-john-coffey/.

Funk, C., et al. 2016. *U.S. Public Wary of Biomedical Technologies to 'Enhance' Human Abilities*. Pew Research Centre Report. Accessed July 26, 2019. http://www.pewinternet.org/2016/07/26/u-s-public-wary-of-biomedical-technologies-to-enhance-human-abilities/.

Hughes, James J. 2007. *The Compatibility of Religious and Transhumanist Views of Metaphysics, Suffering, Virtue and Transcendence in an Enhanced Future*. Institute for Ethics and Emerging Technologies. Accessed July 26, 2019. http://ieet.org/archive/20070326-Hughes-ASU-H+Religion.pdf.

Humanists UK. Accessed July 26, 2019. https://humanism.org.uk.

Masci, David. 2016. *Q&A: Two Perspectives on Human Enhancement Technologies and How the Public Views Them*. Pew Research Centre. Accessed January 25, 2018. http://www.pewresearch.org/fact-tank/2016/07/27/qa-two-perspectives-on-human-enhancement-technologies-and-how-the-public-views-them/.

Mormon Transhumanist Association (MTA). Accessed May 13, 2019. https://transfigurism.org/mission.

Newport, Frank. 2014. *In U.S., 42% Believe Creationist View of Human Origins*. Accessed January 26, 2017. http://www.gallup.com/poll/170822/believe-creationist-view-human-origins.aspx.

Olshansky, S. Jay. 2004. *Don't Fall for the Cult of Immortality*. Accessed February 11, 2018. http://news.bbc.co.uk/1/hi/uk/4059549.stm.

Pessin, Sarah. 2014. The Influence of Islamic Thought on Maimonides. In *The Stanford Encyclopaedia of Philosophy*. First published Thu Jun 30, 2005; Substantive Revision, Wed May 28, 2014. Accessed June 7, 2018. https://plato.stanford.edu/entries/maimonides-islamic/.

Pew Research Centre Report. 2013. *The World's Muslims: Religion, Politics and Society*. Accessed January 16, 2017. http://www.pewforum.org/2013/04/30/the-worlds-muslims-religion-politics-society-overview/.

Index[1]

---

[1] Note: Page numbers followed by 'n' refer to notes.

© The Author(s) 2020
R. Jackson, *Muslim and Supermuslim*, Palgrave Studies in the Future of Humanity and its Successors, https://doi.org/10.1007/978-3-030-37093-0

CPSIA information can be obtained
at www.ICGtesting.com
Printed in the USA
LVHW081803110820
662924LV00010BA/217

9 783030 370923